HOUSING
AND
THE MONEY
MARKET

HOUSING
AND
THE MONEY
MARKET

ROGER STARR

BASIC BOOKS, INC., *Publishers*

NEW YORK

For my father,

Frederick Starr,

in his ninety-seventh year.

Library of Congress Cataloging in Publication Data

Starr, Roger.
  Housing and the money market.

  Includes bibliographical references and index.
    1. Housing—United States.   2. Housing—United
States—Finance.   I. Title.
HD7293.S66   333.3'3   73–91083
ISBN 0–465–03072–6

Manufactured in the United States of America
DESIGNED BY VINCENT TORRE
76 77 78 79 80   10 9 8 7 6 5 4 3 2

CONTENTS

ACKNOWLEDGMENTS   *vi*

PART ONE

Fundamentals

1. The House   *3*
2. The Equity   *10*
3. The Mortgage   *21*
4. The Resources   *35*
5. Money and Its Market   *58*

PART TWO

The Lending Institutions

6. The Commercial Banks   *85*
7. The Mutual Savings Banks   *93*
8. The Savings and Loan Associations   *108*
9. The Life Insurance Companies   *121*
10. The Mortgage Bankers   *138*
11. The State Agencies   *149*

PART THREE

Governmental Institutions and the Future of Policy

12. The Federal Housing Administration   *167*
13. The Federal National Mortgage Association   *182*
14. The Government National Mortgage Association   *198*
15. Policies and Prospects   *209*

NOTES   *236*
INDEX   *243*

ACKNOWLEDGMENTS

JULIET BARTLETT, of the Women's City Club of New York provided the unwitting original stimulus for this book by asking me why mortgage interest rates in publicly-assisted housing were rising so fast. In response, the Citizens Housing and Planning Council of New York encouraged me to give a series of lectures on the subject of the mortgage market.

I must acknowledge the help of countless people who have filled in the gaps in my knowledge of the field. Among them are John J. Brady, Vice President of the New York Federal Home Loan Bank; Saul B. Klaman, Vice President and Chief Economist of the National Association of Mutual Savings Banks, and George Hanc, Director of Research of the National Association of Mutual Savings Banks; Eugene Rubin, then of the New York State Association of Mutual Savings Banks; John M. Wetmore of the Mortgage Bankers Association of America, and Woodward Kingman and others of the Government National Mortgage Association.

Special help was provided by the devoted staff of the Citizens Housing and Planning Council including Marian Sameth, Associate Director; Marvin Markus, Research Director; and James Rouen, Research Assistant. Mildred Black, George Whitmore, Linda Boer, and Donna Anzel cheerfully coped with the preparation of the manuscript.

Valued suggestions were offered by Professor Emanuel Tobier of New York University. The opinions presented, however, are those of the author, who must also express regret for institutional and other changes in the money market which occur more rapidly than paragraphs can be written or type set.

PART ONE

Fundamentals

CHAPTER 1

THE HOUSE

EVERYBODY talks about the housing problem in the United States, and most Americans at one time or another have had to face it in their own lives. All but the very rich find that—to an extent unmatched in the case of other necessities—the search for satisfactory housing imposes on them some measure of compromise between what they feel themselves entitled to and what they must settle for. Many Americans of modest income—far too many—can find only a compromise that leaves them grossly ill-served, with little space, inadequate heat and water, broken plaster, general dilapidation, and a location that seems to emphasize the difficulty of inproving one's economic opportunities or those of one's children.

When Americans complain about their housing, they ask a familiar question: Why is there so much bad housing in so rich a country? Or, to put it another way, why cannot more resources—culled from the very many resources available to the American economy—be allocated to the construction of good new urban housing or to the maintenance of existing housing in satisfactory condition? Why does it seem so difficult to provide legally adequate housing for those families whose incomes are too low to enable them to buy or rent such housing on their own?

The answers to these questions contain a common element: high cost. In an industrialized society, housing is an extremely complex piece of work, by far the most complex that the economy is asked to supply for the exclusive use of a sole occupant or a single family. In the part of the globe in which the United States lies, housing involves more than a roof over one's head, although that specification might suffice for adequate shelter in the tropics. In the temperate zone, housing must shield its occupants against heat and cold, against snow, rain, and wind, against disease and accident, and against fire and burglary. This by no means exhausts the list of the kinds of shelter that housing must provide. Local, state, and national governments have, through the medium of building and housing codes, enacted very specific regulations that tell the builder exactly how, at a minimum, he must provide the shelter.

But housing in an industrialized society is more than shelter. To glimpse the complexity of the housing that Americans demand, one might think of it as a bundle of three packages. In addition to the shelter package, housing must include a utility package, comprising all of those external services without which modern people living in a modern home could not long endure. The utility package, therefore, includes electricity and running water and the system of pipes, wires, and reservoirs that make these possible; it also includes the transportation systems that move people from their homes to their working places, their schools, and their recreation as well as public services like police, fire protection, health, and sanitation.

Finally, if housing is to be of use to anyone except, perhaps, an eccentric descendant of Henry David Thoreau, it cannot stand in isolation, but must offer its occupants a social setting to complete their lives. This social package offers access to a job, the way to earn a living. It includes as well a living environment that reflects the values of the social group to which the residents in a specific housing unit belong. Educational institutions form a very important part of the living environment; second after jobs, Americans tend to try to choose housing on the basis of the educational opportunities its location will offer their children. Most probably, in an industrialized society, preferences in location of housing will be shaped by the coherence of socio-economic classes. People say that they want to live in a "good" neighborhood, a statement that generally means that they want to live among those who resemble them in income, education, and cultural aspirations.

In the preamble to the National Housing Act of 1949 (as amended on frequent occasions), Congress declared not only that every American family should have a "decent" home, but that the home should be located in a "suitable living environment." The crucial word, "suitable," was probably selected in the hope that it would be totally neutral in defining the qualities of neighborhoods. In fact, however, ethnic and racial considerations help to shape the social package, as do the institutions— schools, churches, movie theaters, clubs—that provide people with the opportunity to meet with and react to others, and to the children of others.

Each of these packages is difficult to assemble. The cost of assembling the shelter package is met directly by those who live in it, either through the payment of rent or through the assumption of the costs and responsibilities of ownership. There is little consistency in the way in which the costs of the utility package are met. Many are met in the same way as the shelter package, by direct payment by the housing occupant. Thus, the power bills paid by tenant or owner cover not only the operating costs of the public utility but also periodic charges that pay for the capital investment in generating stations and electric conduits. On the other hand, transportation and garbage collection costs—to name only two—are met differently in different places. In a neighborhood of one-family homes, the public street is put in at the general expense of *all* the local taxpayers, industrial and commercial, as well as residential. In an elevator apartment house, which may contain as many individual units as would be found on four or five blocks of one-family homes, the elevator transportation that substitutes for the public street is paid for solely by the residents of the building; as a matter of fact, each generally pays a share of the property tax on the assessed value of the elevator, while no homeowner pays a tax on the value to him of the public street. (Yet people who live in multiple dwellings do not earn higher incomes than people who live in one-family homes.)

In the case of solid waste removal, the one-family homeowner is frequently entitled to the public service of garbage collection, especially if the home is in a large city. The garbage truck must stop at each house, where the cans of uncompacted and unincinerated waste are hoisted on board. Yet the apartment house resident pays for the internal collection of garbage and frequently for its incineration or compaction. No one has tried to justify this allocation of the costs of the utility package, but a number of writers on urban economics, including Twitchell,[1] have pointed out that no single-family-home neighborhood contributes enough revenues to the municipal government to pay for the costs of the utility services its residents are given.

It follows from the nature of the three packages that housing must be long-lived. The construction specifications written by government to establish standards for safe shelter imply a long life. Moreover, the utility package, with its connections between the individual housing unit and the world, cannot be broken off and reestablished frivolously. Because elements in the utility and social packages—schools and churches,

5

power stations and highways—are themselves costly, they come into existence only when their proposed service area looks as though it will be permanently populated. Thus, municipalities cannot build roads or establish services unless they have the stable tax base that permanent houses ensure, but that tents and trailer camps do not.

Housing is also expensive, by which *we* mean that it can be built and maintained only through the allocation of many resources to its constituent packages. (Of course, when the ordinary man says that good housing is expensive, he means, with apparent simplicity, that the packages cost a great deal of money.) Money provides the mechanism through which resources are allocated to distinct functions in the economic system. A knowledge of money is important to the builder, because he must have an adequate supply of money when he starts to work. On the other hand, those who specialize in the lending of money are particularly interested in the fact that housing is long-lived. This quality helps to determine the way in which money is advanced for housing purposes.

No one can understand housing and its problems without understanding money and its problems. The system by which money is accumulated and then loaned for housing purposes is an integral part of the process by which resources are allocated to housing. Therefore, no one can intelligently correct the inadequacies of the present housing supply without understanding the money system. Yet understanding the limitations of monetary remedies is as important as grasping their potentialities; many schemes for improving the housing supply solely by monetary means have produced unexpected and sometimes unwelcome results.

Understanding the money system as a whole includes the understanding of three major elements: first, the fundamentals of the money market, where the cost of borrowing money is in almost constant fluctuation; second, the institutions that characteristically make loans for housing purposes; and third, the impact of the government on the money market and the institutions.

In the American economy of the 1970s, resources are allocated by private and governmental decisions that are rarely preceded by a calculation of the precise quantities and characteristics of the resources being allocated.

Thus, when officials of the Bowery Savings Bank forecast their allocations to housing for the coming year, they do not resolve to provide home builders with 3 billion bricks, five thousand acres of land, or 6 million man-hours of labor. Instead, they merely predict that the bank's

6

gross cash flows from deposits, interest income, and mortgage repayments will enable it to invest a certain sum of money—say $500 million —in mortgage loans on new buildings during the year ahead. Similarly, when the appropriations committees of the United States Congress decide that low-rent public housing should be built, they do not allocate land or manpower to the builders of these projects. They simply authorize the Department of Housing and Urban Development (HUD) to take money that the government has collected from taxpayers and then arrange, in a very complicated way, to give it to the builders of the housing projects. The needed land and manpower are expected to follow as this money claims them.

The universal acceptability of money as a claim for goods and services means that once a builder has dollars in hand he can trade them for the physical components of housing. True, emergencies like a war may so augment the demand for specific resources—copper and steel, for example—that the modern state can ensure the usefulness of its money only by limiting its universal acceptability; that is, by rationing goods and services. But any such governmental effort to limit the freedom with which citizens dispose of their money creates personal discomfort and, with it, political dissatisfaction. Even those who believe that the universal acceptability of money should be curtailed in the public interest pay tribute to the depth of feeling opposed to such a curtailment.

Historically, we might add, the forces that limit the universal acceptability of money have been considered inhuman by moralists. A barroom braggart may, in tired jest, buy a drink for a friend while telling him: "Your money is no good here." But these words echo a far more ominous tradition: "Your money is no good here, because we don't serve niggers, or spicks, or sheenies, or papists." The suggestion that "inferior" races should "know their place" means that money in their hands is no longer acceptable in exchange for a house, a hotel room, or even a counter seat anywhere they are not welcome.

But if freedom to exercise the universal acceptability of money is one of the most important rights enjoyed by the members of an industrialized society, and if the disposition of money controls the allocation of resources, how is the allocation of resources to housing to be increased? In an economy that combines private and public economic activity, the shift of resources to housing can be accomplished in only two ways—either by making the movement of money into housing so attractive to the private money-holder that he will pursue it voluntarily or else by compulsory government taxation and appropriation.

In every political order, taxation represents the extreme form of de-

priving the private citizen of his right to exploit the universal acceptability of his money. That is why taxation is unpopular. Even in socialist
countries that own and control all means of production and in which
taxation is concealed as the "profits" of the state industries, the state
encourages the movement of private funds into housing through the sale
of bonds, sometimes with lottery chances attached. This, at least, is a
method in use in Poland, Rumania, and the Soviet Union.

In a mixed economy like ours, the political advantages of voluntary
savings over taxation are obvious. Even those who support higher taxes
to achieve public benefits lose their philanthropic smile when the time
comes to file their tax return and sign the check that goes with it. Besides, to accumulate enough money to meet our housing needs solely
through taxation would force the government to set a tax rate so high
that it would inevitably have a depressing effect on the general economy from the time when the taxes were first collected to the time when
enough money would be gathered to pay for the whole cost of the new
housing units. It is doubtful that a free electoral process would produce
a government willing to support so high a tax rate except under conditions of a generally perceived national emergency.

Because it is thus practically impossible to raise the funds needed for
adequate housing by means of taxation alone, we are left with the voluntary pooling of money as the major method for collecting housing
resources. Although it is possible in theory to develop a system of forced
savings, in which the people would sometime get back the money taken
from them, in practice they hardly recognize the fine difference between
forced savings—as in the Social Security System—and taxation—as in the
federal income tax. Both sums are withheld from the average wage
earner's pay before he gets it. In both socialized and mixed economies,
liquid savings are most likely to occur when people are confident that
they can recall their money to active service whenever *they* want it,
and when they can reasonably hope to earn a return on the value of
their accumulations.

To understand the process by which resources become available and
are then allocated to the production and maintenance of housing, one
must first survey how savings are collected by the special institutions
that will make the housing allocations. These institutions were not
formed in deference to a preconceived plan to accumulate resources
and place them in housing. Rather, they grew in response to their institutional needs as these were perceived by their officers, and by the
legislators who controlled them in what they took to be the interest of
the savers and of the general public.

Equally important, the nature of money itself changes. Money can be considered as the mass of universally acceptable, transferable, deferrable claims for goods and services. Once men and women have been paid in money for their goods and services, their choice between spending and saving will determine subsequent allocations of resources. The money that people spend voluntarily may compete with the very purpose of their jobs, or for which their savings are used by the officers of savings institutions. Imagine an automobile worker trained to install filters that will reduce air pollution. He may voluntarily buy a new automobile that tends to increase air pollution. He puts his savings in an institution whose mortgage loans make home construction possible. But the automobile he has bought tends to increase the demand for new roads that can be built only at the cost of actually destroying homes that are in the way. As long as people are free to spend and save with a measure of personal liberty, all projections of the costs and effects of economic programs must contain allowance for an element that is never precisely known in advance. The money originally allocated to accomplish a specific objective may—having filtered through the hands and minds of those who received it—tend to accomplish a different, perhaps even a conflicting objective.

In the discussion of the several types of fiscal institutions involved in housing, this characteristic of money must be kept in mind. Without such recall, the student of housing is likely to grow impatient with all of the indirection and subtlety by which money is lured into pools that feed the housing industry. If the money itself is less than alive, it is nevertheless more than inanimate; and the attempt to curtail its general usefulness involves a curtailment of human freedom that, at this period in history, not even the most unified and ideologically rigid state can achieve without peril to its stability.

CHAPTER 2

THE EQUITY

AS WE NOTED in Chapter 1, a builder of housing must have money available before he starts to work. That is the first essential. The question we must ask is: Where does the builder's money come from? To answer it, we must look to the institutions that collect money for housing purposes.

In simplest form, the builder is a single person who intends to create a home for himself and, perhaps, his family. Henry David Thoreau, erecting his cabin on the shores of Walden Pond, was such a one. So was William Faulkner's fictitious Thomas Sutpen, who established his family seat, Sutpen's Hundred, in the woods of Yoknapatawpha County with a force of wild slaves and bricks baked from the local clay. Literature is amply supplied with heroic figures who build homes for themselves with resources wrested from their environment, but their real presence in the current American economy is quite rare. Few Americans build their own homes with their own resources; only a small minority of American families today enjoy the luxury of engaging an architect to design a home to fit their personalities, at least as they see themselves. According to the annual surveys of HUD and the Bureau of the Census, less than 10 percent of the total annual housing production is built to order for specific customers.[1]

Whether we talk of vacation cottages on a tract near the sea or of mammoth housing projects built for fifteen thousand families at the edge of a city, most American homes are currently built on speculation. This means that the great majority of American builders merely *believe* that people will choose to live in the houses they build. A builder may have researched his market carefully in advance with all of the tools developed by social science; or he may be operating on instinct schooled by experience. In either case, having no firm commitment from anyone to buy or rent the accommodations he is providing, he cannot turn to the future users for the ready cash he needs increasingly as the work of construction progresses.

The profit-motivated speculative builder will expect either to rent or to sell his finished product. But while the profit incentive inspires most of the builders in the United States, some are not interested in profits. Among these are government agencies, including the local housing authorities, that build and own all of the subsidized low-rent public housing in the country. In a sense, they too build on speculation, because they do not know that anyone will choose to live in one of these projects until they have tried to rent it. Sometimes these projects do not meet the market test of eligible renters; they remain empty or they become empty. A number of *nonprofit* private agencies also build housing on speculation in the United States (as in other lands). These include union or neighborhood groups, who may be building for sale to cooperative societies organized by or for their members. Other nonprofit builders may be seeking to assist affiliated institutions, such as hospitals, by providing low-rent apartments for their staffs.

Whatever the purpose of all of these builders, profit or nonprofit, and no matter whether they intend to sell or lease their product, all share one characteristic. They must look to others to provide them with resources. Except in the case of a few cooperatives that will be sold to their future owners before completion, funds to acquire the resources must be supplied by professional lenders.

In general, the funds invested by the builders themselves in their own work are called equity funds. In the simplest possible case, in which everything goes well, the builder will sell his product at a price high enough to repay all of the equity money that he invested, and to give him a profit besides. The remainder of the money that the builder needs in order to construct the house is borrowed from a lender on the security of the house itself. Such a loan, usually secured by the conditional transfer of the title to the house, is called a mortgage. We have now come to the two key words that link housing finance to the money market: *equity* and *mortgage*.

The equity investment in housing confers ownership on the equity investor. Ownership either provides for the owner's possession and use of the housing unit or it confers on the owner the right to sell it or to receive the income produced by allowing someone else to use the housing unit in exchange for a fee called rent. Sometimes, as in the case of a two-family house, ownership provides, in a sense, both possession and income; the owner may live in part of the house and lease out the remainder.

The mortgage investment in housing, on the other hand, confers ownership only in the event that the equity owner fails to make the payments required by the terms of the mortgage note, or defaults in some other serious obligation, such as allowing the building to deteriorate dangerously or not paying the taxes. If we could split a new house into mortgage parts and equity parts, we would find that the mortgage parts are far more numerous. This means that the ability to borrow mortgage money is a talent essential to anyone seeking to build a single home for himself, or to develop tract houses or an apartment complex for ownership and profit, or to develop government-assisted or government-owned housing for social and public reasons.

It may seem that in this respect housing hardly differs from other forms of economic production. In all of them, the ability to raise capital is a crucial entrepreneurial talent. Yet housing *is* different; although housing is a consumer good, *its* capital needs do not precisely resemble the needs of other consumer goods industries. Moreover, according to the president's 1972 Report on Housing Goals, the size of the annual national demand for mortgage capital exceeds all other demands for investment funds.[2] The net mortgage acquisitions of all major lenders in 1972 came to almost $120 billion.[3] Thus, looked at from the supply side, the need for housing capital offers the opportunity to put $120 billion of family and individual savings to work. They might otherwise be placed under the mattress or in the ground, where their removal from the active money supply would discourage activity and employment throughout the whole economy.

Because mortgage loans represent a major investment for the savings of American families, and because American families live in houses, some might wonder why mortgage debt is necessary. Why don't families put their own savings into their own houses, doing away with the whole mortgage institution with one blow? There are several related answers to this question.

One obvious answer is that the families with savings are not necessarily those who need homes. Like income, savings are distributed unequally among families. Age is one major factor in the inequality of savings. Families buy homes at one stage of their lives—usually soon after marriage—but they are likely to have accumulated their greatest savings at a much later stage, perhaps when they are at the point of retirement and have no need for the large house in which they raised their children. Geography also makes a difference. The migration of people seeking jobs in the developing parts of the country creates a large demand for housing, while cash savings may well be higher in the older parts of the country, where there is less competition for investment funds for new industries and governmental construction.

A second reason for the existence of the mortgage institution can be found in the fact that almost one-third of 1972 construction was in apartment houses [4] for families who cannot afford, or do not want, to invest their money in real estate that they occupy. In the case of rented apartments, the size of the project means that the savings of many families must be pooled to provide the necessary funds. Indeed, as we shall see when we examine mortgage institutions, the average savings account in the United States is not nearly large enough to pay for even a single new home.

Third, many families continue to carry mortgages on their homes even though they could dip into their savings to reduce their mortgages or repay them entirely at a net saving of interest cost. Perhaps they prefer to retain contractual rights—like pension or death benefits in life insurance contracts—that would be lost if they were to surrender the contracts to extract cash for investment in their own homes. Perhaps they wish to take advantage of the income tax deductibility of mortgage interest. Perhaps they prefer the greater liquidity of bank accounts or life insurance policies. Money can be easily removed from banks or life insurance policies; money invested in a house cannot.

Money invested in a factory or farm machinery contributes to the production of tangible wealth; money invested in housing contributes, instead, primarily to the satisfaction of its users. Therefore, the provision of housing capital must be regarded as a form of consumer financing. Its purpose is to enable customers to enjoy the use of a product —housing—long before they have saved up the money needed to pay for its construction. Yet it differs from other consumer financing—such as automobile or washing machine loans—because the house itself lasts a much longer time than all other consumer goods that are in general use. (Diamond rings and works of art may last much longer than houses, but, perhaps regrettably, they are not in general use.)

The longer useful life of a house, when contrasted with other items that consumers want to use before they can pay for them, means that a mortgage loan secured by a house can extend over a much longer period than a chattel mortgage secured by an automobile, a suite of furniture, or a motorboat. The typical automobile loan runs for a period of three years; each month, the car owner pays the earned interest and some of the principal until at the end of the thirty-six months the loan will be entirely paid off.

The much greater length of a residential mortgage loan constitutes one of the essential features of housing finance. What is the useful life of a house? While a few castles and other stately homes stand reasonably intact after four or five centuries of use and abuse, it is probably an exaggeration to claim that they are still in use as houses: Only a few rare aristocrats remarkably endowed with cash can afford to heat or paint their vast and chilly rooms at modern cost levels. Many one-hundred-year-old buildings still do provide good housing, but their present quality reflects large amounts of new capital that was put into them over the years to repair defects, to modernize, and to stretch their useful life. Probably, fifty or sixty years should be the longest term over which housing can be expected to survive without substantial reinvestment. Without special security, in the form, perhaps, of government insurance against default, few professional lenders would dare to risk a mortgage loan whose term would exceed twenty years. Of $400 billion of mortgages outstanding in 1973, 31.7 percent was insured by a government agency.[5] If the mortgage on a new house requires full repayment within less than thirty years, the owner, or his tenants, face monthly housing costs far beyond the typical family's means.

We must recognize that while the long term of the housing mortgage makes it possible to repay the principal in relatively small spoonfuls, it also greatly increases the impact of interest cost, which is simply the fee paid by the borrower for the use of the lender's money. In the typical three-year automobile loan, we may assume that interest will be charged at the rate of 12 percent on the loan balance. Total interest charges over the three years will come to about 18 percent of the basic cost of the car. A thirty-year mortgage on a house may carry an interest rate of only 8 percent a year on the loan balance, but the total interest charges over the thirty-year period will come to approximately 120 percent of the original cost of the house; the interest, in short, will overshadow the original cost of the house. So we see that the mortgage interest rate is the single most important element in the cost of housing.

We shall reserve for the next chapter a discussion of mortgages and of the expectations of those who make mortgage loans. (We shall thereafter examine what might be done to lower the interest cost of mortgage loans.) But there is one aspect of the structure of mortgage loans that is crucially important to our present discussion of equity financing. That is the debt-to-value ratio.

The builder who builds housing units in order to sell them knows that he cannot do so unless buyers are able to borrow the money to pay the major part of their cost. The lower the interest rate on the mortgages, and the longer the term of repayment, the more easily the builder will be able to sell his houses, because the lower the necessary income of prospective buyers, the greater their number. Thus, because the builder's profit will depend on the number of homes he can build and sell—the more homes, presumably, the greater his profit—he is necessarily very much concerned with the ratio of mortgage debt to the total selling price of the house. The higher the ratio, the smaller the amount of equity capital the builder needs per house, and the greater the number of houses that the builder can erect with a fixed sum of equity capital.

If the ratio drops, and the builder finds he can arrange for each house only a smaller mortgage than he expected, he will be forced to cut down the size or complexity of the houses he might build, or build fewer of them, or raise the size of the cash equity investment that each home buyer must make, thus cutting down the possible number of eligible buyers. In either case, the builder's profit will be reduced by the state of the mortgage market. A point may come when builders will cancel their plans altogether, because the terms on which mortgages are offered destroy their incentive to invest equity capital.

Of course, the builder may expect to profit from other aspects of his work besides the selling price of the houses. He may, for example, wish to invest in a shopping center adjacent to the houses he builds; in such a case, he might be willing to accept a somewhat smaller profit on each house, because he hopes to receive continuing income from the shopping center. The economic health of the shopping center will depend on the number of families moving into the adjacent development. Even then the availability of mortgage credit at attractive terms will shape the builder's plans. If expensive credit cuts down his home-selling market, the profitability of the shopping center is reduced.

Sometimes such builders may have another, longer-range plan to profit from their activities. They may own very large tracts of land that were acquired at very low prices. By building successfully on a significant part of the tract, they may expect to increase the value of the remaining vacant land to other builders. Here, profit will come from an increase in the value of the land. The economics of building a new town, for example, are largely based on the notion that heavy investment in

basic industrial and public facilities and home construction will stimulate a compensatory rise in the demand for land in and around the
new town. But such a long-range plan also depends for its success on
the ability of the builder—whether a private entity or a public body—
to borrow money to make the original improvements. (No one has yet
convincingly proved that the value of the new town is a real increase
or whether it represents a shift in value that is balanced by the loss in
value of the older cities from which the new town population came.)

The complexity of financing a new town development contrasts
sharply with the investment simplicity of a builder who constructs a
single apartment house or a complex of apartment houses for sale to
their occupants, either jointly, as in a cooperative corporation, or separately, as in a condominium. The profit-motivated builder of either type
of structure derives his reward from the gap between his cost and the
price at which he can sell; his greatest risk is the time lag between
completion of the building and that happy moment when enough customers have appeared so that the cooperative can legally be declared
in effect. This declaration relieves him of any obligation to make good
the deficits of those who were the first to buy apartments and move in.
Here, again, the builder cannot build unless he has been assured of
mortgage terms that will make the building attractive to its future
residents. This usually means a very high ratio of loan to building value
so as to reduce the amount of cash each of the new owners must sub-
scribe. The interest rate may not be so important as the long term of
the mortgage loan, because the builder will advertise the extent of income tax credits from which his customers will benefit. The interest they
will pay will be deductible from their gross income. The amortization
payments, which are simply repayments of the original mortgage borrowing, will not.

The equity investment becomes considerably more important for
builders who expect to profit from the benefits of continued ownership.
In general, there are three such benefits. The first, obviously, is the
profit of earning a high cash return annually on the equity investment
by taking in a higher income from the rents than one pays out in expenses. This income is sweetened by a second benefit: Federal income
tax statutes permit depreciation to be charged each year as though it
were a cash outlay. Depreciation represents that part of the initial cost
of an improvement that must be deducted from its original value each
year so that at the end of its theoretical useful life, it will have no
value remaining on the books of the owners. If a building worth $4
million has a theoretical useful life of forty years, its annual *straight-line*

depreciation is $100,000 per year. If the net income of the building, after paying interest on the mortgage, but before amortization, is also $100,000 per year, the depreciation allowance would offset the income in full; the owner would then pay no income tax on these earnings, out of which he must usually pay the annual amortization of his mortgage loans.

The builder, or the building syndicate, who owns a rental apartment house naturally tries to invest as little of his own money as possible. Obviously, the smaller his own equity, the larger the rate of his profits and the more buildings he can finance with the same investment capital. But the builder is constrained by another set of forces from seeking too large a mortgage or series of mortgages. The larger the mortgage debt, the heavier the interest payments and the greater the need for funds to meet amortization requirements. A builder who uses too much leverage—that is, wields a very large amount of mortgage debt with a very small amount of equity capital—runs the danger of losing his ownership completely if a relatively small drop in rent or a small rise in operating costs diminish his net income below his debt service.

A third possible source of benefit to the owner of rental property lies in the possibility of selling it profitably after owning it for several years. Under present federal income tax laws, the difference between the original cost of the building and its sales price is taxed at capital gains rates.[6] Usually, the difference between the *original cost* and the *depreciated cost* is, however, subject to recapture by the government at ordinary income tax rates.

The tax laws—which, of course, may be changed by Congress—provided in 1973 that the owner of a multiple dwelling that was used to house people of moderate income, and whose rents and profits were subject to control, could derive two special income tax benefits from the ownership.

First, the law stipulated that instead of straight-line depreciation, the owner of a qualifying building could use so-called double-declining-balance depreciation. This means that the effective rate of depreciation would be twice as high as the normal rate. In a building with a life of forty years, the normal straight-line depreciation is 2.5 percent per year on the original cost. In a qualifying building, the rate is 5 percent, but the depreciation is charged against a lower base each year, the base representing the original cost minus depreciation charges already taken. Imagine a building that cost $10 million; straight-line depreciation at 2.5 percent would provide a depreciation reserve of $250,000 in the first year. In a building qualifying for the double-declining-balance treat-

Fundamentals

ment, the depreciation reserve in the first year would be $500,000. In the second year, the cost basis of the building would be reduced by $500,000 to $9.5 million. Therefore, the depreciation allowance in the second year would be $475,000 in the qualifying building. In a building depreciated on the straight-line basis, the depreciation allowance remains a constant $250,000 per year; in the qualifying building, the depreciation allowance diminishes each year.

If a qualifying building is owned by taxpayers who have another taxable income, the depreciation charge can be used to offset the other income and to reduce the income tax that would otherwise be paid on it.

A second advantage provided to owners of qualifying buildings is that they are allowed to treat the recapture of the depreciation at the time of sale as though it were capital gains instead of ordinary income.

These benefits have been so great for people with large pretax incomes that builders have been able to sell the building before or right after construction for considerably more than their invested equity. Even some nonprofit public agencies, like New York's Urban Development Corporation, manage to take what amounts to a profit from the sale of the ownership tax benefits on new developments to long-term, high-income investors. The ability to effectuate such a sale depends on a very high mortgage-to-value ratio. Without this, the investors would have to put up too much equity cash, in covering the development cost, to be willing to pay an additional sum for the depreciation benefits.

In residential rental property held for sale, the builder's objective is to provide a mortgage debt pattern that will make the building most attractive to the prospective purchaser. The purchaser of an existing residential rental building must feel that the return on his equity investment in the building will be competitive with other possible investments, considering the risks as well as the possibility of resale. In making this calculation, the prospective owner must take into account the mortgage market and its interest rates, not only because those rates increase or decrease the profit on his equity but also because the rates of interest that he must pay provide a standard of comparison against which to measure the rate of return he should expect to earn on his own money.

Housing deliberately built for rent is a relatively novel invention of the industrial world; in New York City, for example, the first "tenant houses," a description that was later condensed to "tenements," were built in the 1840s. Until 1900, the ownership of residential rental buildings was of interest only to rather small investors, each of whom owned one or at most a few such houses. With the development of the electric

18

elevator, and other such complexities as flush toilets, central heat, hot water, and electricity, ownership of apartment buildings began to require a more substantial equity investment. Some builders who had started on a very small scale grew big enough to develop many residential buildings with their own equity capital, but most large apartment buildings are erected with equity capital provided by syndicates of investors. Current income tax policies favor the limited partnership, or the Real Estate Investment Trust, as the form of ownership. None of these forms of entrepreneurial investment could exist in the field of residential real estate if it were not possible to borrow large sums of mortgage money. The investors would simply be unable to gather up the large sums of money needed to finance residential construction.

This impression is reinforced in the nonprofit and the governmental sector of residential building. It can be laid down as a matter of principle that not even the most heavily endowed private, nonprofit institutions, such as the ivy league universities of the eastern United States, can build adequate housing without using the mortgage money made available with federal or, sometimes, state aid. If even the wealthy university cannot construct the relatively inexpensive dormitory housing, then it is fruitless to expect hospitals, neighborhood groups, or labor unions to use their own money (if they have any) to provide the funds necessary to construct housing for others. (Many unions indeed have large financial resources, but the general policy of the union usually requires, perhaps not always successfully, that these resources be invested to produce the greatest safe return for the benefit of *all* their members. Using these funds to provide the capital for *some* moderate-income families would require them to be satisfied with a very modest return.)

Thus, all nonprofit housing programs for moderate- and low-income families require the smallest possible equity investment and the largest possible mortgage. Mortgages of 100 percent of cost are authorized under some nonprofit programs for special purposes, but even in these cases, *some* equity capital must be provided by the sponsor, if only to get the architectural plans started and to hire a lawyer who will help arrange the mortgage financing. There are, in addition, some programs —both government and private—that provide so-called seed money grants, repayable only under certain circumstances, to finance the initial working capital needed by a nonprofit agency. In the case of government-owned housing, as in the federally subsidized low-income public housing program, initial planning advances are made to local housing authorities by the federal government. This constitutes their equity capital. It is ultimately repaid to the government when an authority borrows enough money from the public to cover all the costs of development.

The nonprofit and government builders of housing are, by definition, interested in large mortgage loans that will keep the equity investment small, long-term mortgages, and low interest rates. To see how difficult this prescription is, and the circumstances under which it might be achieved, it is necessary to look at the other side of the picture—the mortgage loan itself and what its maker wants.

CHAPTER 3

THE MORTGAGE

IN THE previous chapter, we examined in very broad outline what benefit the equity investor expects from his investment in housing. As we noted, most of these expectations depend on the arrangements that can be made for borrowing money against the value of the housing—that is, on a mortgage loan. But what does the lender of mortgage money expect when he makes his loan?

Not surprisingly, the lender of mortgage money has two objectives that differ from the borrower's. First, he hopes to earn as high a rate of interest as possible. Second, he hopes to lend safely—he wants to get his money back as promised. Obviously, the first objective squarely confronts the hope of the borrower for low interest rates. As in any business transaction, the two sides ultimately agree only because each of them is under pressure. The mortgage lender—who is called the mortgagee because the property that constitutes the security of the loan is conditionally transferred *to* him when the mortgage loan is agreed to, or closed—usually is under some pressure to make loans because only by making them can he earn income on his own savings or the savings that have been entrusted to him by others. The borrower or builder, who is called the mortgagor, obviously needs the money to satisfy his personal housing requirements or to carry on his building business. The pressures on each side may be uneven. When building demand is slack, the lender may be extremely anxious to close new loans; when money is tight, the builder may be hard pressed to borrow at any price.

It is impossible to select a stipulated rate of interest and proclaim that this is the *true* mortgage rate that would come about when the pressures on mortgagees to lend are precisely as heavy as the pressures on mortgagors to borrow. In the United States during the last twenty-five years, interest rates on mortgage loans for residential properties have rarely been less than 3 percent a year, or more than 10 percent a year.[1] This seven point spread may seem fairly narrow, but not when we remember that a 10 percent rate of interest is more than 3 times as great as a 3 percent rate. In the first year of a $25,000 mortgage on a new home, the 10 percent mortgage would require interest payments of $2,500. The 3 percent mortgage would require interest payments of only $750. Obviously, many families who can afford to pay interest of $750 per year on their home would be unable to pay interest of $2,500 on the same home. This fact, of course, has important consequences for the builders of homes, to say nothing of those who might want to live in them.

The impossibility of fixing a true mortgage rate that is permanently equitable has not prevented state legislatures from adopting laws against usury in an attempt to set maximum interest rates. Historically, these rates have been set at 6 percent on real estate mortgage loans. Legal interest ceilings on smaller consumer loans, which are much riskier and more expensive to make per dollar loaned, have been set higher, while loans to corporations have been exempt from regulation altogether. But in recent years, in response to a general rise in interest rates, usury ceilings have been raised in most if not all states.

State usury laws are merely a special, institutionalized expression of the feeling of many borrowers that the payment of interest serves no very useful purpose, and that the economy would be more humane if interest were limited or abolished. A state law that restricts lenders to making all, or a substantial part, of their loans within a specific radius of their establishments would appear to be inspired by the same natural sense. By limiting the scope of each lender's market, the legislators hope that lenders will be forced to extend credit to borrowers who might otherwise be considered too risky, or to lend generally at rates lower than they might be in a less restricted market.

To a limited extent, antiusury laws are probably effective. They keep interest rates down on loans made within a state, but unless all states move to pass identical laws (which is most unlikely, as long as some states need housing capital more than others), they merely encourage lenders to explore opportunities for making loans elsewhere. If the federal government passed an antiusury law affecting mortgage rates (assuming that it could do so constitutionally), it would tend to drive lending institutions to explore other uncontrolled forms of investment —bonds or stocks, commercial real estate, landownership, or foreign securities. If *all* interest rates were controlled by law within the United States, investment funds would move abroad. Laws limiting the investments of lenders in whole or part to specific geographic areas do tend to lower the earnings of the lenders, and to influence savers to place their funds elsewhere. Generally, such laws hurt small savers more than large ones, who are more sophisticated in finding investment opportunities, or better able to pay others for finding them on their behalf.

Coming now to the second major objective of the lenders in making mortgage loans—safety—we find that it cannot be absolutely separated from the question of interest rate. There are some mortgage loans that are too risky to make at any rate, but there are others that lenders feel they can make at, say, 9.5 percent, but not at 7 percent, because they are too risky for a 7 percent rate.

This distinction may seem irrational to the casual observer. After all, if a $1 million mortgage loan is not likely to be repaid, how will the extra 2.5 percent interest help the distraught lender? Yet there is a certain logic in the rate differential, provided that one imagines that the difference is intended to compensate the mortgagee for added costs that might be incurred in collecting late payments, and for lost earnings on payments that come in after the due date and that could have been reinvested during the unpleasant wait. The added interest income earned on many risky mortgages can be used to build up a reserve against which a few future defaults would be charged. There will probably be only a few real losses, except in the course of a major economic catastrophe, or of unusual stupidity or venality on the part of a mortgage loan officer.

Differential interest rates are not, however, the principal answer to the risk of nonpayment. The most obvious assurance of mortgage loan security must be the prospective ability of a specific mortgagor to meet the payments required in the mortgage note. When a lender issues a mortgage commitment to cover individual homes, so that the builder of the tract of homes can obtain temporary financing before he begins construction, the prospective mortgagee stipulates in his letter of commitment that he will issue permanent financing on each home only if its buyer meets the mortgagee's standards of credit worthiness.

Institutional lenders, such as savings banks, consider homeowners' credit worthy only if their regular earnings are big enough to cover comfortably all living expenses plus the mortgage carrying costs. Because individual mortgagees apply different rules in calculating the credit worthiness of the mortgagor, it is impossible to assert a single national credit standard. In general, however, mortgagees require that the household earnings reach or exceed five times the annual mortgage payments and taxes. Some mortgagees regard the earnings of anyone other than the father of the household as temporary and hypothetical: Wives may, they think, give up work to have another child, or for any other reason. Young members of the family may, and probably will, move away to establish households of their own. In some cases, these bland and reasonable rules may be applied unfairly to women who are as deeply dedicated to their careers as men can be. Similarly, the rules may cloak a measure of conscious or unconscious prejudice against non-white mortgagors, under a purported fear that discounts the high earnings of nonwhites as so unusual that they may be subject to wide swings. An "equal opportunity lender" is one who pledges not to allow this type of misapprehension to occur.

In the case of mortgages on apartment houses, the lender may specify that the permanent mortgage will not be closed, or that a part of the funds involved may be withheld, until a stipulated percentage of the apartments are rented at a stipulated average rental. In order to meet these terms in an unfriendly market, builder-owners will sometimes offer concessions to lure new tenants into the mortgage premises. These concessions may consist of a temporary reduction of rent for a number of months at the beginning of the lease. (Of course, the permanent rent, which begins at the end of the concession period, is high enough to be acceptable to the mortgage lender under the terms of the commitment.) Another form of concession may be a free, onetime service, performed for a new tenant who agrees to enter at an acceptable permanent rent. The onetime service may be in the form of free wall-to-wall carpeting, a vacation trip to Europe, or a mink coat. In any case, the objective is the same: A tenant who can be tallied by the owner as part of the percentage of occupancy demanded by the mortgagee.

Finally, in an effort to maintain the safety of their loans, mortgagees may refuse to permit the transfer of the mortgage liability to the new owner at the time a property is sold, thus continuing the liability of the first owner under the existing mortgage even though he no longer has an interest in the home. This refusal to release the seller can be a considerable embarrassment to the original mortgagor. His continuing liability for future defaults on the mortgage of his old home may make it impossible for him to qualify for a mortgage on a new home. If rigidly enforced, the hardships imposed by nonrelease would impede the transfer of real property and, therefore, seriously undermine the sales price of residential real estate. Because this would ultimately affect the value of mortgaged real property, mortgage lenders are not usually sticky in giving mortgage releases to sellers of mortgaged premises, provided that the buyer comes within the qualifying range of income. Consent to the transfer of a mortgage liability has become easier to grant since the general use of an amortizing mortgage. If the terms of a mortgage have required periodic repayment of principal (amortization), the outstanding debt at the time of sale will have been reduced below its starting level. Therefore, the new owner will find it easier to qualify than the first owner did. If the resale purchase price is higher than the original price when the mortgage was put on, the mortgagee's security is enhanced by the increase. If the sale price is considerably higher, the purchaser will not wish to continue the old mortgage, but may seek a new, larger one from the same lender, or another one.

In the final analysis, satisfactory earnings on the part of the mortgage are not enough to ensure the untroubled slumber of mortgage officers. For mortgage officers are not in the personal loan business; they are in the property loan business. No other type of property shares the two major qualifications of residential real estate: It is permanent in nature, and it is the object of universal demand. These two qualities make possible the financing of residential real estate so large an infusion with borrowed money, secured by the intrinsic value of the collateral property.

We have already noted that housing is a long-lived piece of consumer goods and that it can be compared, in this respect, to diamond rings and works of art. But the permanence on which mortgage officers rely in making loans of real estate refers not only to the longevity of the dwelling but to the fact that the property is permanently fixed in a specific place. This enables them not only to lend on the security of the property but to permit the property owner to retain possession of the house even while it constitutes loan collateral. This is very different from the way bankers treat stock certificates or pawnbrokers treat jewelry.

A twenty-carat diamond ring may be worth as much as a small house, perhaps as much as a rather large house. But mortgage officers will not (in fact, as a matter of law, they cannot) lend money on a diamond ring. It passes so readily from hand to hand that if the borrower defaults in his loan payments, the lender may not be able to establish who owns it. A pawnbroker who lends money on a diamond ring slaps it into his safe until the loan is paid.

The final resting place of a house is an immovable parcel of land, identifiable by metes and bounds. Ownership of the parcel is recorded in official documents, and so are the conditional transfers that are set up in mortgage documents. While the possibility of erroneous ascription is not totally eliminated, it is reduced to the point at which title insurance can be procured very cheaply to eliminate entirely the risk of error.

The universal demand for residential property underscores the platitude that while everybody needs a place to live, no one actually needs a diamond ring, however friendly girls may proverbially find them. Although certain artifacts, like Rembrandt's painting of Aristotle, are worth notorious fortunes simply because they are unique, the value of housing as collateral is largely due to the fact that everyone must have it.

There are, of course, significant exceptions to the general rule that because everyone needs a house in which to lay his head, housing is the object of universal demand. If a residential building is designed to look strange or "ahead of its time" or idiosyncratic to a specific owner, its mere permanence will not encourage the mortgage officer to believe that he will be able to sell it readily in satisfaction of a defaulted note. The mortgage system thus tends to inhibit experiments and novelty in architecture, in the social package of the house as well as its design. If prejudice against racial minorities tends to keep white families from moving to an integrated area, the resale value of buildings in such an area is likely to be lower than that of similar buildings elsewhere. More important, the mortgage officer is likely to *think* that the resale of integrated housing will be difficult.

The very nature of mortgage lending in a modern economy—the process of entrusting someone else's money into the care and custody of a third party—pricks the caution of the mortgage officer. His responsibility to the savers who have confided in him leads him to sniff for possible changes that may undermine or restrict universal demand for the residential collateral. Unfortunately, the fears of mortgage officers tend to be self-fulfilling. When lenders fear to lend in an area, their fears are often confirmed because the shutting off of new capital resources discourages purchasers, and this in turn discourages costly maintenance and rehabilitation. It is sometimes difficult to decide which came first, the actual deterioration of an area or the fear on the part of mortgage lenders that the area was deteriorating.

Once a mortgage officer has, on behalf of a lender, satisfied himself that the mortgagor will be unlikely to default on his obligation, and that the housing collateral is permanent and universally in demand, one might imagine that his fears of risk would have been allayed. This is not the case, however. Every experienced mortgage officer knows that he may be wrong about both the borrower and the collateral. The mortgagor almost never has enough assets in hand at the time of the mortgage closing to permit him to avoid ever having to earn money to meet the monthly payments and his other living expenses. Mortgage officers are not paid to ruminate about the unforeseen metamorphoses that characterize the human condition: the plagues, the famines, the personal disagreements, the wars, the temptations, the weaknesses that interfere with a mortgagor's future earnings and turn a sound credit risk into a will-o'-the-wisp. Nor can mortgage officers spend their time considering changes in human taste that may, in a strikingly short time, make unfashionable the most dearly beloved styles of architecture, location, or room arrangement. The mortgage officer does know that neighborhoods change and that such changes may adversely affect not only the price that houses can command, but their value as loan collateral.

The mortgage officer's major protection against such vicissitudes is to insist on making only relatively small loans against a relatively large current value of housing. If, for example, a mortgage officer lends only 50 percent of the present value of a house, as that value is determined by professional real estate appraisers, he can comfortably look forward to recapturing the bank's investment at a forced sale even should the mortgage loan go into default. Both house and surroundings can lose a significant amount of attractiveness before reaching the point at which no willing buyer can be found for a house at one-half its original value.

Unfortunately for the sleep of a mortgage officer, a 50 percent ratio of mortgage loan to value will not usually satisfy either his employers or the borrower. From the point of view of most builder-borrowers and the owners to whom they may sell, a mortgage covering half the sale price still leaves a cash gap too large for the borrowers to bridge with their own fiscal resources. If buyers can't get a higher loan-to-value mortgage, the probability is that the housing can't be built if new, or sold if already in existence.

It is more surprising that a low loan-to-value mortgage is unattractive also from the lender (we are here distinguishing the lender as a whole from the personality and character of the mortgage officer alone). Remember that the lender derives its income from the interest charged the mortgagor: The larger the loan, the greater the interest income. The lender's costs do not increase proportionately with the size of the mortgage loan, however. Costs that must be charged against interest income do not include the original costs of placing the mortgage; these, including the title search, the bank attorney's fee, the recording costs, and a number of other items for which nonprofessional house buyers are not usually prepared, are charged to the buyer at the time the mortgage is closed. But beyond these, the lender has continuing costs in connection with its mortgages. These costs include the salary and other emoluments of the mortgage officer and his staff; the printing, postage, and clerical work of sending out notices of payments due; the checking of insurance policies and premium notices, tax bills, and handling the escrow payments to meet these charges, which the modern mortgage frequently requires the mortgagor to deposit with the lender; the occasional inspection of the premises to ensure that they are not deteriorating rapidly and that casualty losses like fire damage are properly repaired with the proceeds of insurance policies. All of these activities are comprised in the job of servicing a mortgage; axiomatically, it costs no more to service a large mortgage than a small one on the same premises, while the reinvestment of the larger increments of amortization that come back with each regular payment may be a bit simpler also than in the case of a smaller mortgage.

A third party, the United States government, also encourages the extension of mortgages on a high loan-to-value basis. The government hopes thereby to achieve better housing for all of the people and to provide a high level of employment in home-building and allied industries. In fact, to encourage mortgage lenders to make high loan-to-value mortgages, in 1934 the government established the Federal Housing Administration (FHA), which insures lenders against loss in making mortgages that bear an extremely high relationship to the value of the housing that secures them. In some circumstances, laws permit the FHA to insure mortgages up to 97 percent of allowable costs (which may even exceed 100 percent of out-of-pocket costs). But FHA-insured mortgages, which provide that the government will make good the lender's losses in the event of a default, constitute a minority of all the outstanding mortgages in the United States.[2]

If the lender and borrower agree on a loan-to-value ratio, even without FHA intervention, the process of establishing the dollar value is relatively simple. In the case of completed buildings, mortgages depend on the assistance of professional real estate appraisers to establish a fair value. The establishment of the value of an incomplete structure is much more difficult, although essential, if financing is to be supplied to a builder as construction proceeds. Many lenders who make mortgage loans on completed residential structures do not consider themselves qualified to lend on buildings under construction. As might be expected, the greater risk in this type of loan and the limited number of lenders willing to make them result in much higher interest rates on construction mortgages than on permanent mortgages; effective rates 5% higher than the rates on permanent mortgages are not unusual. In fact, when mortgage money is readily available, the spread between the construction mortgage rate and the rate on other types of corporate loans enable Real Estate Investment Trusts to borrow money from lenders who refuse to make construction loans in order to lend it profitably to builders who require them.

The lender of construction money wants to keep the ratio of loan to value so low that if the borrower defaults before the building is completed another builder can be found to finish the structure without exceeding the reasonable limits of permanent financing. To do this, the lender relies on a staff that analyzes the sequence of costs in the construction so that a reasonable schedule of payments can be worked out, geared to an accurate determination of the percentage of completion. This calls for efficient (and incorruptible) inspectors and a careful analysis of the qualifications of the contractors engaged in the work. Finally, as the building progresses, the mortgage officer of the construction lender holds back a substantial part of the money due at each payment date.

Notwithstanding devices that increase the safety of mortgages, three major and continuing objections to mortgage lending make the interest rates on mortgages higher than on other types of borrowing. The first, as we shall see, is the long term of the mortgage instrument. No matter what changes take place in the neighborhood, the individual property, the money market, or the market interest rate, the lending institution cannot demand prepayment. Meanwhile, the savers who entrusted their money to the mortgagee may insist on withdrawing their savings or closing their accounts. In a market in which savings are invested on long-term, low interest rate mortgages the lender is helpless to raise the interest rates paid to its depositors.

The second objection is closely related to the first. The mortgage itself lacks a continuing market. If a lender buys bonds that may run for the same long term as mortgages, there nevertheless exists a market where bonds can be sold long before maturity; although the seller may have to accept a below-par price, bonds at least can be liquidated, while mortgages cannot. In the natural course of events, mortgages are governed by many different laws that vary from state to state. Each reflects the credit, not of some easily examined industrial giant, but of an unknown private citizen. Consequently, no private market has developed by itself—like the New York Stock Exchange—in which mortgage holders can sell their mortgages to raise necessary cash.

The third objection to mortgages is the amortization process that provides for continuing small repayments. These cannot be reinvested easily. In fact, they cannot be reinvested at all unless the lender has so large a mortgage portfolio that repayments can be assembled into sums large enough to make at least one new mortgage loan. While the repayments remain on hand, or in the commercial banks in which mortgage lenders keep their accounts, they earn little or no interest. This, too, discourages the formation of a national mortgage market and helps to make mortgages a less attractive choice whenever the demand for loans picks up and offers alternative possibilities to lenders. Ideally, the mortgage officer would meet these objections by writing each mortgage to cover only a brief span of time. This would give him the opportunity to review changes every year, both in the condition of the building and its surroundings and also in the money market. Obviously, if interest rates rise over the year, the mortgage officer would write a renewal mortgage only on condition that the interest rate be increased to protect the lender against having to pay higher costs for its own money.

In this natural desire for a short-term mortgage, the mortgage officer runs into everyone's opposition, including other officers of his own lending agency. While it is true that the short term gives the lender an opportunity to review the condition of the collateral, this right, in practice, turns out to be expensive and not very reliable. Even if the lender's inspectors discover that the property has deteriorated, there is precious little that a mortgagee can do about it without foreclosing on the loan, itself a difficult process. If a mortgagee simply refuses to renew an expiring mortgage because of market conditions, the mortgagor will almost certainly be unable to find another mortgagee to lend him the money. The lender would then be in the rather awkward position of having to take over direct ownership and control of the property, probably the last thing in the world it wishes to do. While the possibility of higher interest on the new mortgage is seductive, the lender may instead find itself in a market in which lower interest rates prevail. If this is the case, the borrower could replace the mortgage quite easily elsewhere, because the lower rate implies an adequate supply of mortgage money. On a long-term mortgage, the lender can protect itself against an unwelcome prepayment by imposing a prepayment penalty that discourages the borrower from seeking to replace a high interest mortgage with a new mortgage at a lower rate.

In England, long-term mortgages customarily carry a variable interest rate, which may change annually in accordance with the fluctuations of an agreed-on benchmark, like the Bank of England discount rate. In British practice, the amortization schedule of a long-term mortgage varies inversely with the interest rate, so that the actual debt service each year over the life of the mortgage remains unchanged. In years when the interest rate is low, the mortgage repayment speeds up; when interest rates rise, the mortgage repayment slows down. Similar mortgage practice has often been suggested in the United States, but it has not yet been adopted. Lenders are apparently afraid that borrowers will take advantage of interest rate drops, but refuse to allow the lenders to take advantage of interest rate rises.

Following the debacle of the great depression, the United States government intervened very strongly on behalf of long-term mortgages on the grounds that they relieve homeowners from the threat of a lender's sudden refusal to renew a short-term mortgage, thus depriving the owner of his property in a forced sale.

Obviously, a long-term mortgage must provide a repayment schedule, which is called amortization. The Federal Housing Administration pioneered in the widespread development of long-term (twenty-five and thirty year) home mortgages with a very high loan-to-value ratio and a provision for total amortization over the life of the mortgage.[3] These so-called self-amortizing mortgages provide for equal monthly payments, including both interest and principal, over the life of the mortgage. At the onset, almost all of the payment is absorbed by interest, but even the small portion of amortization in the first payment reduces the outstanding principal of the loan. Therefore, slightly less interest is due to the lender in the second payment than in the first; each successive equal payment consists of a little bit more principal and a little less interest, until the final payment consists almost entirely of principal.

In the noninsured sphere of apartment house mortgaging, the mortgage terms are likely to be shorter while the amortization schedule provides less than complete self-liquidation over the terms of the mortgage. Most private lending institutions do not want to write extended loans on major properties, but expect to renew a mortgage at or before its expiration at the then current interest rate. If the loan were required to be fully self-amortizing over the typical ten- to twenty-year period, the rent structure would be so high as to be unmarketable. Because the amortization part of each payment of debt service is not considered a business expense, and must therefore come from the owner's taxable income, a fully-amortizing, short-term apartment house mortgage would be fully as unpopular with the owner as with the tenants.

Finally, the mortgage officer of the lending institution expects to enjoy a sense of security because of the impact of proprietorship on the owner who is in possession and control of his property. Faith in the sense of ownership is based on the observation that if the owner-debtor has what he believes to be a significant economic stake in the housing, he will be at least as deeply concerned as the mortgagee to maintain it in good condition. If ownership did not imply lasting concern for the good condition of the property, mortgagees could not permit the mortgagor to retain possession and control when the debt is up.

The mortgage instrument generally used in the United States combines the desire to protect the lender's resort to resale with the idea that the borrower of mortgage money should retain the rights and obligations of ownership. Two distinctive influences traceable to British law have determined the shape of mortgages. These influences are the common law,[4] which grew up as the accumulated custom of early English history, and the decisions of the Courts of Equity, which were themselves founded on the principles of civil law that relate to the laws of countries other than Britain.[5]

The common law theory of mortgages dates from the *gage* of land in the Saxon and early Norman periods.[6] These gages are mentioned in the Doomsday Book of William the Conqueror, in which all ownership of land was recorded. A gage, derived from the French word meaning hand, referred to the transfer of some of the incidents of ownership of a piece of land as security for a debt incurred by its original owner. The gage was a hand laid on the land in order to protect the interest of one who loaned money to its owner. Under common law, two types of gages were in existence. If the lender took over immediate control of the property, collecting and retaining the rents and issues from the land to recoup his loan, the transaction was known as a "live" gage. If, on the other hand, the borrower kept control of the land and was committed to making specific payments from its income, the transaction was known as a "dead" gage, which in French became a *mortgage*,[7] *mort* being, of course, the French word for *dead*. The live gage was an effective conveyance of land to the lender for a limited period. During that period the creditor was supposed to extract enough rents and profits to pay the debt, after which title to the land reverted to the former debtor. The mortgage was a conditional form of conveyance in which the creditor did not actually take on ownership unless the debtor failed to live up to the condition of his pledge.[8] Obviously, modern one-family housing could not be financed under the live gage system, because the borrower would lose possession of his home. In order to make housing finance work on the debt principle, a sound mortgage system had to be established by the courts.

In all of the states, what makes the mortgage debt system work is the assumption that the debtor in possession of the property, and the creditor that has loaned money, share a common interest in the longevity of the property and in its proper care. In all of the states, however, partly under the sponsorship of the federal government and partly through the operation of state agencies, the ratio of mortgage debt to the total value of the property continues to rise. This is fitting and proper because the smaller equity requirement makes homeownership easier for families of modest means—both in one-family houses and in mutually owned cooperatives and condominiums. Lower equity requirements become essential in reducing the rental level for low-income families through a system of debt service subsidy. Obviously, the higher the loan-to-value ratio, the more effective an interest subsidy becomes. The lower the equity requirement, the easier becomes the stimulation of rental housing ownership by investors.

Ultimately, there looms the possibility that high loan-to-value ratios will reduce the owner's actual investment until the debtor in possession no longer thinks of himself as a true owner of the premises. A co-operator whose down payment is nominal tends to think of himself as a mere renter, without a continuing stake in the soundness of the apartment building. If rents must rise to meet operating costs, his own long-range ownership benefits may seem less important than the immediate increase in rent. He will collaborate in withholding mortgage debt payments, using the money to pay other bills or refusing to pay rent. Perhaps a strong sense of cooperative membership can compensate for the disappearance of the feeling of ownership. Perhaps in some cooperatives, the communal sense will prevail, but, despite the words of the old militant union song, solidarity does not seem to last forever.

In housing, generally, the economic consequences of a serious decay of the common interest between mortgagor and mortgagee have scarcely been examined systematically. If a thin slice of equity investment fails to inspire ownership interest, the implications for the entire system of private savings would be very serious. If the residential properties in which American citizens live begin to deteriorate with unexpected speed, potential mortgage money will be frightened into other investments. The interest rate will rise. It would be very costly to make good the housing deterioration that would result from a general maltreatment of property by owners who hold only a minimal investment in their homes. Such a turn of events would dictate a new order of American priorities. Housing repair would inevitably take precedence over such desirable objectives as environmental conservation and mass transit.

There are limits to the resources of the American economy. It would be tragic indeed if, thanks to an overstretching of the mortgage system of capital allocation, major increments of resources of manpower and materials had to be devoted to rescuing from accelerated decay large parts of the housing stockpile that would ordinarily be expected to provide good homes for a much longer period.

CHAPTER 4

THE RESOURCES

TOGETHER, the equity investor—public or private—and the mortgage investor—institutional, personal, or governmental—provide the money that mobilizes resources for housing. We have already noted that money is used as a not altogether satisfactory measure of the quantity of resources that will be allocated to the improvement of housing conditions, or to the satisfaction of other human needs. As a measure, money is imprecise because its own value is subject to fluctuation. Therefore, it is also important to recognize that the number of dollars that a national economy will make available in a specific year for housing purposes stands as an abbreviated catalog of the specific resources that housing requires. These might be summarized under five headings:

One, a stockpile of existing housing. Although some existing housing may not meet the standards that professional experts consider advisable, or that have been established by local or state law, existing housing generally constitutes the most important single resource for improvement in housing.

Two, land.

Three, labor capable of producing the building materials, transporting them, and constructing the housing itself.

Four, building materials and the industrial agglomerates with which they are produced and transported.

Five, enough other goods and services (money) to satisfy the demands of the people and the enterprises that directly or indirectly produce housing.

Because the last of these is probably the most obscure, we had better deal generally with it at the outset, returning to a more specific discussion at the end. It expresses the apparently simple fact that those who work in the construction and operation of housing require food, clothing, shelter, and recreation for themselves, and that if these needs are unsatisfied, they will not construct housing very long. If an economy has achieved full employment, it obviously cannot find more labor internally with which to increase its housing production; if it suffers from less than full employment, steps taken to increase housing production may put some of the unemployed to work. This will not only increase the number of people employed directly in housing construction; it will also probably increase the number of people engaged in providing services to the newly engaged house builders. The effect of a larger housing output on general demand and employment throughout the economy must be calculated in one way or another before a centrally planned housing production program can be taken seriously.

A further implication of the fifth resource—the goods and services demanded by the house builders—is that if a national economy produces enough goods and services that are in demand elsewhere, it can buy the resources it needs for housing, even land. Many northern European countries, for example, currently import much of their housing construction labor from the less industrialized southern European countries, paying for the labor with money earned in the export of industrial products. After World War I, the United States imported bricks from Belgium to be used in the construction boom in New York City. As a major creditor nation, the United States was easily able to pay for the bricks; New York builders found it was cheaper to bring bricks from Antwerp as ballast in empty freighters coming west to load general cargo than to barge them from the brickyards of Newburgh sixty miles away. When India was a part of the British Empire, the water closets of its finer homes were graced with earthenware fixtures baked in the kilns of the English midlands, and paid for, no doubt, with money earned by the export of rubies and burlap. Those families from the continental United States that were encouraged (during the depression) to homestead in Alaska could not have received their land grants if the United States had not purchased Alaska from the Russian emperor eighty years earlier. The purchase was paid for in gold; ironically, the czar of all the Russians did not know that enough gold would be found in Alaska itself to pay for the purchase many times over. We need not even bother to list the countries that have obtained residential land for their citizens by force of arms.

36

As an extreme case of the housing power of unadorned money, we might wish to imagine the situation of a turbaned potentate of the Middle East, one of those benevolent tyrants so favored by writers on political philosophy. If this ruler's son had been sent by his father to London University, where he might have happened to take a course in tropical architecture, it is not inconceivable that he would return to his emirate convinced that his people, like it or not, would be better off abandoning their tents made from the tanned hides of camels and moving into new rigid homes with jalousies and concrete floor slabs. Assuming, first, that the emirate contains no single item on the long list of housing components—not merely no copper wire or steel hinges, but neither trees for joists nor limestone for portland cement—and second that the citizens of the emirate have resolutely turned their backs on the notion of actually working on the construction of housing, could the benevolent despot still proceed with his program? The answer is "Yes," provided only that deep down below the sands of his realm lie vast pools of crude petroleum of such high specific gravity that the rest of the world stands ready to acquire it at the highest price. In short, if a national economy lacks all of the first four necessary resources for housing, it can make good the deficiency if only it has enough money, the fifth resource. But money does not consist of paper bills, no matter how gorgeously engraved; it consists of the production of goods or services that others demand. A nation that is poor in general will be inevitably poor in housing, too, even if it has all of the resources that are needed for housing production. It will be busy exporting whatever resources it can in order to feed and clothe its citizens. Its citizens will be struggling to produce food, clothing, and exportable goods. They will not have the time to spend on building housing, and if they had, no one would be able to give them the food to live on.

The First Resource: A Stockpile of Existing Housing

Our mythical Middle Eastern potentate helped us to understand the significance of general resources if housing is to be improved. He may also be of help in pointing up the significance of a stockpile of existing housing. By examining his fictional history, we can learn that an existing stockpile is of great value economically to those who would improve the housing supply. It is, at the same time, of negative value politically, because the better the stockpile, the greater the difficulty in gaining political support for housing programs.

If our sheik, upon his return from London University, had been able to convince his subjects that permanent European-type housing is the sole essential ingredient in their long-term happiness, the entire population would have demanded new housing. No one would have continued to be content with his camel-leather tent. Because no one was living in any other form of shelter, the entire population, converted to a belief in the supremacy of permanent homes, would have been impatient for improvement. The sheik's Draconian insistence that all the foreign exchange earned by the export of oil was to be spent on the import of housing materials and labor would have met with universal approval.

Let us, however, consider the situation ten years later. Suppose that our sheik originally planned to put his whole population in houses within twenty years. Within the first five years, 25 percent of the population would have become satisfactorily housed. Would this group continue to support the dedication of the nation's foreign exchange earnings to housing? Possibly, but not probably. Having themselves attained decent housing, at least some of the 25 percent would have come to the conclusion that continued emphasis on housing was not in the national interest. Having now been satisfied, the lucky ones might well promulgate in protest of the sheik's continued housing emphasis a whole list of valuable imports denied to our potentate's subjects because of the concentration on housing development. Five years later, 50 percent of the population would have become well housed. While we may assume that a few dedicated citizens would continue to propagandize for housing the unfortunate "other half," we may also assume that five years still later, when only 25 percent of the population would remain unhoused, a considerable majority of the entire population would now agree that the ruler's emphasis on housing production was more of a personal quirk than a sincere dedication to the needs of the country.

In the United States in 1968, Congress and President Lyndon Johnson agreed on a federal housing program with a target production of 26 million housing units in ten years, an average of 2.6 million housing units per year.[1] While many economists questioned whether or not the nation was capable of forcing the production of so many units without creating inflationary demand in the economy in general (resource number five on our list was uncertain), this program called for the production of only a 2.5 percent addition to the existing stockpile each year. Surely, the American economy was capable of producing that much housing; surely, poor families living in substandard conditions stood in demonstrable need of better housing. It seems to be a political fact, however, that because existing housing provided adequate accommodations for the great majority of Americans (75 percent, if one is to take the national policy at face value), the nation in the first year after the adoption of the national housing goal was in the same position as the Middle Eastern potentate in the fifteenth year of his Draconic housing program. Fewer people needed housing than were satisfied with what they had.

The political problem can be expressed quite simply: only a small part of the population can be expected to benefit directly each year from the United States national housing program; namely, 2.5 percent. Furthermore, the principal beneficiaries originally will be families excluded from the electoral majority. They will be black families, poor families, old people—those who still needed housing in 1968. This stands in contrast to the much greater economic problem of housing the American population immediately after World War II. Then, newly formed families at every income level needed housing; other families faced the results of a shortage that had developed as a result of underproduction during the depression and war years, and housing became a highly popular political issue. As all but some of the poor and racial minorities improved their housing, the newly housed discovered that housing was not so significant a social issue. How does one find political support for housing expenditures when—having already been satisfied—the former supporters of housing programs decide that building more housing on a large scale is not only economically wasteful but fails to solve social problems that it had been expected to eliminate? Housing programs, the newly housed decided further, threaten the stability of neighborhoods, and might well produce "new slums."

It is probably no accident that a surge of interest in the usefulness of older housing, in rehabilitation, replaced the emphasis on production of new housing that had been characteristic of the years when important political segments of the population wanted new housing.[2] At any rate, setting politics aside, there are many serious technical questions about the usefulness of the existing stockpile in solving residual American housing problems, specifically urban housing problems.

First among those questions is the condition of existing housing. What is the remaining useful life of different types of structures? Is it cheaper, more humane, less impersonal, and less destructive of sound social patterns in the city to rehabilitate older buildings than to destroy and replace them?

Obviously, the existing housing stock in the United States varies widely in quality; no one can lay down a set of rules that will apply to all buildings equally. Although the Internal Revenue Code prescribes a useful life for residential buildings of forty years, the number is intended as a taxpayers' compromise rather than as a practical rule of thumb. The Dakota—New York's first luxury elevator apartment house—is going strong after a hundred years of service, including care and replacement. Some buildings, such as the dumbbell-shaped, six-story tenement houses of New York City, built before the 1901 Tenement House Law proscribed their further construction, failed to meet reasonable standards of light and air even at the time they were built. Yet among those same tenement houses today, there are significant differences in quality. Some buildings were long ago rehabilitated to quite decent standards, and for a much lower number of occupants than originally anticipated. Others, which have been modernized by the installation of plumbing, heating, and electrical work not originally contemplated, may yet have generally deteriorated to a point at which they are no longer useful.

People who ask how much housing in the United States is generally unfit to live in are understandably surprised by the evasive answers that their question provokes. It is a fact, although probably a regrettable one, that there is no simple way in which to define a substandard house. The Bureau of the Census has tried to develop formulations that would answer the question with a degree of objectivity, but it has found that subjective considerations intrude to make the judgments somewhat unreliable. In 1950 and 1960, for example, the bureau categorized housing units as either *sound* or *deteriorating*, and which then either lacked or did not lack all plumbing facilities. It also set up another category for housing units, *dilapidated*, about which its enumerators were not required to find out whether or not they contained plumbing facilities. Between 1950 and 1960, the categories of sound and deteriorating housing that lacked some plumbing facilities, together with all the dwelling units marked as dilapidated, dropped from 17 million to 11.1 million.[3] Expressed in percentages, 37 percent of all American housing units lacked essential plumbing or were dilapidated in 1950.[4] In 1960, this figure dropped to 19 percent.[5]

In 1970, the bureau abandoned the attempt to classify housing units as dilapidated. The 1970 census thereupon reported that only 7 percent of the total number of year-round housing units lacked some plumbing facilities.[6] While the figure is not strictly comparable with the 19 percent reported in 1960, because there may well have been units in 1970 that would have been called dilapidated even though they had plumbing facilities, the figures do tend to show consistent improvement in housing conditions.

Figures on overcrowding are similarly encouraging. Specialists in housing standards have customarily described as overcrowded any dwelling unit with more than one person per room (statistically, this is rephrased so that any unit is overcrowded that has 1.01 persons or more per room). The number of overcrowded units has gone down steadily in the United States from 1940 to 1970, and has declined even more sharply as a percentage of all housing units. Slightly over 20 percent of the nation's housing units were overcrowded in 1940; [7] only 8 percent were overcrowded in 1970.[8]

In any case, even though the general improvement of American housing is correctly represented by the Bureau of the Census, pockets of bad housing remain, particularly in the cities, particularly for low-income families, and particularly for families that have been victims of racial or national prejudice. It may also be true that satisfactory city apartments cannot be found by new families, or by unmarried young people, because of rapidly rising costs of multiple-dwelling construction and operation.

Many groups have argued that the older buildings constitute a more valuable resource as buildings than as sites for new construction. From this springs a demand that structurally sound buildings be protected by law from demolition. But if provision is not made for income adequate to keep the structurally sound building in good condition, such a law would not be very helpful in improving housing conditions. It should furthermore be noted that the structural soundness of a building is less important now than it was years ago. This does not mean that a housing economist no longer cares whether a building teeters on its foundations in a wind or gives evidence of being in imminent danger of collapse. On the contrary, structural *un*soundness remains every bit as important as it ever was. But today the structural elements of a building constitute a far smaller part of its total cost than was the case in the tenement-house era. When the nation's older houses were built, many included neither heat nor hot water nor electricity. In urban tenements, a single sink was provided in the common corridor on each floor, generally shared by four families. Obviously, the cost of the foundations, walls, and floors represented almost the total cost of the building. Over the years since that time, the utility package that has had to be inserted into residential buildings has come to account for a larger and larger part of its total cost. Because the pipes, wires, and heating elements are integral—inserted into the structure of the building—the structure itself may be greatly affected by the repair of the utility package. The work of restoring the repair might be as great as if the structure were essentially unsound. Perhaps future buildings may be designed so that those elements most subject to wear and tear can be repaired without affecting the fundamental structure. Bathrooms, for example, might be so placed in a structure that when they require major repair a total bathroom could be inserted to replace the defective unit, much as the oil filter in an automobile engine is changed without dismantling the whole engine. Until that day arrives, however, the structural soundness of a building reveals little about the relative economy of rehabilitating or demolishing it. Other, less tangible factors—public psychology, aesthetics, the scale and variety of the cityscape—are more pertinent than economics to the question of whether or not to rehabilitate the structurally sound building.

It is possible, however, to outline a few general conditions that must prevail if the present housing stock is to provide a major resource for the general improvement of the level of housing quality in the United States. The first requirement is that mortgage funds must be available to refinance obligations on existing housing. It is not enough to provide mortgages for new buildings; the gross flows of income into savings intermediaries, representing not only new deposits but the earnings and repayments on investments, must be sufficient to refinance apartment house mortgages as they expire, and as people choose to sell their private homes, most of which are now financed with self-liquidating mortgages. In multiple dwellings, we noted, mortgages are rarely if ever fully amortized during the term that the mortgage runs. The expectation, as we also noted, of both lender and borrower is that a new mortgage loan will be made at the expiration of the existing loan, perhaps big enough to include funds necessary to repair any defective systems that can be repaired without drastic alteration of the basic structure.

New housing programs frequently depend for their success on the marketability of old houses. The simplest illustration would be so-called Golden Age apartment houses for old people who are unable to keep up their own homes on retirement incomes and with diminished physical strength. Their ability to use the new housing for the aged depends on their ability to sell their existing houses, which depends on the availability of mortgage money adequate to support the current sale value of the house. The ratio between mortgage loans on new properties and those on existing properties varies widely from one type of mortgagee to another, a variation that we will have opportunity to examine in detail. In general, taking into account all types of mortgagees, the yearly volume of loans made on old properties is much greater than the volume of loans made on *new* properties. In 1972, the volume of new mortgages on old residential properties was almost twice the volume of mortgages on new properties, according to the Department of Housing and Urban Development.

A second requirement that must be satisfied if existing housing is to be considered a serious resource is that the flow of income to the owner of the housing must be adequate to support the maintenance required to keep it in good condition. The income must be accompanied by a disposition on the owner's part to invest funds for proper maintenance. This disposition, which is essential if existing housing is to be a valuable resource, depends not only on the character of the owner but on the conditions in the neighborhood, which must be stable enough to make reinvestment in the housing stock reasonable.

A third requirement for successful utilization of the existing stockpile is a reasonably founded set of high hopes for the future. The owner of the property and its residents must share a belief that the neighborhood will probably improve in attractiveness, commercial facilities, public maintenance, and freedom from crime. A single infusion of money in building rehabilitation, or even a continuing set of infusions, will not protect a neighborhood against deterioration.

Finally, it is clear that some realistic threat must face both owner and occupant (whether they are the same person or different people) of some unpleasant consequence of failing to maintain the property. The threat to the owner may be the threat of law enforcement, or the market threat that potentially rentable apartments will become useless without reinvestment. A legal threat to the tenant for destroying property is unfortunately unconvincing. Even if the law provides that tenants may be penalized for damaging a building, the possibility of pinning the damage to a specific tenant is very slim. Any legal change in the relationship between tenant and owner must be viewed not only from the point of view of the so-called justice to the tenant; any proposed change in landlord-tenant relationships must be studied with respect to its effect on the economic stability of the residential property (if either private or public investors are to use funds wisely in good maintenance). Probably the most effective sanctions or threats that can be levied against the user of residential property is peer pressure, whether this is expressed by the fear that one's lawn will be distinguished as containing the only crabgrass on the street, or that one's apartment house neighbors will complain about the garbage that drops out of the soggy brown paper bag on its way to the incinerator door.

In landlord-tenant law, there has been considerable work intended to favor the tenant against the landlord. When this movement started, it had plentiful justification. The model leases that were traditionally drawn up by lawyers for real estate boards have generally imposed major obligations on tenants, while the owner of the building has been required to perform very little. State courts have generally supported leases of this type and imposed on tenants the absolute burden of paying rent no matter how inadequate the service and maintenance, unless the tenants vacate the premises, while asserting the claim that they have been evicted, in effect, by the landlord's deficiencies.

Consumer advocates, together with the so-called poverty lawyers, have banded together to redress the balance. In response to such pressures, new statute law has modified the absolute obligation to pay rent and imposed new obligations that stipulate that the owner maintain the premises in good condition, and conveys to the tenant the right to withhold rent if the owner fails in his duties. Certainly, there is justice, perhaps even wisdom, in redressing the lopsided pro-owner legal position, particularly in such matters as the failure to provide heat, a condition that rarely arises from acts by the tenant. Yet even if a readjustment of landlord-tenant responsibility seems both just and benevolent, its practical effect could be destructive if it unexpectedly undermines the ownership interest of those landlords whose good motives might keep existing rental housing in good condition. As a resource for housing in the United States, existing housing may become even more important in the event that a change in the legal obligations of landlords and tenants discourages private and public agencies from undertaking new rental housing construction.

The Second Resource:
Land

Next after the stock of existing housing, the most important resource for a national housing program is land. Obviously, if existing housing does not meet reasonable standards, and cannot be modified to fit them, new housing must be built for the existing as well as for the future population. It must be built *somewhere*.

This does not appear to be an impossible challenge, for the United States is one of the least densely populated of all industrialized countries.

Only one major nation—the Soviet Union—has a population density lower than that of the United States—twenty-eight persons per square mile as against 56.6 in the United States (according to 1970 census data). Russia, of course, includes the vast, sparsely populated area of Siberia, so that the Russian land mass is almost two and a half times as large as the American. China, the country nearest in size to the United States, has about four times as many people per square mile, 224. The European countries have even less land per person. The United Kingdom, for example, has almost 590 people on each square mile, approximately ten times as many as in the United States; the Netherlands crowds more than 900 people per mile, exceeded in Europe only by Monaco at a freakish 40,000.[9]

It seems clear enough from these gross figures that if the United States will run out of any commodity on the scale that would require rigid controls over its use or abuse, land is one of the least likely to require price regulations. But the abundance of land in general does not mean that land for housing is cheap. In fact, the president's Fourth Annual Report on National Housing Goals, published in 1972, describes land as "the most rapidly rising element of housing cost." [10]

There are primarily two limitations on land as a resource for housing. The first limitation is imposed by the fact of location. Even those who long for total isolation are making a specification that may be hard to fulfill. But the prevailing wish—to live where one can make a living—imposes even more imperious limitations on the suitability of location. The demand for housing land, and, consequently, its basic market value, reflects its location with respect to jobs, recreation, and schooling opportunities.

Countless commentators have pointed out that the rise in the market value of vacant land generally results from a growth in industrial and commercial activities in the vicinity. Only rarely has the landowner himself contributed significantly to this growth; the rise in the value of his holding, therefore, represents not only a cost to the ultimate resident of whatever housing may be placed on the land, but a reward to the owner for no specific contribution other than that of having kept it from being developed at a lower price. What to do about this is not so clear. Henry George suggested that all vacant land should be taxed at very high rates, while improvements should not be taxed at all. This does discourage the holding of vacant land, but it also generates tremendous pressures to develop land prematurely for prospects that often turn out to be illusory. In Great Britain, the national government has purchased large tracts of vacant land on which it has encouraged the building of new towns, including industrial and commercial establishments as well as housing. The economic motive in this program is to capture for the national government the accretion in land value that otherwise may bless the descendants of a potato farmer whose fields become suitable for apartment houses.

The location value of a land site is inevitably the reflection of the number of possibly incompatible uses to which the land might be put. In a totally free economy, the prospective users will bid for the land, with the highest bidder emerging victorious. In a mixed private-public economy, the auction will be limited by laws, as in the case of zoning ordinances, that bar certain uses from certain land sites. In a socialized economy, the same debate over the appropriate use for a specific site may arise, but it will be limited by the governmental plan for the area; this, in turn, may be shaped by a political decision that settles a conflict between commissioners. In all of these systems, the housing use of the land resources of the nation is clearly dependent on the resolution of locational conflicts.

But location is only the first of the two major limitations on the land resources for housing. The other limitation is cultural and reflects the ancient fact that a spatial location is not merely a matter of convenience; it also denotes social class and establishes for the society as a whole the notion of what is a suitable background for social intercourse, for life itself. Thus, zoning regulations limit the size of buildings and the density with which they can be concentrated on land areas of specific sizes. Sometimes these regulations are arbitrary, and merely codify social prejudices. Yet they may also prove beneficial, preventing the development of housing forms and industrial arrangements that are ill-conceived and will lead to premature deterioration. As government believes itself forced more and more to intervene in affairs previously outside its jurisdiction, in order to conserve or bring into existence a social vision of the world, more and more restrictions are imposed on land use. Aesthetic regulations have sometimes followed the zoning restrictions on land use, bulk, and density. Environmental standards have now been codified, which in some cases have excluded from federal subsidy large areas of the city in which people are living and presumably want to continue living. Whereas, in the early flush of enthusiasm for housing, the right of condemnation was invoked in order to obtain housing sites at moderate cost, government has increasingly noted the burden borne by those to be relocated from such housing sites. Their compensation has risen sharply—both for residential and business occupants—so that for most of these people, it is a far, far better thing financially to be condemned for a public purpose in housing than because a private entity wishes to buy it and build something else on it.

Nor are these the only considerations that limit the amount of land that might be made available for housing purposes, or that establish its cost. There are extralegal restrictions on the use of land that are sometimes more effective than law itself. Such a restriction came into being as a practical political matter to stop the construction of public housing in Forest Hills, a section of the borough of Queens in New York City. The law was all on the side of building such housing, but the political objections had become so noisy that city government was forced to vitiate its own contracts. Nor, similarly, can any more public housing be built in certain sections of Chicago, not because the housing would violate existing zoning or other municipal land use laws, but because the federal courts, in this case, have ruled that the concentration of more low-income, largely black families in those areas will tend to perpetuate an undemocratic denial of equal opportunity. In response to this, the Department of Housing and Urban Development issued criteria that have the effect of ruling out the use of land for subsidized housing in many of the areas in the central cities in which vacant or underutilized land exists.

All of these serious questions of public policy must be considered in measuring the adequacy of the nation's land for housing purposes. On a map, the United States looks so large that the suggestion that there is a land shortage seems absurd. When the area is reduced to those sections in which people wish to live, and when these sections are further reduced by the cultural factors we have briefly summarized, it is easy to see why the land resource is so much smaller than it appears and why the cost of land for housing is rising more rapidly than the cost of any other component.

The Third Resource:
Labor

The 1972 presidential housing message endeavored to calculate whether or not an adequate supply of trained and competent construction labor would be available for the housing goals set by Congress. The report stated that to meet the goals an increase in residential on-site, full-time construction manpower of 9 percent over the 1971 total would be required.[11] This would mean that 3.1 million construction workers would be needed in 1973,[12] including both residential and nonresidential construction. It should be obvious, after what we have already said about the utility and social packages, that nonresidential construction of schools, roads, sewage treatment plants, and other sanitary facilities is essential if housing construction is to be made possible. The total expansion of the construction labor force predicted in the president's message includes a projected drop in the segment of construction workers who are busy in nonresidential activities, as the federal highway program nears completion and the office building construction boom of the late sixties dwindles off.

Historically, the construction industry has been able to expand its work force readily in response to increased demand, because many industrial jobs involve skills that are similar to if not identical with the job requirements in construction. Construction workers, at least in the higher paid, more specialized categories such as structural steel erection and elevator installation, are quite mobile, travel great distances, and establish temporary headquarters in locations where long-range construction is under way. But this should not mislead anyone about the highly localized nature of the building trades unions among the carpenters, the brick masons, the electricians, and the other craft trades that make up the bulk of building labor.

Unquestionably there exists now, and will exist in the foreseeable future, a human pool that can easily supply the additional 9 percent of full-time jobs (this means a somewhat greater number of workers, because of sickness, absenteeism, and other frictions) and make good the inevitable losses through retirement, death, and shifts to other occupations. The problem in marshaling the labor resources for an expanded housing program revolves about the difficulties of turning the numerical bodies into an effective working force at the point at which its efforts are needed.

Perhaps the most formidable of all of these difficulties is the decentralized structure of the building trades unions. Organized on a craft basis, in which each local establishes its own basic wages and working conditions, frequently in response to pressures from other trades as well as employers, the building trades unions resist national efforts to shape their policies. This is particularly true in such policy matters as the admission of newcomers to union status, and it has certainly prevented many black and other minority group workers from entering building trades employment and, even where the outright ban has been broken, has discouraged others from trying.

Of importance also is the outdoor nature of the work that makes employment and payrolls irregular. To overcome the weather by encouraging factory assembly of entire housing units or major components runs into trouble because of the questions it raises in the minds of the local unions who fear impairment of their geographic monopoly and a shift in the allocation of work among crafts.

At a time when professional accreditation clearly carries prestige connotations in American life, which were hardly noted before, the building trades have not offered much attraction to those individual workers who have some choice of occupation. The apprenticeship programs have been charged with not training young men to do skilled work with a minimum of costly preparation, but instead programs have been deliberately designed to discourage applicants. Another, but by no means the last, of the difficulties in meeting the recruitment needs has been the very criticism of the building trades that have been made by those seeking to ameliorate the present situation.

The greater the criticism of the trades, the more likely they are to close ranks and resist change; but without criticism from the outside, the chance that they will change their fundamental views of recruitment is nil. The casual nature of construction employment, the "tough" nature of the work, and the chancy and sometimes very high profits made by contractors (no one but the contractor notices the losses or remembers them very long) tend to make the adversary position less amenable to changes that would be highly desirable economically.

One must conclude, in looking at the manpower resource for housing, that while it is unquestionably *there*, its full mobilization under present social and political conditions will be both difficult and expensive.

The Fourth Resource:
Building Materials

Although the world seems well supplied with men who believe that the future of housing construction lies in the use of materials hitherto shunned—domes made of plastic sheet at one end of the spectrum and a return to natural materials like thatching at the other—no one believes any abrupt changes will take place within the next few years. The materials that are important to the construction of housing and to the network of supporting facilities that we have called the utility package will be substantially the same materials that have been used for construction since the beginning of the postwar boom.

Nevertheless, over those twenty-odd years, changes have taken place in the relative importance of some building materials. The production of gypsum products, including the wallboard that has replaced many plaster walls, had tripled between 1947–49 and 1972; the production of mill-work, which includes door and window frames made of wood, increased only by 11 percent, according to the Construction Review, the Bureau of Domestic Commerce, and the Current Industrial Reports prepared by the Bureau of the Census.[13] These shifts in demand, impelled largely by the desire to save field labor, have not generally resulted in shortages. Productive capacity has grown in those fields in which housing demand has increased; in fact, it might as easily be said that the increased demand for the labor-saving product was stimulated by the increase in industrial capacity and the consequent sales promotion efforts by the manufacturers.

In 1973, the most important materials used in American housing construction remained as in 1947: lumber, gypsum products, iron and steel, portland cement, heating equipment, copper tubing, brick, glass, and plumbing fixtures. Although shortages have occasionally developed in one or another of these materials, particularly when construction spurted in a part of the country that lacked adequate production facilities for bulky or heavy components that are costly to ship, building materials supply has not generally been a limiting factor on housing production. One might in confidence predict that the United States economy will not be hampered in meeting its housing goals by material shortages, provided that adequate financing is available.

These cheerful words are subject to a number of sobering conditions, however. First among them is the matter of price. Overcapacity of domestic production of steel, and a fairly high level of imports of some types of building steel, such as concrete reinforcing bars, have dampened price increases in this component, but whenever the economy booms, stimulating a large increase in the demand for many types of steel products, all of which are made from the same basic pig iron, the prices of steel products rise.[14] Adding new steel-making capacity is a time-consuming and very expensive affair. If housing production is to be maintained at a high level when the general economy is booming, it will be difficult to maintain the price stability of housing components like steel because of the vast amount of capital required to expand their production.

A second type of pressure on building material prices arises from the collusive efforts of producers or distributors to control or limit competition. Some of this is simple and understandable. Local distributors of a product like ready-mixed concrete recognize that the price that they charge constitutes a relatively small part of the total cost of an individual house; at the same time, they know that price cuts will not enlarge their sales and will weaken their own financial stability. Because it is relatively difficult for a new producer to enter into this business, and because long-distance shipments of fluid concrete are impossible, the dealers in ready-mixed concrete in a given market need not fear that a price arrangement will invite new entrepreneurs into the business.

Finally, combinations in restraint of trade are encouraged by the lack of differentiation among the products. One dealer's ready-mixed concrete is very much like another dealer's; the specifications, such as the amount of portland cement in each cubic yard of material and the type of sand, stone, or gravel used, are not established directly by the customer, who might be influenced by advertising. They are, instead, established by consulting engineers in accordance with building code requirements, at least in the case of large-scale housing construction. Because the products are so nearly identical, sellers are readily able to enter into formal or informal price agreements.

At the same time, however, in a local area, there are forces that tend to support competition, rather than suppress it. While the dealers in a specific market area may understand that their long-range interest will be adversely affected by price cutting, they cannot always afford to take such a long-range view. The cash position of an individual dealer, his continuity of work, or his relationship with a specific contractor may impel him to cut his price on a specific job. Agreements to support prices are, of course, illegal; and in the real world, they are difficult to maintain in the face of the natural mutual suspicion of disparate interests. The largest dealer in a market area may be heard complaining—in confidence, naturally—that his business suffers from too much weak competition that cannot be relied upon to keep prices up. If he had two or three well-financed competitors, he could count on them to avoid ludicrous price cuts. Business enterprises that are big enough to carry large and formal organizations, accurate cost accounting, and public stockholders who may note that the profits earned run below the industry average in relationship to total sales are more likely to avoid price cutting than small local dealers.

For these reasons, the most serious anticompetitive pressure to raise housing component prices comes from the large basic producers of materials like portland cement, glass, plumbing fixtures, copper tubing and wire, and asphalt. The federal government has sometimes intervened to break up obvious collusive efforts to fix prices, as in the portland cement industry, which not only maintained a common sales price but insisted for years on limiting the methods of delivery so that the natural geographic monopolies were encouraged. In all except the most blatant cases, illegal price fixing is difficult to establish. After a major producer publicly announces a price change, all other producers follow suit—a general practice in the cement and lime industry—but this set of facts, taken by itself, does not prove that they agreed illegally among themselves to maintain a common price level. There is nothing in general law that makes it unlawful for a basic producer to raise its price when it finds that its competitor is doing so.

Competition from abroad, including the import of such basic items as steel and portland cement, has been of help in limiting price increases, at least in certain housing markets located near the coasts of the United States, where transshipment by rail or truck may be unnecessary or relatively inexpensive. When ocean shipping conditions are favorable to the importer, bulk materials may be carried a very long distance. The case of Belgian brick has already been noted; recently, concrete blocks in the eastern United States have been made of pumice imported from the Aegean Sea, an even longer trip, but one that has been economically justifiable in competition with domestically produced lightweight concrete materials.

Of even greater importance in combating the collusive price fixing of housing construction materials is the opening up of local building codes so that a variety of materials may be permitted for the same purpose. Although code revision sounds easy, it turns out to be a very complicated issue, involving real considerations of safety. The dangers of fire, accelerated deterioration, or even collapse under wind pressure are real. Unfortunately, in practice, the real issue of avoidance of danger is complicated by the vested interests or long-time habits of those who believe their income to be threatened by the introduction of new materials. There are frequent close ties between the unions and the specialist subcontractors who share the fears of the unions over the loss in work that might result from technological change.

The basic producers of materials like the rigid pipe in which electric wires must in some cities be run also fear that a change in codes will undermine their present advantage. Even professionals like architects, engineers, and lawyers fear that a change in building codes will affect their costs or the value of their work. The issue is further complicated by the fact that requirements differ from city to city so that no general improvement is easy despite the extensive work by national professional societies, by the national government, particularly through its Bureau of Standards, and by some states that have set forth uniform building codes that local governments have been encouraged to adopt. Finally, there remains a serious problem in public administration: Assuming that building codes are made much more flexible so that competition among the suppliers of different types of materials will be increased, who will assume the responsibility for testing the new materials and assuring their continuing consistency?

A third area of difficulty for housing material prices in the future has been given added importance by the environmental conservation movement. The prices of those materials produced by mining or extraction may be significantly affected by the growth of new regulations on landscape restoration.

Areas surrounding American cities have been pockmarked by the sandpits, quarries, and emptied claybanks from which building materials have been taken. Alternative locations where the public objection to extractive excavation is more muted are, by definition, much farther from the housing market, while transport costs for these heavy, bulky materials are very high.

Some of the housing materials industries—of which portland cement and asbestos products are two obvious cases—involve major smoke and dust nuisances that are costly to control. Other industries, such as the manufacture of asphalt tile, are smelly. The insistence that these nuisances be cleared up amounts to an insistence that the cost of housing increase, and that greater amounts of capital be provided to build it. While it is still too early to tell whether or not the environmental movement will cause an increase or a diminution of total economic activity (inevitably following the stalling of the energy industries for conservation reasons), the connection between the two—conservation and economic activity—is probably more significant in assessing the housing material resources than any other social or economic factor.

The Fifth Resource:
Money

We are now again at the subject with which this examination of housing resources started: money. If Americans are to build 2.6 million new homes per year, employing more than 1 million people in full-time jobs on the building sites, many others in the production and transportation of components, and still others in the production, distribution, and sales of the goods and services demanded by those employed as a result of the housing construction, the nation must be reasonably sure that it produces enough goods and services to fill the sum total of these demands. If it does not, then the establishment of a national housing goal merely enshrines futility. Without the goods and services needed to achieve the goal, and sufficient to satisfy the demands generated by this housing activity, establishing a ten-year housing goal of 26 million units is hardly more practical an enterprise than tacking mailboxes on palm trees of a tropical paradise and expecting air mail letters dropped into these boxes to be placed on airplanes without having made any provision for recruiting mailmen from among the happy islanders who are busy fishing, dancing, and posing for anthropologists.

The problem of estimating the availability of total resources is somewhat more difficult than that of estimating the availability of any single material or human resource. In describing this task in the previous paragraph, we considered only the question of whether or not the economy actually *has* the strength to supply the needed wealth. This falls short of the complexities of the issue, because the true question is whether or not the economy *might* or *will* have that power.

If the productive plant of the United States were operating at a modest fraction of its full capacity, current performance would be of little help in measuring its potential. Yet moving from fractional utilization to full utilization cannot be instantaneous. The estimator must develop a theory —explicit or assumed—to describe how fast he thinks a labor force can be mobilized and inventories built up. All of the frictions that seem inevitable in a human economy must be taken into account. As a flaccid economy begins to stir with life, jobs may open up in precisely those areas where employment is already high; yet many of the workers who are unemployed elsewhere may be reluctant to move. The unfamiliarity of workers with new jobs, or even with working at all, may hold production far below its theoretical maximum. The entrepreneurs, whose willingness to invest in new plants or larger inventories may have been undermined while business was slack, may choose to sit on their savings, refusing to take advantage of government schemes that encourage them to go into debt. Racial prejudice may slow up the promotion of skilled workers to levels at which they are needed to bring the economy to its maximum performance. It might slow the recruitment of minority workers for service in an area into which they might be afraid to go.

These frictions, together with many other social and psychological factors, add difficulties to the problems of forecasting the performance of an economy. But whatever assumptions the economist makes about the difference between the present and the future, his predictions about the capacity of the economic system start with one calculation: the present rate of saving.

Savings comprise that part of the income of a person, a family, or an enterprise that is not spent on current consumption. Therefore, it includes both cash savings and savings in the form of purchase of equipment that will not be totally consumed within the current year. For the purposes of housing economics, we must be primarily concerned with cash savings, which represent part of the stream of income paid to people and enterprises for the production of goods and services. Relatively few Americans place their savings in the mattress. They entrust them—probably through the intermediation of an institution, perhaps directly—to others who will make use of the productive capacity that provided the saver with the income out of which, in turn, he set aside the savings. If this process of transferring savings for the use of others did not take place, the total activity of the economy would trend downward.

As we noted at the outset, housing mortgages constitute a primary outlet for the individual and family savings of Americans. If, perhaps because other forms of investment paid much higher interest rates, Americans decided not to put their savings into housing, resources would become available for housing only if they could be diverted from elsewhere, a difficult and perhaps an impossible job given the current limits on governmental authoritarianism.

Therefore, to estimate whether or not the economy of the United States is capable of building 2.6 million housing units each year, the economist must look at the current rate of savings. He must predict what portion of the savings will flow into institutions, like savings and loan associations, that make residential mortgage investments.

But this is just the beginning. The economist must also decide whether or not the rate of savings will continue at its previous level. In the United States over the past twelve years, the rate of personal savings has ranged from slightly over 8 percent of total disposable personal income to about 5 percent.[15] The *highest rate* of saving takes place when the economy is in a slump and total income is relatively low, as in 1971; the *lowest rate* coincides with boom conditions, when people are optimistic about their jobs and their future and are not afraid to spend money. Thus, in order to estimate both the rate of savings and the total amount of income that, when multiplied by the *savings rate* provides an estimate of the dollar amount of savings, the economist must estimate the gross national product for the year for which he is forecasting. This involves him in an analysis of the money supply, a phrase that we will discuss in the next chapter. Money supply, as we will see, is closely related to the policies of the Federal Reserve Board, and both affects and is affected by the rates of interest charged by the Federal Reserve Board on money borrowed by its member banks.

These computations give the economist an idea of how much money will be saved in the year for which he is predicting. His next problem is to find a way to forecast how much of the savings will go into housing and how much, in dollars, housing will need.[16] The housing economists who helped the president prepare his 1972 housing message determined the amount of money that would be available for housing by, in effect, estimating how much of the total savings in the following year would be deposited in the savings and loan associations, the mutual savings banks, and the commerical banks. Then came an estimate of what the demand for capital funds would be on the part of the government and private companies that raise money for their capital needs by selling bonds. After subtracting the funds that each of the savings institutions would put into the various types of bonds, the economists predicted how much would be left to put into mortgages, breaking the sums down on the basis of the past performance of the institutions with regard to one-family homes or apartments, new loans, existing loans, and construction loans. The economists also included the money each of these institutions would receive in the form of repayment of existing mortgages.

The economists who worked on the 1972 report predicted that in 1973, enough savings would be available to meet the requirements of housing production at the 2.6 million level, but that this could be achieved only by the use of federal agencies to borrow money from the public, which would supplement the otherwise inadequate flow from the traditional mortgage lenders.[17]

In accepting the cheering words that the nation could afford to invest $73.8 billion in housing in 1973, the reader might wish to articulate a few of the unspoken reservations. First, the $73.8 billion will be inadequate if housing costs rise faster than the gross national product. This will happen if the resources needed for housing become more expensive; if, for example, land costs soar, or production frictions increase, or labor productivity changes downward, or building materials components rise unpredictably.

Second, the savings will not be available for housing if the nation decides, either consciously by the political process or half-consciously by the economic process, that resources should be allocated elsewhere (assuming that the gross national product grows no faster than the economists predicted). Thus, the nation cannot have *more* guns *and* housing;

more highways *and* housing; *more* large-scale environmental expenses *and* housing. A great consumer boom, picking up the price level and encouraging people to spend money because it will be worth less in the bank, will distort the projected savings ratio and force the allocation of resources to consumer goods.

Third, the savings for housing will not be adequate if the intrinsic cost of housing becomes higher either because it will cost more to produce the same house or because, for any of a dozen reasons, higher standards for housing are imposed by local and national governments or by public opinion. In short, the possibility of meeting the housing goal depends on balancing the use of one of the nation's resources against the others. This balancing—whether in reponse to national political pressures or the domestic marketplace or the currents of international trade or finance—takes place in the money market and drastically affects housing production and cost. Naturally, then, we must next look at money.

CHAPTER 5

MONEY AND ITS MARKET

HAVING examined the goods and services needed for housing, we can move to a more detailed examination of money itself. Remember that it is the price of the money that accounts for the greatest single part of the cost of housing. Any program that is designed to meet the nation's most serious housing need—homes for the low-income families and, most particularly, those handicapped by racial and national prejudice—must start with an effort to reduce the price of money. As in the case of any specific "good" or "service," the price of money depends not only on demand but on supply, and one of the major objectives of government financial policy is the provision of a proper money supply.

If the money supply is too big, there is no special value in retaining liquidity. People will then tend to think that it is losing value too fast to be worth the amount printed on its face. The danger in such a condition is that when people receive money, they will hasten to buy goods, enabling sellers to raise their prices still further and making the dollars seem increasingly less desirable. In such circumstances, saving money appears not only fruitless but positively dangerous: The savings lose their value faster than would purchases.

If the monetary supply is too small, rather than too large, housing builders, and manufacturers generally, will have trouble borrowing money with which to expand production. People generally will be reluctant to spend, and savings accumulate as savers sense that sellers must continue to cut prices.

The regrettable difficulty of regulating the money supply by conscious governmental activity explains why it became unacceptable to allow the forces of nature to regulate it. Over the centuries, gold alone was an almost universally acceptable claim for goods and services. For a relatively stagnant economy had a relatively stable population—phrases that describe the condition of western Europe from the fall of Rome to the Renaissance—gold worked. It was easy to recognize and impossible to counterfeit. It resisted chemical interaction with other elements, providing the quality of deferability because it refused to deteriorate, rust, tarnish, or gassify. One could save it forever. It was itself industrially nearly useless so that, its value as money being greater than any other, it did not disappear from circulation. Yet it was decorative and so in demand for adornment that its value was not merely conventional.

The trouble with gold as money was that men did not discover it rapidly enough to keep pace with a growing world population. As more people survived infancy to perform productive labor and to demand payment for their efforts, as trade among nations increased, and as kings and other potentates recruited larger armies and decorated more elaborate palaces, the supply of gold became inadequate to the needs of the economy. Nor could the supply of gold be stretched indefinitely to provide a larger coin supply. There is a natural minimum size below which one cannot manufacture coins; when the coins become too small, not even misers can count them, and ordinary people lose them.

By the nineteenth century, a vastly increased industrial work force required payment in cash (instead of in *kind,* as farm laborers had). The invention of machines made factories necessary. Those who built and equipped the factories required payment long before the factories produced salable goods. In the absence of a sufficient gold supply, banks in England and America found that their customers were happy to give the bankers their own promissory notes, which were not generally acceptable as claims for goods and services, and take back a somewhat smaller amount of the bankers' promises that were, if not universally, at least more generally acceptable. Central banks, which extended credit to the national government in return for its own promises to pay, issued their notes, and these too became universally acceptable, all adding to the supply of money.

In the United States, the check has become the most convenient and generally used method of tendering payment for goods and services. The bank accounts against which the vast volume of checks are written every day are called demand deposits; put the other way, demand deposits consist of promises from banks to their customers to pay, on presentation of a check, the money owed by the banks to their depositors. Because a check, properly filled out, can pass from hand to hand with almost the same freedom as the printed currency of the United States, the demand deposits against which the checks may be drawn must be considered as much a part of the money supply as the rectangular pieces of paper that we call currency and that bear the engraved portraits of prominent (and deceased) Americans. As a matter of fact, demand deposits constitute about 80 percent of the money supply of the United States; [1] the currency—made up of bills and coins—constitutes the rest.

Demand deposits come into existence in two ways. The first occurs when a bank customer mails or hands money to a bank teller, together with a properly filled out deposit slip. The deposit may be in the form of currency or checks. The significance of the deposit is that the customer thereby lends money to the bank at no interest on condition that the bank allow it to be withdrawn at any time by check without notice.

The second method of originating a demand deposit occurs when the bank makes a loan to a customer by crediting his account with the proceeds of the loan. Because we have defined the money supply of the nation as the sum of the currency in circulation plus the demand deposits, the money supply is increased by the loan to the same extent that the customer's demand deposit balance is increased.

Under the same sort of pressure as that which influenced the growth of the money supply, the national treasuries of the industrial nations have struggled with the problem of finding the money to carry on their business (and to encourage a flourishing economy that will support the tax burden). They have found themselves continuing the practice of Renaissance princes who reduced the gold content of their coins and then demanded that their creditors accept the new coins in place of the old.

The process of developing a money supply separated from the limitations imposed by gold did not come about through the abstract theorizing of economists. We have seen how the industrial revolution made a large money supply necessary. To Americans, the political potency of a change in the money supply can best be recalled in the dramatic words of William Jennings Bryan who warned against "crucifying Mankind upon a Cross of Gold." Behind the revivalist rhetoric lay the very real economic troubles of the farmers who had gone into debt to open the West to agricultural development. They were in the position of having to discharge debt for land, machinery, seeds, and living expenses, with dollars that were costlier than those they had borrowed. The money supply had remained relatively unchanged while economic activity and population increased dramatically, making each dollar more difficult to earn. The blessings of a flexible money supply in stimulating industrial and agricultural expansion, employment, and a higher standard of living should not be underestimated. Neither should the dangers.

Perhaps the greatest danger in a money supply that is subject only to self-imposed limits, rather than the limits of nature, lies in the great difference in assets ownership that, despite the progressive income and inheritance taxes, continues to separate individual Americans. This difference offers a sound ethical basis for the demand that those who have relatively less are entitled to relatively more, no matter how favorable may be the comparison between the standard of living of poor Americans and the poor of any other large nation. But a scheme of redistribution must first come to terms with the fact that the productive capacity of any economic system is limited and that some types of redistribution actually reduce the total productive capacity of the system. To make matters more complicated, the demands on the system have become more specialized. Those who want better housing for families living in big city slums cannot explain their demand intelligibly to the advocates of national defense expenditures, nor can the advocates of better defense, however serious their intent, make themselves clear to the housing demanders. Chopping away at any group's present share by open political action is so difficult that in the end the pressures for more real wealth become pressures, instead, for more money.

Great self-discipline is required to avoid abusing the apparently magical power to create more money. Use of the term self-discipline implies the existence of a unified, national self, whose reality in political terms may be seriously questioned. The ability to create money is dangerous enough; it becomes more dangerous when each interest group in America fancies itself as the embodiment of the general will. Each demonstrates a readiness to spend or invest or speculate in foreign currencies without regard to the effect on the money supply and the relative cost, therefore, of such expensive commodities as urban housing. A nation must not lose the strength to keep its money supply under control, nor succumb to the temptation to use monetary flexibility as a substitute for taxation and the more difficult task of reaching consensus on the use of government assets. A national government must not imprudently issue claims on its goods and services, claims that its productive capacity cannot satisfy. As those who have received the claims press for payment, or at least encourage the issuance of still more claims, the government finds that it has dangerously undermined its ability to buy the products that it needs to maintain its productive capacity at high speed. But it should be possible—though difficult—to follow a course of expanding the money supply without allowing it to produce a dangerous inflation and to control that expansion without closing off the hope of economic improvement from the poor who still inhabit slums.

Because demand deposits constitute 80 percent of the national money supply, the crucial institution involved in the determination of its size—and hence in the establishment of interest rates—is the bank in which demand deposits exist.

There are several different kinds of banks in the United States, and we must distinguish at the beginning that we are now talking only of commercial banks. Standing by itself, the title is somewhat confusing, because few if any commercial banks include the word commercial in their name. Frequently, they call themselves national banks, which means simply that they are commercial banks that are subject to national, rather than state, supervision. All commercial banks share one characteristic: They encourage their customers to maintain demand deposits, permitting them to draw against these deposits by writing checks that may be payable to third parties. No commercial bank is permitted by law to pay interest on demand deposits. In addition to demand deposits, commercial banks *may* (and most of them *do*) encourage so-called thrift, or time, accounts. These may not be drawn on by checks payable on demand to third parties. Because these are not demand deposits, commercial banks are permitted to pay interest to their time and thrift depositors. Commercial banks are profit-making institutions owned by stockholders, although some are affiliated with nonprofit institutions such as labor unions (the Amalgamated Bank of New York, for example, is affiliated with the Amalgamated Clothing Workers).

If banks are to operate profitably, their officials must avoid two missteps above all others. First, they must avoid making loans to customers who are unable to repay them. Second, they must avoid leaving money idle, or, nearly as bad, they must avoid renting it out at a price that is lower than need be. For the rest, the job of running a commercial bank is not vastly different from that of running any other business enterprise; its managers must try to keep down their operating costs, but not by being so stingy that they repel customers. They must have a sharp sense of the money market at any given moment, an instinct for knowing whether its price, as expressed in interest rates, will go up or down and, correspondingly, whether the demand for loans will increase or decrease. They must judge whether the customers who seek to borrow from them face good times or hard ones. This sense of the future is one of the familiar requirements of anyone in business. A characteristic peculiar to banks—because the stuff in which they trade, money, is so universally coveted and so volatile in its movements—is that they must take an inventory *every day*. That, of course, is what the bank's staff does when the doors close to the public in the middle of the afternoon.

The statement that a bank must avoid keeping its money idle is probably an unfortunate one. It implies a concreteness that is fatal to an understanding of the money supply and, ultimately, to the effect of changes in that supply on housing. Hearing someone speak of a road contractor allowing his equipment to stand idle, the listener imagines a yard crammed with rusty bulldozers, scrapers, graders, and cranes. When one speaks of money being kept idle at a bank, the words reinforce a wholly inappropriate image of a shoebox, or a tier of shoeboxes, each marked with the name of a customer, in which old checks and ten-, twenty-, and fifty-dollar bills are lying about like unemployed road machinery, waiting for an alert loan officer to scoop them up and rent them out. The "money" that a bank seeks not to leave idle is very different: Its existence is far less corporeal, and it is subject to a law that comes straight from Wonderland—the more money a bank lends, the more it has available to lend.

This remarkable procedure seems to defy all natural experience. In all other circumstances, the more money you loan out, the less you have to loan in the future. The basic difference is that, in distinction from ordinary experience, the bank does not merely lend its *own* funds. It also lends the funds that others have, in effect, loaned to it by depositing money in the bank. When it credits a depositor's account with the proceeds of a loan, the bank is simultaneously borrowing back, in the form of a deposit, the very same sum that it had just loaned out. As a result of the simultaneous loan and deposit, it remains able to lend the same deposit balance all over again, less only a reserve that it must set up against the new deposit.

Almost everyone who stumbles on this process for the first time cries out that the borrower who lends his loan back to the bank by keeping its proceeds on deposit does not intend to keep the deposit in the bank very long. He borrowed it not to oblige the bank by increasing the bank's ability to lend to others but to increase his own power to pay other people what he already owes them. He will draw the money out soon, almost immediately in fact. Of course, the bank knows this too. It is true not only of the borrower's account but of all its accounts, that they could all be closed without warning at any time. They simply aren't.

The bank also knows that people do not continuously demand proof of liquidity if they have confidence in the institutions to which they have entrusted a deposit. Furthermore, the reserves established by the bank against its deposits and capital funds will tend to protect it against sudden demands for funds by too many depositors simultaneously. Finally, there is at least a possibility that the recipients of the checks drawn by its depositors will turn out also to be depositors or that the people whom they will pay are depositors. Naturally, when they deposit their checks, they are then lending the money back to the bank.

In any case, when the borrower does draw a check against the proceeds of his loan and sends the check to his creditor, the happy recipient will, of course, deposit the check in a bank account, which has the effect of increasing the amount of that second bank's loanable deposits. Thus, whenever a bank makes a loan by adding to a customer's demand deposit, it increases the money supply of the nation as a whole; whenever it accepts payment for a loan by charging the loan against a customer's demand deposit balance, it reduces the money supply.

This explanation does not satisfy the persistent questioner who asks what happens if the bank is disappointed by its customers; that is, what happens if so many checks are drawn against its total demand deposits that the bank's own account at the Federal Reserve Bank or at its own commercial bank is in danger of being overdrawn. In fact, the bank is somewhat prepared for this.

In the first place, the bank may borrow money from the Federal Reserve Bank or from one of the commercial banks at which it may have an account, provided that the notes that its customers have signed are satisfactory to the Federal Reserve Bank or to another commercial bank as collateral for a loan.

In the second place, it may have bought some securities at a time when the demand for loans was slow. Now that its depositors are seeking to withdraw their funds, the bank may decide to sell its securities, receiving payment in the form of checks that it will deposit in its Federal Reserve Bank account or its own account at another bank. There it will defray the charges that are accumulating in the form of checks drawn by its customers and sent by third parties to their banks for collection.

Third, when it sees the possibility of a severe draft against its reserve accounts, or its accounts with other banks, a bank may seek to augment its balances in those accounts by raising funds that will not be subject to such drains. This might come from selling more stock to the public, or by shifting customers' accounts (with their permission, of course) from demand deposits to thrift accounts, which provide in small print that the bank may require sixty days' notice before giving its depositors their money back, or to time accounts, which also pay interest but from which money may not be withdrawn before a stipulated date, or to certificates of deposit that are, like bonds, negotiable instruments that promise large-scale lenders that their bank will give them their money back with a stipulated amount of interest, but only at a stipulated future time.

The most important single restraint on the unlimited expansion of the money supply lies in the prudence of commercial bankers themselves. They must assure themselves that the loans they make will in fact be repaid. Of course, the standards they use may be subject to criticism; they may be far less shrewd than they pretend to be. Or they may be altogether too shrewd so that their lending policies fail to take into account the social desirability of loans that, although they cannot be justified by traditional standards, may nevertheless be valid in times that change faster than the perceptions of bankers. We will not pause to mediate this argument, merely remarking that a loan that goes into default has, ipso facto, done its borrower very little good; that the desire for profit tends to expand rather than contract the horizons of lenders; that interbank competition probably helps expand horizons; that bankers read the newspapers, are subject to the pressures of public opinion, and are sensitive to costs of unpopularity; that competition among banks is somewhat more difficult to evaluate than competition in other enterprises, inasmuch as all banks sell precisely the same commodity, money on demand; and, finally perhaps, social goals in the economic sphere are likely to require the infusion of tax money by government action. Those who criticize the wan appearance of banking's social programs rarely present practical remedies that might win the approval of those who are likeliest to pay for them—the stockholders.

Whatever may be the net of these random comments, even the least sophisticated observer knows that bankers cannot expect the money they lend to remain forever on deposit in the account of the borrower. Although all banks depend on the improbability that every depositor will develop a simultaneous unannounced need for all of his money, some reserves must remain on hand—in cash or in nearly liquid form. And in this calculation, the long-term, hard-to-sell asset of a residential mortgage cannot be regarded with very much affection.

In deference to his own prudence and the mass of laws and regulations, a bank's loan officer typically decides to recommend that the first investment of idle funds be made in treasury bills. Treasury bills are short-term promises by the United States Treasury to pay round-number sums of money (usually not less than ten thousand dollars per bill) at the end of a specific period of time from the date of issue. The terms usually run 45, 90-odd, or 182 days. The bills are easily sold because at maturity they are payable to the bearer at face value. They can readily be sold on the private market before their due date, but never for so much as their face value. The difference between the sale price of a treasury bill and its face value represents the interest equivalent that the buyer demands for the use of his money between the date of sale and the date on which the bill matures.

New treasury bills are offered for sale once each week by the New York Federal Reserve Bank, acting as the agent for the United States Treasury. The bidders—who are large banks or specialized dealers—offer to buy a stipulated amount of bills at a stipulated price below their face value. The bid price represents the calculation made by the bidders as to the current value of money, and is a very sensitive indicator of the trend of the interest rate. Bidders will offer a low price when they think interest rates are going up, because they will expect to earn high rates elsewhere; they will offer a higher price when they expect interest rates are going down, because they will be less able to earn high rates elsewhere.

If a bank is satisfied that its liquidity is assured by the soundness of its loan portfolio (so that it could sell its customers' obligations to other banks in a time of difficulty) and by an adequate supply of treasury bills, it might purchase long-term government obligations, on which the interest is usually higher than on treasury bills. Because interest rates may rise more readily over the longer term of these obligations than over the short term of treasury bills, the risks of a loss on a sale before maturity is greater—they are less liquid. The same is true of the obligations of government agencies, whose interest rate is likely to be still higher; or the obligations of state and local governments, whose interest is exempt from federal income tax, and sometimes from state and local taxes as well.

In all of these investments of idle funds, the loan officers of a bank are guided primarily by the desire to earn income, but this also requires that they remember their liquidity. If they are heavily invested in relatively nonliquid assets that they cannot sell hurriedly, they may have to make short-term loans from other banks, including their Federal Reserve Bank, that are expensive and may wipe out a large part or all of the greater profit anticipated from higher interest rates.

The development of bank policy is further complicated by more subtle matters. Banks may charge very high interest rates on consumer loans such as automobile loans. These have now become very important to commerical banks, although for years they were considered dangerous and undignified. Lately, bank policy has sacrificed both dignity and a measure of liquidity in order to increase interest income. Accounts receivable financing, in which banks lend to customers against the security of sums of money owed to the customers, used to be frowned on by commercial banks; it was considered risky and ungentlemanly because the collateral of an accounts receivable loan is much more difficult to evaluate than stocks and bonds traded on a public exchange whose prices are listed daily in the newspapers. Nevertheless, accounts receivable financing has been growing as a commercial bank activity, and a number of banks have acquired subsidiary companies that do nothing else (one company that is very active in the consumer loan and receivable-financing field has acquired a large commercial bank, demonstrating that the process can work both ways). Commercial banks have been reluctant to finance production expenses unless the manufacturer-borrower has an extremely good credit standing and other resources, but construction mortgage financing—i.e., advancing money to builders as their work continues—has become more important for those banks with a technical staff capable of handling it.

Other factors, too, enter into the determination of bank policy. Commercial banks have a physical locale, where their headquarters is located. This breeds a natural interest in the prosperity of their home city. Banks have recognized some civic responsibility or perhaps a long-term self-interest in the promotion of local industry and the maintenance of local housing. On the other hand, interbank borrowing and customer relations frequently suggest to bank policymakers that they should lend to out-of-city customers who reach them through correspondent banks with whom they maintain relationships. The flow of credit or, more properly, the creation of money is so critical an activity to the American economy, it determines to so great an extent the issue of who will prosper in what part of the country and who will not, and the policies of banks sometimes seem so arbitrary to the outsider, that intensive government supervision has been inevitable. There is still some regulating to do. Nothing seems to prevent the extension of large sums of money to corporate conglomerators with which these gentlemen buy up the stock of other companies, sometimes with beneficial effects for all concerned, sometimes with disastrous effects for themselves as well as everyone else. For this kind of monster wheeling-and-dealing, some of it international in scope, the major city banks are wonderfully well equipped. Yet they frequently must bring in country cousins, their correspondent banks whose deposits are very high in relation to their commercial loan opportunities. A big corporate transaction may involve the mobilization of many small banks by a few larger ones. Intensive commercial loan correspondent business in the smaller cities tends to push the smaller banks out of lower-earning home mortgage investment. The large city commercial banks generally limit their mortgage investments to construction loans and short-term situations.

In 1971, according to the Call Reports of the Federal Deposit Insurance Corporation, the total loans and investments of the nation's commercial banks stood at $517.2 billion.[2] Commercial and industrial loans were the biggest single item on the list of investments, amounting to about 22 percent of bank loans and investments. Municipal securities, real estate loans (including construction mortgages), and treasury securities together with securities issued by agencies of the federal government each amounted to about 16 percent of banks' total investments. Consumer and "other" loans came to about 14 percent each.

In 1971, time deposits in commercial banks were $100 billion higher than demand deposits,[3] having shown remarkable relative growth in the postwar period. Obviously, the rate of interest charged by the banks to their loan customers, including real estate, were the highest rates that the banks could charge in the face of their joint competition. A floor under that rate is established by the cost of the money to the banks—the competition for time deposits and the effective rate that can be earned by a bank when it simply puts its idle funds into treasury bills.

This brings us to an examination of the Federal Reserve System, which is the nation's primary organ for controlling the actions of the nation's commercial banks with reference to the money supply.

The Federal Reserve System came into existence in 1913 by an act of Congress. It had become abundantly clear to the national legislators that a central bank was required that would supervise the crucial banking operations of the country. It would provide, as well, regional reserve banks in which the commercial banks could maintain their own demand deposit accounts. Interbank transfers of checks could be expedited through changes and credits to these accounts. The twelve regional banks act as the banker for the commercial banks in their area in much the same way as the commercial banks act for the public. But behind the service function lies a regulatory function.

All the commercial banks that choose to be regulated by the federal government, rather than by the state, must become member banks of the Federal Reserve System. The member banks own all the stock of the Federal Reserve Banks, each being required to invest 3 percent of its capital and surplus in the stock of its regional Federal Reserve Bank.[4] By statute, a member bank is entitled to a 6 percent annual dividend on its stock in its Federal Reserve Bank; in fact, the Federal Reserve System—performing for the member banks many of the income-producing functions that all banks perform for their depositors—has earned substantially greater profits than it has had to pay out in dividends. The excess profits were initially used to accumulate a substantial surplus that the Federal Reserve Banks hold in the form of government securities, or each other's notes, or Treasury gold certificates, or the obligations of member banks. Earnings above the 6 percent statutory dividend level are now turned over to the United States Treasury.[5]

The affairs of the Federal Reserve System are managed by a board of governors with seven members appointed by the President and confirmed by the Senate. Each of the regional banks operate with some degree of autonomy within the general framework of law, as interpreted by the board of governors, and within the policy guidelines laid down by the board.[6]

The system, in short, involves a typically American compromise between national and regional interests, and between government and private enterprise. The fact that the system as a whole mirrors the profit-making system of private commercial banking probably reassured the legislators that it would not follow a policy of restricting credit unduly. After all, the more money that the Federal Reserve System lends to its member banks, the higher its profits are likely to be.

From the early days of the republic onward, American agrarian and small commercial interests—and their representatives in Congress—feared that a central bank would restrict expansion of the money supply (they did not use precisely this term, but the meaning was identical) so that big bank creditors could easily extort high interest rates from borrowers and make the repayment of loans onerous. The design of the Federal Reserve System was intended to allay this fear. A succession of financial panics, brought on in part by an imprudent and uncontrolled expansion of credit, made some forms of central banking finally acceptable to the congressional majority. This has not kept the system immune from criticism over the years, both by those who fear that it has made money too scarce and interest rates too high, and those who, in other periods, feel that it has made money too cheap in an effort to woo popular support or to keep down the Treasury's borrowing costs.

To most of these criticisms, the Federal Reserve Board replies, if at all, with the disclaimer that it is not interested in achieving any specific economic goal for the benefit of any one segment of the population, or any one institution. Its function, its spokesmen say, is to provide an institutional setting in which the amount of credit and its cost can be adjusted to the needs of the economy in an orderly fashion. Its role is primarily to prevent the occurrence of panics due to unnecessary hardships of market adjustment or improvident bank management. The Federal Reserve System, for example, can aid the shift of liquidity from one part of the country where it is in excess to other parts where it is needed; it can discourage the possibility of cornering a market in funds or foreign currency; it can expand the money supply to meet peak periods of commercial activity, such as the pre-Christmas season, contracting the supply later on to prevent the disturbances that might be caused by an oversupply of bank credit and currency; and it can exercise pressures on the commercial bank system in an effort to increase or decrease the money supply to help ensure a high rate of employment and high levels of production, or whatever other goal the national interest may seem to favor.

The maintenance of a policy of strict neutrality in money matters, which these statements would suggest, is as difficult as the maintenance of a neutral tax policy that does not favor one type of monetary gain over another, one type of income recipient over another. We shall examine it later for its implications for housing and other sections of the economy, like agriculture, which have been closely tied to the availability of low-cost credit. Before attempting judgments, one had better look at the way in which the Federal Reserve System actually functions in its relationship with the commercial banks.

Having elected to join the system, a bank must abide by Federal Reserve Bank regulations that require it—subject to change within the limits of the law—to keep a reserve equal to a 15 percent fraction of its demand deposit liabilities. The Federal Reserve System recognizes only two kinds of assets as acceptable reserves. The first is legal United States currency held in the vaults of the bank every night at the close of business. This probably constitutes a small part of the bank's required reserves. The only other admissible reserve is the bank's own demand deposit balance in its regional Federal Reserve Bank account. At the close of business every Wednesday, each member bank must be in balance. That is, its vault cash and its Federal Reserve Bank deposits must be equal to at least 15 percent of its demand deposits plus 5 percent of its time and thrift deposits. The regulations permit slight temporary overdrafts, but they must be cleaned up the following week.

It is crucial that neither one of the two acceptable reserve items—cash or the demand deposit balance at the regional Federal Reserve Bank—earns interest. The Federal Reserve System's effectiveness depends on the hypothesis that every bank directs its efforts to earn as much profit as possible. This need will discourage it from maintaining in its account at the regional Federal Reserve Bank a balance any bigger than it is required to keep. If a bank finds itself with excess reserves, or idle funds, it will seek to put these to work by making more customer loans (thus, increasing its own deposit liabilities to the extent permitted by the condition of its own reserve account balance) or by lending to other banks (thus, drawing down its reserve account balance) or by investing in treasury bills or other securities permitted by law (thus, also drawing down its reserve account balance).

If the member banks as a whole find themselves Wednesday after Wednesday with little excess reserves, their condition suggests that the economy is very active. The high rate of activity naturally produces a high level of demand for loans by businessmen and others. Each loan increases the deposit liabilities of the banking system, as we have seen, and each one thousand dollar increase in such deposits requires a corresponding one hundred fifty dollar increase in the minimum balance in the regional Federal Reserve Bank.

If, contrariwise, the member banks of the Federal Reserve System find themselves Wednesday after Wednesday with substantially higher reserves than their deposit level requires them to keep, their condition suggests that business activity may be slowing down. The reserve balance in a regional Federal Reserve Bank account becomes excess when the bank's demand deposits decline, because each decline in the demand deposit liability of a bank lowers the minimum level of the reserves that the bank is required to maintain. Usually, a decline in the demand deposit may be attributed to the repayment of loans by business customers of the bank who instruct the bank to charge their accounts with the amount needed to pay the loan. Such a simultaneous reduction in the loan asset of a bank and its deposit liability does not reduce the balance in the bank's reserve account in the regional Federal Reserve Bank. Thus, the reduction in demand deposits to repay the loan makes excess that part of the bank's reserve balance that had been necessary to cover 15 percent of the deposit liability.

We have already noted that the primary limiting factor on a bank's ability to make loans is the level of demand for loan accommodation by credit-worthy customers. There are times when business is slack and unemployment high. In such an atmosphere of fear and deflation, no customer seems credit worthy, either to the bank or to himself. At this point in the business cycle, the dynamic goal of Federal Reserve Bank policy must be to make lending as easy as possible. By helping to create excess reserves, the Federal Reserve System assists in lowering interest rates, until some business enterprises become attractive because the cost of servicing the debts incurred to accumulate their capital has been greatly reduced. Housing, for example, becomes attractive to more buyers or tenants when interest rates are lowered until the final product is much cheaper. It seems correct to say that while low interest rates alone are not enough to restore consumer and investor confidence, they are an essential part of a recovery program.

There are other times when business is booming, when the employment of skilled workers is high, when consumers pant to buy automobiles and deep freezers, and when retailers believe they must carry large inventories of goods and must pay for them. In the rosy glow of high consumer income and demand, all borrowers look good to themselves and to the banks. At this point in the business cycle, the dynamic goal of the Federal Reserve System must be to limit the expansion of bank credit and the money supply. The system hopes to maintain reasonable stability of prices and to protect against overexpansion of productive facilities that will turn the boom into a bust. When the economy reaches this level of activity, the fractional reserve requirement becomes the most important limiting factor on the making of loans and the growth of the money supply.

To illustrate this, let us take the case of a specific bank whose customers continue to assert a demand for loans despite the bank's attempt to choke it off by higher interest rates. Realizing that it will have to increase its loans or lose customers permanently, the bank will adopt the strategy of bolstering its reserve position. The bank's choice of tactics to fulfill that strategy will depend on the management's view of the nature of its problem, on the actions of the Federal Reserve System, and on general conditions in the money market. Will the shortage of reserves continue, or is it likely to abate on the receipt of a large, expected influx of deposits? Is Federal Reserve System policy likely to favor tighter or looser monetary controls in the near future? Are interest rates in a steady long-term upward trend, or have they neared an interim peak?

If the bank management concludes that its reserve shortage is temporary, it may simply decide to borrow the additional reserves it needs. A perfectly legal procedure, borrowing reserves helps to ensure that the supply of bank credit is made available wherever in the United States the maximum demand for credit is felt. A member bank of the Federal Reserve System may borrow reserves from two sources. First, it may borrow from the Federal Reserve System on the security of sound assets, usually consisting of treasury bills but possibly including other government securities or the obligations of the largest business enterprises in the nation.

The Federal Reserve Board has made clear that while every member bank has the power to borrow from the system, this power is regarded as a privilege rather than a right. Banks are expected to own the assets they require to conduct their normal business.

As an alternative to incurring the embarrassments of borrowing from the Federal Reserve System itself, member banks may borrow additional reserves from each other; those banks with excess reserves, of course, lending them to banks with prospective shortages in their reserve accounts. Because the reserves that are transferred consist of demand deposits at regional Federal Reserve Banks, the reserves are called federal funds. They can be transferred by checks drawn by the lending banks on their regional Federal Reserve Bank accounts and deposited by the borrowing banks in *their* accounts. In the case of transfers of federal funds between banks in different parts of the nation, the Federal Reserve System teletype network is used to effect instantaneous transfers.

Naturally, the banks that loan federal funds to other banks charge interest for the use of their money. The rate is established by negotiation, frequently assisted by a few major dealers in New York City and Chicago, who "make markets" in federal funds, finding such funds for banks who need them, finding borrowers for banks who have the funds to spare. The interest rate bears some relationship to the rate the Federal Reserve Bank charges its member banks when they borrow from it. Usually, however, the federal fund rate is higher than the Federal Reserve Bank discount rate because the banks that need to borrow additional reserves are under pressure *not* to use the Federal Reserve Bank discount privilege. They can, in a sense, be made to pay for their desire to escape criticism.

Every day, banks and government securities dealers throughout the nation watch the federal funds rate, regarding it as a sensitive indicator of the direction of movement of interest rates. Obviously, a high rate means a shortage of reserves and a high level of business activity.

If bank management concludes that interest rates will continue their upward movement, and that the demand for credit will continue to be strong, threatening to make the bank's reserve position permanently inadequate, the bank will look for more permanent ways to meet its reserve shortage. It will probably undertake to bolster its reserves by selling some of its assets, starting with its most liquid assets, its treasury bills, if it owns any.

A continuing market in outstanding treasury bills is made by a few large banks in New York City, together with a handful of very important securities dealers who buy and sell these bills for their own account, using large amounts of bank and nonbank credit to carry their inventory. Bank credit, of course, means bank loans. The nonbank credit consists of loans from large corporations and state and local governments that may find themselves with demand deposit balances that are temporarily greater than their immediate need for funds.

The same dealers who make the market in federal funds (including the banks that act as dealers) also make the market in treasury bills and other government agency securities. It is inevitable that except for unusual circumstances that might cut down the supply of one of these instruments, but not the others, all of the interest rates on Federal Reserve Bank discounts, on federal funds, on treasury bills, and on other government and government agency obligations move in the same direction at the same time. Without such liquidity, America's tremendous growth in the national product and high personal standard of living would have been much harder to achieve.

Nevertheless, there are disadvantages to the liquidity, particularly affecting the holders of long-term obligations, such as mortgages. The ease of movement from one type of investment to another means that as interest rates go up, investment funds generally flow into the investments that yield the highest safe returns. The flow away from mortgage lending is accentuated because there are several limits on the interest that can be charged to the borrowers of mortgage funds: the limits of housing consumers' incomes; the limits imposed by the FHA as a condition for insuring mortgages; the limits imposed by state usury laws. Just as all lenders can move their money back and forth between treasury bills, other short-term government securities, high-grade, short-term commercial paper, short-term bank paper, as in certificates of deposit, and the federal funds market, so the managers of thrift institutions find themselves increasingly attracted, in a high-interest, money-tight phase of the business cycle, by these nonmortgage investments. The depositors in some thrift institutions (those in New York City are peculiarly vulnerable) have grown increasingly sensitive to the high rates of interest they could earn by direct ownership of many of these instruments (treasury bills are not usually sold in denominations smaller than ten thousand dollars, precisely to keep small investors out of them). In order to keep their depositors from removing savings, the managers of thrift institutions must try to lift interest rates to the point where they are competitive with other options open to their depositors. All of the possible solutions to this predicament are bad for the mortgage market: High mortgage interest rates raise the effective cost of housing and loosen the demand for it; a shift from mortgages to money market investments cuts down the availability of funds for housing; a low payout by the thrift institutions stimulates an outflow of savings and, therefore, also cuts down the availability of mortgage money.

Although the money market is therefore crucial to the workings of the American economy, it cannot be found anywhere in the same physical sense that one can find the Flea Market in Paris or the Farmers' Market in Los Angeles. It is a loose network of dealers, bankers, and treasurers of public and private corporations talking in very large round numbers over telephones. Participants move in and out of it, following the pressures of their own needs for liquidity or desires for investment income. The Federal Reserve System is very much a part of the money market; it is far and away the most important single factor in the market, followed by the Treasury of the United States with its vast need for credit and its tremendous flows of tax money coming in and disbursements going out to pay government contractors and public employees.

At any given moment on a business day in New York City, one of the large money market dealers may hear from a major bank wishing to sell $25 million in treasury bills to bolster its reserve position. The dealer will make a price that will reflect the pressure to sell and that may raise the implicit interest rate. Then he may offer the bills in smaller lots to smaller banks to whom the return will appear attractive.

Then a call may come in from the treasurer of a large nonbank corporation who finds that its construction of new plants is going slower than expected and who therefore does not need for fifteen days some $50 million in demand deposit balances that is earning no interest. The dealer may work out an arrangement to sell the corporation $50 million of his treasury bills coupled with a commitment to buy back the same bills in fifteen days, at a stipulated price that will give the corporation a gain roughly equal to the current interest rate on $50 million for fifteen days. With the $50 million, the dealer will pay off one of his own bank loans, saving himself the interest he was paying on the loans.

A call may come in from the fiscal officer of a major federal agency that provides credit to farmers for the purchase of land. The agency wants a reading on the current federal funds rate, because it is preparing to float a large bond issue and wants to assure itself as to the best timing and probable interest cost. The dealer makes a note to himself that these new agency securities will be very attractive at current interest rates to mortgage-making institutions that are hampered in raising interest rates by state usury laws. The dealer calculates how big a position he can afford to take in the securities when they come out and which of the possible investors he has spoken to in the last week might be interested.

The dealer hears from the Federal Reserve Bank of New York acting as fiscal representative of a foreign country that has large bank balances in two major New York banks, thanks to a recent major sale of raw materials. The foreign country is interested in a quote on medium-term government securities. Obviously, it is comparing American interest rates with yields it can earn elsewhere in the world. Its decision on whether or not to invest in American securities is big enough to exert a noticeable effect on bank reserves. If it draws its checks to American securities dealers, they will be deposited in American banks and find their way inevitably into the banks' reserve accounts; if the money goes abroad, none of it will be available to bolster American bank reserves.

Throughout the day, sales and purchases, borrowings and lendings will take place as the actors in the money market on that particular day express their needs. The dealer in the money market will feel the pressure of their net efforts; he will sense whether or not the pressure to sell and to borrow exceeds the pressure to buy and to lend. The dominance of one set of pressures over the other will determine the immediate future course of the economy.

The manifold activities of the money market are far more complex and intricate than could be set forth on paper, because so many different actions are under way simultaneously, while none of the actors is precisely sure what all of the others are doing. The Federal Reserve System tries to make sure that none of the day's transactions will cause a radical shift in bank reserves that would suddenly impede bank lending. It holds in its hand three tools that may have major effects on the money market.

The first of these tools is the reserve requirement. Our discussion of the limits of credit expansion in boom times indicated that the reserve requirement could be of crucial importance. The Federal Reserve System has the power to raise or lower the fractional reserve that the member banks must keep in noninterest-bearing reserve accounts or in currency. A rise in the fraction has an immediate, gross effect on a bank's ability to lend, assuming that in boom times it has no shortage of prospective borrowers. If the fractional reserve requirement were raised from 15 percent of demand deposits to 20 percent of demand deposits, the amount of lending of which a bank is capable would be reduced by 25 percent. As an example, let us consider a member bank with $15 million in its reserve account. The 15 percent requirement would enable it to carry bank deposits of $100 million. With the same $15 million in reserves, a 20 percent reserve requirement would permit the member bank to carry bank deposits of only $75 million. The reduced ability to lend that would follow the increase in the reserve requirement would probably also stimulate higher interest rates. The bank overhead would be spread over a smaller volume of loans, putting it under great pressure to realize higher income per unit loaned. The second major tool of the Federal Reserve System is the discount rate. By raising the discount rate, which is the interest rate at which member banks are privileged to borrow from their regional Federal Reserve Banks, the Federal Reserve System hopes to make such borrowing more expensive. Even though member banks may not continually borrow from the Federal Reserve System, the discount rate may be effective in raising interest rates generally. Certainly, the federal funds rate of interest will move upward with the discount rate because the two are roughly competitive.

But the federal funds rate also affects the treasury bill rate. If banks can earn a higher rate of interest lending other banks their excess reserves, they will not be attracted to the purchase of treasury bills until they can earn a commensurate return on them. The demand for bills would drop until their yield increases. Thus, a rise in the discount rate would probably stimulate a rise in all the other interest rates in the economy.

The movement of the discount rate seems to have a less important effect on the quantity of the money supply than it had previously. High tax rates mitigate the effects of interest on corporate and other business borrowers.[7] The development of such credit devices as federal funds makes borrowing at the Federal Reserve Bank discount window only one of several alternatives open to bank officers who need to expand their reserve position. The tremendous amount of treasury bills in the hands of bankers and dealers, rather than in the safe deposit vaults of the general public, has helped to create a truly national market for credit. The importance of Federal Reserve Bank credit is thus diminished, except, perhaps in a psychological sense.

If the Federal Reserve Bank wishes to move in the opposite direction, to stimulate a business revival by lowering the interest rates in the economy, its manipulation of the discount rate is probably even less effective. The very nature of a depressed economy is reflected in the fact that no one needs to borrow money. Interest rates are low without intervention of the Federal Reserve Bank, and the ability of the bank to push economic activity by keeping interest rates low has been compared to trying to push a ball with a string.

The third tool of the Federal Reserve System is by all odds its most effective and most flexible. This is the activity known as open market operations. Under the direction of the Open Market Committee, specialists in the employ of the bank are constantly active in the New York money market, buying and selling treasury bills and occasionally other government and government agency securities, and bankers' acceptances (trade obligations guaranteed by one or more banks). The purpose of the Federal Reserve System's open market operations is to smooth the operations of the money market, to prevent wide and panicky swings that might exaggerate and thus defeat the purpose of long-term Federal Reserve System policy. Open market operations also provide assistance—either on the buy or sell side of the market—that will enable the market to adjust comfortably to the stresses of changing levels of economic activity.

Two points are implicit in this discussion of the Federal Reserve System and the three tools through which it controls bank reserves and, hence, the money supply for any purpose in the economy, including housing.

The first point is that the Federal Reserve System relies for its effectiveness on the economic motives of the major actors. If it creates bank reserves, it expects that the desire for income will propel bankers to invest their excess reserves in loans or money market instruments. If, on the other hand, it wishes to cut back on economic activity, it can do so by the Draconic measure of increasing reserve requirements and literally shrinking the money supply by force. It would appear, therefore, to be in principle more effective in stopping economic expansion than in stimulating it. This probably can be taken to be a special case of the general proposition that governments are more effective in preventing things than in stimulating them.

Unquestionably, if the Federal Reserve System managers were under pressure to do so, they could stop economic expansion in its tracks. No one wants them to do this. On the other hand, while everyone claims to want the Federal Reserve System to provide full employment with reasonably stable prices, its managers can't seem to accomplish this. The resulting measures, or half measures, to restrain expansion without stifling it, cannot become full measures because they would succeed better in creating stable prices than in maintaining full employment. These half measures work even less well in current circumstances than they worked not long ago. Interest rates are no longer the mild total depressant they once were. Large groups of consumers have banded together in labor unions to demand wage increases that take the sting out of the higher prices caused by interest rate increases. Manufacturers take advantage of the higher costs to tack on a little extra in the sales price. Some types of capital-intensive products are put under great pressure by higher interest rates: Housing is an example.

But the lowering of interest rates along with an increase in the money supply will not guarantee that, once having been flattened, housing production will rise again. What stimulates the producers and their consumers to sudden activity? At other times, what plunges them into corresponding apathy? These two questions are as mysterious as the reason why trout will rise to a fly with no restraint at all at one moment, but sulk underwater a minute later. It must be said for the Federal Reserve System, and its monetary tools, that without an administered flexibility in the money supply, there can be little hope of achieving full production in the economy, especially including those capital-intensive activities like housing construction. But monetary management alone will not achieve this objective.

The second point to be noted about the Federal Reserve System's monetary tools is their blindness. Monetary policy that acts to increase and restrict the monetary supply is essentially indiscriminate: The influence of the policy is felt by everyone who needs money or wishes to profit from those who do need it. In its blindness, it cannot distinguish between those who would use money for purposes that moralists might consider constructive—the provision of fire-safe housing in American cities, for example—from those who would use money for purposes that moralists would consider trivial—the acquisition of stock in a company as part of a merger that will benefit the promoters and their investment bankers alone. It sometimes seems that monetary policy works perversely. The weight of restrictive monetary policy—intended to slow down the creation of money, alleviate rapid price rises, and encourage economic stability—seems to fall most heavily on the shoulders of those who can least afford it: The families that need better housing, but do not qualify for special subsidies. The investor-speculators can carry a high interest burden somewhat more readily, though the investor-speculators themselves might claim to view the matter differently.

It should be stressed, however, that blindness is sometimes a virtue. The blindness of the lover to the blemishes on milady's cheeks has been extolled by poets; successful marriages probably require blindness (and a touch of deafness) on the part of both parties if they are to survive.

So, in the management of an economy, it is useful to have policies that, if not self-executing, at least avoid bearing a label indicating that they are intended primarily to aid one part of the nation rather than another. Generally, monetary policy avoids direct politicization. While a move to restrict monetary growth and raise interest rates does bring complaints, from some members of Congress, that bankers are being enriched while borrowers suffer,* the criticism cannot be reduced to the same geographical basis on which the Congress of the United States is elected. Once, of course, it was possible to think of the East as the land of the bankers and the West as the land of the borrowers, but reports of the wealth in Texas, Oklahoma, and California have made this geographic allocation obsolete.

At any rate, it is impossible to draw a statute that will limit any single state's share of the immediate benefit or cost of a change in monetary policy to 15 percent of the nation's benefit or cost. This limitation characterizes many statutes that confer housing subsidies. While generous tax allocations for better housing in the slums of a few major American cities might win the support of Congress, the possibility is no certainty. One might argue persuasively that what moralists consider socially desirable becomes acceptable to a majority of their countrymen only when they fail to understand exactly what their representatives are supporting. While this supposition cannot be proved, it does suggest that anything that works should be cherished even if it involves doing the right thing for the wrong reason.

In an effort to remedy the partial blindness of monetary policy, the Federal Reserve System has been permitted by the Congress to exert powers that not only expand or contract credit but that open or close channels into which it may flow. Thus, to offset the charms of marketable stocks and bonds as collateral for loans, the Federal Reserve Board may establish limits on the amount of credit that may be extended by banks against the market value of stocks for the purpose of buying more stocks. The regulation is intended to prevent the extension of so much credit on stocks and bonds that the prices of those securities will be artificially inflated, sucking more and more credit into investments that only indirectly increase productive capacity.

The Federal Reserve Board also directly controls the flow of credit into consumer financing and establishes limits under Regulation "Q," which impose a differential by law between the interest rates that commercial banks may pay on time and thrift deposits and the interest

---

* The criticism fails to note that banks are borrowers too. The common stocks of banks do not boom during high interest periods.

rates that may be paid by thrift institutions such as mutual savings banks and savings and loan associations. The intent of this regulation is to discourage savers from removing their funds from the mortgage-making institutions, and it is undoubtedly of some help in this connection. Yet it by no means offers absolute protection to the mortgage market. The clearest single fact that emerges from an examination of the activities of the money market is that all parts of the market are related. Whenever government agencies offer their securities for sale, they are potential competitors for the funds held by mutual savings banks; whenever the major city banks seek funds to support major loans to their customers, they offer to small city banks an alternative to mortgage investment.

Money, as any of the commodities that it purchases, will flow to the renter or purchaser offering the highest price. The Federal Reserve System has injected a measure of orderliness into the process by which money flows. It has also, as we shall see, provided a measure of relief to thrift institutions by permitting commercial banks to lend them funds in time of stringency and to discount their paper at the regional Federal Reserve Bank window. But unless the Federal Reserve System were able to dedicate its work entirely to keeping interest rates low in all parts of the market—as it did in the period following World War II when it was solely concerned with the cost to the United States Treasury of carrying the national debt—it cannot alone provide the cheap real savings that housing programs for the low-income, urban families require.

It may help to remember that cheap credit did not solve the farm problem by itself, although it was a necessary part of a solution that included many other more painful measures. In the same way, housing requires a healthy money market and a generally expansive money supply, free from the pressures and distortions of foreign affairs and the lure of security loans. But these alone will not provide housing with the capital it needs at the prices that moderate-income families in the city can afford.

PART TWO

The Lending
Institutions

CHAPTER 6

THE COMMERCIAL BANKS

THE commercial banks are so important a part of American economic life that their absolute size overwhelms the relative importance of their several investments. Thus, commercial banks devote only a small part of their portfolios to real estate investments as a whole—20 percent would be a high estimate of the national ratio of real estate investments to total assets. Residential mortgages constitute only a part of the total real estate investment; the residential mortgage portfolio of commercial banks constitutes, on a national average, less than 15 percent of the total assets of the banks. Nevertheless, the total assets of the commercial banks are so huge that even the small part dedicated to residential mortgages makes this sector the third largest holding of such mortgages in the United States.[1]

As a matter of principle, commercial banks tend to avoid residential mortgages because of their lack of liquidity, their long term at fixed interest rates, the reinvestment problem they present as the principal sums return in small amortization payments, and the cost of servicing. Regulatory agencies have generally discouraged the investment of commercial bank assets in real estate; in fact, national banks were not permitted to invest in any real estate until the passage of the Federal Reserve Act of 1913. Today, regulations continue to restrict the amount of a bank's assets that may be invested in real estate mortgages, the minimum terms of repayment, value to loan ratio, and the length of the mortgages. The trouble with real estate from a bank examiner's perspective is that the value of the real estate as security is very difficult to determine accurately. Every parcel of real estate differs from every other parcel. Real estate appraisal may be an art or a science. In either case, experience confirms the impression that appraisers are reluctant to publicize opinions that frustrate the needs or desires of the clients who engage them.

Yet commercial banks have obviously been making real estate loans for a number of reasons, the most significant of which is that banks located outside major commercial centers may have relatively fewer opportunities for the business and personal loans that comprised 30.9 percent of all commercial bank assets in 1970.[2] The real estate loan share of all commercial bank assets in the same year was 12.6[3] percent; almost one-half of these loans were on commercial, not residential, properties. Residential mortgages may be the best investment available to some banks despite their disadvantages. The lack of competitive local loan demand probably makes smaller commercial banks in the smaller population centers turn more readily than large banks in large cities to residential real estate mortgages. But even big banks find themselves sometimes making residential real estate mortgages in preference to other more attractive commercial loans, because they feel that promoting the physical development of their environment is in their long-term economic interest.

Implicit reinforcement of the theory that the relatively smaller commercial banks make most of the residential mortgages is provided by the statistics on Federal Housing Administration and Veterans Administration (VA) guaranteed mortgages. In 1971, commercial banks used FHA and VA mortgage insurance to cover only 14.3 percent of the mortgages they held,[4] while mutual savings banks used government insurance on 48.5 percent of their mortgages.[5] Presumably, mutual savings banks, concentrated in the larger cities, are forced to make out-of-town as well as out-of-state mortgages. The difficulty of accurately appraising the remote property that secures such a mortgage makes government insurance attractive. But the small commercial bank, lending primarily to nearby homeowners, feels it can safely rely on its own judgment of property values: The officers know local real estate values well enough at least to provide a rough check on its appraiser's report.

An interesting aspect of mortgage lending by commercial banks is that these banks make loans on existing properties more readily than do the mutual savings banks. Commercial banks in the smaller cities, which lend to smaller business enterprises than do banks in big cities, may insist upon a residential mortgage on the home of the small businessman as security for what would ordinarily be considered a commercial loan.

This is suggested as one possible explanation for the rapid turnover of commercial bank mortgages on residential property. In 1970, for example, when the mutual savings banks and the commercial banks held approximately the same total amount of residential mortgages in their portfolios—$40 billion, more or less [6]—the commercial banks originated almost twice as many mortgages as the mutual savings banks; [7] presumably, twice as many had been paid off. It seems likely that those residential mortgages that are used to fund business enterprises can be retired faster than normal residential mortgages.

The size of the residential unit financed by the commercial banks as a whole also reflects the tendency of the smaller commercial bank to carry a larger proportionate share of their residential mortgage portfolio. At the end of 1970, 92 percent of the commercial bank mortgages covered properties with four or fewer units, a higher concentration in small buildings than we find in the residential mortgage portfolios of the mutual savings banks, the savings and loan associations, and life insurance companies.[8]

Thanks to recent changes in the tax laws, we now must take into account developments that have opened new opportunities for participation by the commercial banks in the housing field.

First, there have been significant structural changes in the mortgage market. Mortgage banking has grown tremendously since World War II, in response to a large development boom accompanied by a widespread shift in population. Mortgage bankers usually originate mortgage loans in the areas of the country that are growing too fast to develop local banks to provide the capital needed for building. The mortgage banker intends to sell his mortgages to some large national institution—perhaps a life insurance company. What he needs is temporary financing to enable him to make mortgage loans pending the sale of those loans to a permanent investor.

This temporary financing is provided by commercial banks, either local or remote. For the commercial bank, the loan is protected not merely by the mortgages held by the mortgage banker but by the promise (the technical word is commitment) of the permanent investor to buy the mortgage within a stipulated time. Local resources may be enough to cover one year's local demand for mortgage money, but there would ultimately be a serious shortage of local capital unless the national money market, by honoring its commitments, replenishes the local bank's balances by purchasing the mortgages originated locally.

If interest rates drop while the local mortgage banker continues to hold a mortgage originated with borrowed money, the mortgage will be more attractive to a permanent investor because its interest rate has become higher than the current market rate. Sensing this, a mortgage banker, relying on the security of the commitment, can hold the mortgage he has on hand in the hope of getting a higher price than that established in the commitment. Even a small difference in price makes a big difference to the mortgage originator because so much of the money he uses is borrowed. If, for example, a mortgage banker borrows 90 percent of the money with which he makes a pool of mortgage loans, a two-point rise in the final price of the mortgage means a 20 percent gain on his own capital investment.

The process of holding mortgages for a favorable market opportunity or while waiting for the permanent investor to make good on his commitment has, in an expression of pseudoconcreteness, been called the warehousing of mortgages. Commercial banks finance this warehousing, and find it tasty business. Some have already begun to wonder if the profit of the mortgage banker and the profit of the commercial banker who provides his warehousing capability might not be merged. Already investment-banking firms have begun to acquire mortgage-banking firms. Commercial bankers and their lawyers are consulting state and federal rule books to see whether or not this might be worthwhile for them and legal, as well. This new enthusiasm for the mortgage-banking field reflects far more than the commitments of privately owned holding companies. It reflects the development of a very large though informal market in which mortgages can now be bought and sold, usually with the help in one form or another, as we shall see, of the United States government.

An even newer field in which commercial banks are beginning to think of playing a significant part is that opened up by a new institution altogether—the Real Estate Investment Trust. The Real Estate Investment Trust is a corporate entity that lies somewhere between the familiar corporation and a limited partnership. Its purpose is to pool the resources of a number of individual investors (at least five hundred, of whom some may be corporations); thus it is larger or more widely held than the typical limited partnership. Yet the liability of each member of the trust is limited, and, most important of all, the profits of the investment trust are taxed only as they are distributed to the participants. Ninety percent of the profits must be so distributed every year; even better, the losses that the roseate-billed investors hope will be paper losses consisting mainly of depreciation, are also pushed through the trust so that each investor may apply his share of loss to his own income taxes.

Commercial banks are considering organizing Real Estate Investment Trusts under the aegis of their skilled real estate departments. There is no reason why a commercial bank should not lend money to a trust if the loan had proper collateral. This would not be a direct investment in residential real estate, but if the trust were in turn investing in residential real estate, the loan of the commercial bank would have been of great help to it. Ordinarily, the Real Estate Investment Trust's investment is in ownership of properties, but there is no legal reason why it should not also invest in mortgages; some of them do, in fact, particularly in those mortgages—usually on commercial or highly specialized property—in which the mortgagee not only earns interest but also gets a share of the equity profit. If the spread between the interest rate on the mortgage and the rate at which the trust can borrow is sufficient, the trust can earn a very considerable amount of income on a highly leveraged basis. In fact, trusts that specialize in mortgages find that they can leverage their own capital with six or more times as much in borrowed funds. Naturally, the profitability of this depends on their making mortgages with higher interest rates than they have to pay on their own borrowings. The entry of a large number of trusts in this field, all of whom would be trying to acquire attractive mortgages with high yields, would have the effect of bringing mortgage yields down, as one trust after another would settle for a little smaller spread, rather than no spread at all. In their search for borrowed money, the trusts are busy tapping sources—including pension and welfare funds—that do not ordinarily invest in mortgages. We have yet to see whether or not any of this high-spirited financial pinochle will eventually gather a big enough kitty to help solve financial problems in residential construction. Their relationship with the commercial banks is still evolving.

Another area of commercial bank activity in the field of housing has scarcely been mentioned in the public press. This involves the discount window of the Federal Reserve System. During the severe credit shortage of 1969–70 many mutual savings banks found themselves with insufficient liquidity. People were coming into the banks and demanding their deposits in cash, many of them with the hope that they could place their savings in the thrift department of a commercial bank, picking up a color television set for their pains. Others had dreams of future indolent wealth, to be achieved by investing in corporate bonds at 8 percent instead of savings accounts at 5 percent. In any case, the banks could scarcely expect to raise money by selling mortgages that had been made at 4½ percent years before. Voices were raised in Congress to demand that the Federal Reserve System move to the rescue of the "people banks" (as savings banks in New York State call themselves in commercials) by opening wide the discount windows of the Federal Reserve Banks to savings bankers bringing mortgages, undoubtedly sound, for discount.

The board of the Federal Reserve System reacted to this in approximately the same way as the board of governors of a golf course would react to a proposal to use the greens every summer as Sunday picnic grounds for slum dwellers. They hastened to remind the congressmen and others that the Federal Reserve System's facilities are open to members only. (If any financial institution could borrow at the windows, who would be willing to submit to the regulations that Federal Reserve System membership involves?) The Federal Reserve System also refreshed Congress's recollection of its familiar slogan: Discounting at the Reserve Bank is a privilege, not a right. How could this discipline be enforced if Congress suddenly took action to ensure that those who did not even enjoy the privilege would be invested with the right?

The proposal disappeared. In the meantime, the Federal Reserve System had suggested to its commercial bank members that *if they* loaned money to mutual savings banks on notes that were secured by the pledge of assets, those notes would be considered acceptable collateral at the discount window. The same—or practically the same—increase in liquidity was achieved by this discreet method, following the rules and avoiding the establishment of a precedent that might later prove somewhat embarrassing.

Finally, and most important, some commercial banks have begun to play a large role in construction financing, secured by a first mortgage on the land and the incomplete building. Usually, a commercial bank making the mortgage requires that the builder have a commitment for a permanent mortgage on completion; some banks insist that the commitment be in the form of an agreement to purchase the construction mortgage. Yet, in some cases, where the borrower enjoys a very high credit rating and the proposed building strikes the bank as entirely sound, a construction mortgage may be made without a formal take-out arrangement.

In the recent housing boom, construction mortgages have produced a remarkably high yield for commercial banks. The yield is made up of an interest rate on the nominal loan installments, as well as fees for special legal work and technical inspections, and sometimes a commitment fee in advance on the total projected sum of the construction mortgage. The yield is made richer because the nominal payments on which the borrower pays interest are greater than the actual advances made. The bank holds back a stipulated percentage of the installment to protect it against the dangers of lending on an incomplete building.

But although losses on construction loans have been minimal, the risk remains. What happens if the total cost of construction exceeds the agreed upon construction mortgage plus the builder's equity? Or if the builder goes into bankruptcy and is unable to finish the building? Some banks seek to protect themselves by insisting on performance bonds, which are contracts between the general contractor (or his subcontractors) and a surety company that commits itself to complete the building; and payment bonds, which purportedly guarantee that anyone who might have a claim for goods and services provided to the building will be paid in full. But such bonds are expensive, not enforceable if the building deviates from the structure described in the bonding documents. Many banks that specialize in construction mortgage financing rely on their own inspection teams to see to it that the actual cost of completing the building will be less than the amount still payable under the construction mortgage agreement.

All of this sounds easy, but it requires experience and talent. At the beginning of the work, a schedule of payments is devised, under which stipulated percentages of the total mortgage (less the agreed upon withholding) are paid when certain typical events have taken place: the completion of the foundation, the completion of the framework, the completion of the rough plumbing lines. But the balance of costs in the construction industry is dynamically unstable. A strike, a jurisdictional change, a managerial failure on the part of a subcontractor may throw the percentage out of kilter. The bank may have paid out 90 percent of its construction loan only to find that the last 10 percent of the building will cost 30 percent of the total expense. This is an area of housing finance in which clever people or a well-organized bank should be able to make a profit with only minimal adverse effects on the ultimate housing cost: The interest on the construction adds only a small amount to the total cost, at least if the work is done with dispatch.

One response to such a situation—the possibility of profit at high risk— is to suggest that the government assume responsibility for it. The FHA now insures certain types of construction loans; and in multifamily mortgages, the Federal National Mortgage Association (FNMA), as we shall see, commits to buy them. But for government, the risk may outweigh the profit. New York City's Municipal Loan Program, involved in the rehabilitation of older buildings, necessarily offered construction loans. The loans went into default, in some cases, to help contractors in the early days of jobs, when the city had consciously overpaid them. When buildings remained unfinished, or later, in default of city mortgage loans, the press led a major outcry against rehabilitation in general. In the public furor over the losses in the program, government housing programs for rehabilitating buildings were roundly condemned. At the same time, commercial lenders in the same area of rehabilitation (of better buildings, to be sure, but old buildings equally difficult to estimate in advance) had been functioning successfully for years. This does not prove that government is always wrong in housing; but it is at least evidence that blending risky construction lending into even riskier social purposes provides opportunities for scandal and misuse of public funds. Before running those risks, a moderately prudent government would try to ensure that the ownership and management of the building to be rehabilitated are good enough to keep it alive after the unwitting public has swallowed the rehabilitation costs. Even more cautious governments would refuse to undertake such programs altogether, unless they had a clear mandate from the public to speculate with its funds. Even such a mandate—if it could be obtained—would fade very quickly in the face of losses and foreclosures. The mortgage system is based on the notion that debts will be repaid; if there is a greater chance that they will not be, grant subsidies are probably better public policy. Acceptance by the government of vast mortgage payment arrears in rehabilitated buildings occupied by low-income families may well encourage better-off families to overlook paying their mortgages too.

CHAPTER 7

THE MUTUAL SAVINGS
BANKS

THE mutual savings banks, of which the oldest American example dates back less than one hundred fifty years, testify to one of the miraculous achievements of the industrial revolution, the unprecedented ability of ordinary working-class or artisan families to save money. Savings, if they could be accumulated before the 18th century by peasants or urban workers, were accumulated in kind, not in cash: a bit of land, the tools of one's trade, the household goods. Nor was there anything in the descriptions of working-class life in England in the early nineteenth century to suggest that lightening of the burden of poverty could ever be brought about by a social metamorphosis whose first impact, in the period of capital accumulation, was generally severe, brutal, and unpromising.

In the United States, particularly, capital was needed to finance the opening of a continent and to make industrialization possible. It was, therefore, inevitable that capitalists noted the growing accumulation of money in the hands of those who had never held it before. The accumulation in the possession of any one working-class family was too small to provide equity capital for a business venture at a time when the art of corporate organization was in its infancy. Widespread stock distribution through investment bankers with sales staff was not even dreamed of, and the mutual fund—which now provides an opportunity for those with modest savings to acquire a thin slice of a number of enterprises—still lay far over the future horizon.

It did not take the stock market collapse of 1974 to make them wonder if widespread equity ownership in established enterprises is indeed a satisfactory use of savings. Here libertarian principles intercede to ask whether or not people of modest means should be provided with the same facilities for stock investment that wealthier investors have. Deferring all questions about principles and trying to replace them with questions about practice, let us agree that investment funds in new enterprises, or in the novel activities of existing enterprises, are easier to raise when there exists a marketplace in which such investments are readily salable. Are the costs of maintaining the marketplace less than the costs of attracting capital *without* ready liquidity? Or may this whole question be answered by time itself, as the prices of stocks go so high in relation to their earnings and dividends that the smaller investors lose interest in them? Would this affect the rate of savings altogether, as people might feel that money was continuing to lose its deferability and the stock market losing its promise of keeping pace in a world of rising prices? Or would it simply mean that buyers of mutual funds would sell their shares—as many are being said to in 1974 —to put their money in bonds or in deposit accounts. Or are these changes the result of merely evanescent shifts in public psychology and business climate?

These questions are latter-day versions of the questions asked by the prominent citizens of the eastern seaboard cities between 1850 and 1875, when the mutual savings banks experienced their first heady growth. It was impractical to urge working people to put their money into business investments; yet the streets were full of promoters of dubious enterprises, swindlers, confidence men with gaudy stories of quick fortunes to be made elsewhere in the country. The mutual savings banks offered a response to the problem of how to protect the savings of the newly industrialized working classes—a welcome problem compared with their previous poverty. The answer involved an irresistible brew of human motivations: prestige for the banks' founders and successor trustees, a sense on the part of these same gentlemen that they were doing good, no investment needed on their part—the savings banks were to be owned by their depositors—though the sense of ownership is quite attenuated. Most important of all, the activities that the founders and successor trustees of the savings banks carry on are pleasant, one might almost say easy. The banks make mortgages, buy bonds, and generally deal in abstracts. One senses that one is doing good and important work without having to become personally involved with the grubby details of why a borrower can't make his mortgage payments, and why a neighborhood, once good, has now sadly deteriorated.

Looking at the successful record of the mutual savings banks, many people ask why similar nonprofit ownership would not be applicable in the housing field. The differences are important.[1] In comparison with savings banking, the ownership of housing is grubby, even if large government mortgages make cash investment by the founder unnecessary.[2]

One sees not the grateful smiles of depositors whose savings have been fruitful and multiplied (slowly, of course), but instead the surly anger of the tenant in 13B whose kitchen sink has stopped draining three times in the past month. The prestige of having created an apartment house—without any investment, through the magic of a 100 percent mortgage—disappears when the tenants move in or when the cooperators commence a lawsuit on the grounds that the finished building is less than its sponsor promised it would be.

Finally, it should be remembered that as successful as the mutual savings banks have been in fulfilling their purpose of safeguarding the savings of families of modest means, and providing them with a regular return within the limits of prudence—the institution hardly spread beyond the original industrial states of the East. In the rural states in the nineteenth century, family savings had not yet accumulated. When the midwestern states beyond Indiana began to industrialize, the established commercial banks fought the introduction of mutual savings bank legislation—successfully, too. It is inescapably clear that the mutual savings banks today face severe problems. The investment and savings climate has changed drastically, particularly in the past ten years, while the powers of savings banks have changed relatively little since their original legalization. Because the mutual savings banks supply very important amounts of mortgage money for residential purposes—not only in the states in which they are organized but throughout the United States—the future form of the mutual savings bank is vital to the housing industry.

In discussing the commercial banks, we stressed their absolute size. In discussing the mutual savings banks, we find ourselves in a smaller universe, but a universe organized about a single comprehensible principle.

The total assets and resources of the commercial banks of the United States stood at $486 billion at the end of 1970;[1] these were distributed very unevenly among more than twelve thousand banks located in every state and in the District of Columbia.[2] The assets were by and large invested in loans and discounts to corporations and individuals, in securities of federal, state, and local governments, and, as we have seen, in real estate mortgages to the extent of less than 20 percent of all assets.

Also at the end of 1970, the assets of the mutual savings banks of the country stood at $79 billion,[3] approximately one-sixth of the assets of commercial banks. These assets were distributed among only 494 mutual savings banks, one twenty-fourth as many as the number of commercial banks.[4] The mutual savings banks are legalized to do business only in eighteen states and Puerto Rico.[5]

Whereas commercial banks may be chartered by the states or the federal government, there is no federal law permitting the chartering of mutual savings banks. All are, therefore, directly regulated by the states in which they are located. Unlike the commercial banks, which may join the Federal Reserve System whether they are chartered by the federal or the state government, the mutual savings banks are not permitted to join. They are, however, regulated as to reserves and investments by the local state governments. They may join the Federal Home Loan Bank (FHLB), as we shall see.

In any case, the federal government is well aware of the existence of the mutual savings banks, and they are permitted to join the Federal Deposit Insurance Corporation (FDIC), which insures deposits up to a maximum of twenty thousand dollars for an individual account. As a condition to writing the insurance, the FDIC inspects the mutual savings banks, and, among other prerogatives, the FDIC has always had the right to set ceilings on the rate of interest that can be paid on different types of accounts. One might surmise that in establishing its ceiling rates on the interest that mutual savings banks may pay on their deposits, the FDIC has not been unaware of the ceilings that the Federal Reserve Bank places on the interest that commercial banks may pay on demand deposits (zero interest, to repeat), and on their time and thrift accounts. In 1966, direct federal regulation of all interest paid by commercial banks, mutual savings banks, and savings and loan associations was established for the first time.[6] The regulations provide that commercial banks may not pay so high a rate of interest as mutual savings banks and savings and loan associations. Because the differentials are subject to change, as are the ceilings, it is fruitless to commit them to memory. The purpose of the differentials, in any case, remains clear: Its purpose is to shield the deposit growth or stability of the thrift institutions from the competition of the commercial bank. Because the residential mortgage market offers the final resting place for most of the deposits placed in the thrift intermediaries—the mutual savings banks and the savings and loan associations—it is theoretically the mortgage market that benefits from the higher ceilings permitted on the interest paid by the thrift intermediaries. In theory, more money will flow into the mortgage market because the intermediaries that make mortgage loans can pay higher interest rates than the commercial banks that do not make mortgage loans as the cornerstone of their investment policy. Because every benefit must be paid for somewhere, we find that the depositors in the thrift and time departments of commercial banks pay for this benefit. They earn less than they would if they took their money and trotted around the corner to the nearest mutual savings bank (provided, of course, that they happen to be keeping their money in a mutual savings bank state). Meanwhile, some managers of thrift institutions wonder whether or not the commercial bank time depositors are paying *enough*. The managers would argue that the difference in permitted interest rates is too small to protect the thrift institutions. In any case, there is nothing to prevent savings bank depositors from withdrawing their money altogether, and buying bonds or treasury bills. In 1974, they were doing this at such a rate that in one month alone the savings banks lost half a billion dollars in deposits.

Commercial bank thrift depositors differ from mutual savings bank depositors. The discussion of the mutual savings bank began with the notion of *family* savings. Throughout its history, the savings bank has emphasized its service to families and to natural persons (as contrasted with corporations and business partnerships). The variation in laws from state to state makes any sweeping specific description impractical, but many states limit by law the kinds of persons who may open accounts in mutual savings banks; in some states, some corporations may do so, provided they are not profit making. There are no such general restrictions on commercial bank time depositors. Most savings bank states also place a ceiling on the balance that may be carried by any single depositor in any single savings bank. The regulations reflect a political reality, the tussle in each of the savings bank states between the commercial banking interests and the mutual savings bank interests, each of which is happy to be free to accept deposits without limit in the interest of the depositors' freedom, but each of which seems ready to seek to impose restrictions on the other, in the interest of its own freedom from objectionable competition. The right to open branches is another subject of intense competition between commercial and savings banks.

The competition for savings between commercial and mutual savings banks has become significant in the years since World War II. In the early postwar years, the demand deposits of commercial banks were at a high level relative to the requests for loans, and the commercial banks did little to encourage the growth of savings on which they would be forced to pay interest. With the passage of time, the demand for loans increased, making a growth in deposits not only desirable but necessary. The interest payments required to attract time deposit accounts were offset by the advantage of a much smaller required reserve by the Federal Reserve System.

As liquidity decreased with the boom years of the 1960s and the Vietnam war, interest rates rose and corporate treasurers with large balances in their demand deposit accounts began to wonder why they should keep so much company money idle without earning interest. All of these factors combined to increase commercial bank interest in developing interest-bearing deposits; it is now an important part of commercial banking. The commercial banks appear to be spending significant sums of money in advertising those of their characteristics that make their time and thrift accounts competitive with mutual savings banks.

The First National City Bank advertises with a jingle to assure listeners that it is the *only* bank they ever need. What is the point of this curious claim? How many families have more than one commercial bank in which they keep demand deposit checking accounts? The percentage must be infinitesimal. The slogan makes sense only in a mutual savings bank state, where many families traditionally keep the household savings in a passbook-type account with one of the mutual savings banks, while they pay their household bills with a nonminimum-balance checking account at a commercial bank. The First National City Bank is not blatantly urging such families to withdraw their savings from the Bowery Savings Bank or the Dry Dock Saving Bank, but the import of the message is to suggest that such a change would simplify life: only one bank to visit. You deposit your paycheck, get some cash, and put aside your savings without stepping out into the blizzard or onto the heat of the midsummer pavements. The message probably works.

Similarly, the Chase Manhattan Bank explains on television that *all* of the household fiscal data will henceforth be provided on a single statement. The point is that instead of having to look up that dreary old passbook from the mutual savings bank when you want to know how rich you are, you can look at the monthly checking account statement for the bad news about how much money your family spent, and then find reassurance at the bottom of the page. Here, in a separate tabulation on the same sheet of paper, you will find the statement of your thrift account as well, solid as Gibraltar and growing just about as quickly.

The increased attention paid by the commercial bankers to the profits that lie hidden in the family thrift account has frightened mutual savings bankers and caused legislators, economists, and other deep thinkers to ponder the roles of these two forms of financial intermediary. The course of the mutual savings bank industry since World War II justifies their sense of alarm, despite the fact that at the end of 1971, total deposits in mutual savings banks had reached $89 billion.[7] This was more than five times the total deposits in 1945. While this may seem a comfortable rate of growth, two major difficulties were concealed behind the number. First, the mutual savings banks were growing less rapidly than the commercial banks and the savings and loan associations.[8] Second, the annual growth has been subject to wide swings, in one year dropping to a true net outflow of cash deposits, masked only by the crediting of accrued interest to the balances already on deposit.[9]

The 1972 National Fact Book of Mutual Savings Banking describes the significance of the swings:

The substantial 1966 and 1969 reductions in the industry's saving flows, for instance, largely reflected its weakened competitive position in savings markets and underscored its increased vulnerability to rapid changes in financial market conditions.[10]

Precisely the same events were repeated in the last quarter of 1972 and in 1973: Interest rates rose precipitously while the Federal Reserve System tried to stifle a boom by cutting down (unsuccessfully, it appears) on the growth rate of the money supply.

The impact of these swings has been felt in the residential mortgage market, because residential mortgages constitute one of the three major investment areas for mutual savings banks. The other two fields are corporate securities and government securities, including primarily federal securities and an increasing amount of federal agency securities. These latter are the direct obligations of special government agencies, such as the Federal Home Loan Bank Board, of which more anon. The federal agencies are obviously given debt-incurring power by the Congress—obviously, because they would not be able to incur debt without it—but the debt is not officially guaranteed by the United States government. Because most soothsayers believe that the federal government would not allow one of its agencies to go into default, the bonds have almost the same investment rating as United States Treasury securities. Their sum outstanding has increased dramatically since the end of World War II, in spite of the fact, or perhaps because of the fact, that they are regarded by many monetary specialists as a weak and craven way to incur government debt without appearing to do so, complicating a sound evaluation of money supply trends.

The concentration of mutual savings bank assets in mortgages and long-term bonds reflects the relatively slow turnover of mutual savings bank deposits. Industry spokesmen frequently complain that their industry "borrows short-term and lends long-term," meaning that its depositors are free to withdraw their balances at any time, but the money to pay them must necessarily be bound up in long-term obligations in order to earn the highest interest rates commensurate with safety. Interest on long-term obligations tends to be higher than interest paid on short-term obligations.

Uncertainty grows with the remoteness of the future event, diminution of the value of money increases over time, and the long-term obligation poses a problem of liquidity. In theory, at least, the borrower of money at long term must pay enough interest so that the lender who accommodates him will not be afraid of the cost of raising cash by borrowing before its maturity against the security of the debt. Despite the presumption that long-term money is more expensive than short-term money, there are occasions on which short-term money becomes more expensive. These are unusual and worth mentioning, if at all, only to cast some doubt on any economic statement whose originator claims it to be universally true. This unusual inverse relationship comes about when short-term interest rates get so high that no one believes they will remain at their current levels very long.

Looking back at the end of World War II, we can trace the shift in investment policy on the part of the mutual savings bank, and relate the shift to changes in the economic climate of the nation. The 1945 peace appeared to end a period of unprecedented savings accumulation. Four years of industrial expansion to provide war material had kept employment at levels that exceeded the theoretical level of full employment because new people were drawn into the work force. Consumer goods were in short supply, so short that demand had to be curtailed with rationing, while residential construction had been at a standstill. Of the approximately $16 billion in invested assets of the mutual savings banks at the end of 1945, less than 30 percent was in real estate mortgages, including nonresidential mortgages.[11] More than 70 percent of the assets of mutual savings banks were invested in bonds.[12] Almost 64 percent were in United States government bonds alone.[13]

Within five years after the war, 1950, mortgages amounted to only 36.8 percent of mutual savings banks assets.[14] Within ten years, or 1960, this figure had nearly doubled, climbing to 65.8 percent; [15] five years later, mortgages comprised 73.1 percent of savings bank portfolios.[16] The net flow of savings bank money into mortgages continued to rise, though somewhat unevenly, through the 1950s (dipping in the recession of 1959) and reached a peak of $4.3 billion in 1964.[17] (Net flows, incidentally, consist of all the money invested in new mortgages during a specific year less the capital sums paid back to the lender by the borrowers of previous mortgages.) The net flow represents the actual increase in mortgage lending in a given period.

In 1965, the net flow of mortgage money from mutual savings banks dropped slightly: In the later 1960s, as money tightened, the drop accelerated. In 1970, the mutual savings banks were able to provide only $1.06 billion in new mortgages on properties containing one-to-four dwelling units; this was a 60 percent drop from the situation of six years before.[18] The drop in larger apartment house lending was even more dramatic. The savings banks provided only 20 percent of their 1964 net flows.[19]

The drop in apartment house lending may be somewhat exaggerated by an unusually high figure for the years from 1963 to 1965, when New York City was experiencing an apartment house construction boom stimulated by fear of the restrictions imposed by a new zoning ordinance. The savings banks, concentrated in the older industrialized parts of the United States, as we have said, are especially concentrated in New York City and are quite susceptible to local situations.

In fact, the pressure on mutual savings banks to invest their mortgage funds in local, or in-state, mortgages is heavy and persistent. It reflects both outer pressure and the natural inner tendencies of the bank trustees. The outer pressure reflects a feeling of impatience with conditions in the cities in which mutual savings banks are located, and the sense that these banks, with their impressive resources, should be required to use a fair share of them for the improvement of local housing, more particularly low-income housing. There is ample legal precedent for a requirement that state-chartered mutual savings banks invest a stipulated part of their assets within the state; and this suggestion rises again, from time to time, even in those states that had such a requirement but later repealed it. The inner pressure from the trustees of the bank reflects their interest in the immediate surroundings of the bank, and in the city in which it is located. Trustees would seem to be impelled to serve in that capacity in part from a genuine dedication to their city, and this dedication has been indicated by a number of slum-rebuilding developments in the older cities to which savings banks have contributed (the word is loosely used, of course) mortgage money. Several historic housing cooperatives that were erected in New York City by the United Housing Foundation were made possible by savings bank mortgages written at a rate of interest that was below the going rate. Of course, this was by no means the only factor required to keep the rent down: The city offered real estate tax abatement as well.

There are, of course, contrary pressures. Of relatively minor importance is the pressure to prove to the Congress and the national banking authorities that the mutual savings banks are *national* institutions, benefiting the entire country in their operations, and that they therefore should not be subjected to restrictive or unfair national legislation. In 1970, 39 percent of savings bank mortgage loans were on out-of-state properties;[20] only about one-quarter of these were made by savings banks in other states where savings banks are legalized. The remaining three-quarters of the out-of-state mortgages, amounting to about 30 percent of all savings bank mortgages, were made in states where no savings banks exist.[21]

Of greater importance, probably, than good national public relations in determining the amount of out-of-state lending is the question of locating the highest yield with safety. Those who argue that savings banks should not be required to invest in-state point to the interest sensitivity of savings bank depositors. They argue that the depositors will move their money to other depositories, or "disintermediate" altogether, if the earnings of savings banks were adversely affected by a geographical limitation on mortgage investment. Proponents suggest that a significant part of savings bank deposits are not interest sensitive, and would not move elsewhere even if a geographic limitation were imposed on a given percentage of the total mortgage portfolio. The difference of opinion attracts little attention in times of ample mortgage money; it heats up when money is tight, interest rates are high, and depositors are indeed considering moving their funds in search of higher yields. Recent government activity on behalf of the secondary mortgage market may relieve somewhat the pressure to regulate the geography of savings bank mortgages, but the issue continues to be raised.

Many other arguments still rage in the sphere of mutual savings banking. The subject matter of all the arguments is roughly the same: Can the mutual savings banks usefully survive in their present form? Will they continue to lose their share of liquid household savings as in the fifties and sixties? If the answer to either question raises doubt about the future of the savings banks, what changes might be made, and what will be their effect?

Three of the most dramatic years in the history of the mutual savings banks have been 1969, 1970, and 1973. They demonstrated with the pith of a morality play the problems faced by these banks when credit is tight, as a result of natural forces plus deliberate policy: Interest rates are high and depositors are itchy for higher returns. In 1969, as we briefly noted, withdrawals exceeded deposits in total savings bank accounts, and only the accrual of interest saved the banks from a net loss in deposits. This drop in gross deposits runs counter to the general and universal trend in American life. Personal income in 1969 actually exceeded that of 1968 by $60 billion.[22] Personal outlays and taxes rose by the same amount, leaving a net saving generally of 6 percent of the gross national income.[23] The problem for the mutual savings banks was their failure to attract their share of this saving, a problem accompanied by cries of pain from the other side of their account books—from people demanding mortgage money for new housing construction.

A review of the gross loss in deposits should also encompass several auxiliary propositions. Previous changes in the income tax law required savings banks to report the interest earned by depositors, who, consequently, incurred a tax liability, the size of which depends on the total tax situation of the depositor. In any case, this tax cannot be deferred to maturity, as income tax on certain types of government savings bonds may be deferred. The banks will have to expect a certain loss of interest deposits as depositor-taxpayers prepare themselves to meet the Internal Revenue Service.

A second serious and continuing problem that was raised to crisis proportion by the 1969 events was the long drop in the share of total savings deposited in mutual savings banks as contrasted with the share deposited with other intermediary institutions. Was this the result of demographic changes as population moved from the savings bank states to the western states? Or was it the product of increased investment sophistication, as depositors "disintermediated" in the search for higher yields in the bond or commercial paper market? The year 1970 offered a temporary answer, as the mutual savings banks (except in New York State) experienced a significant deposit gain that in 1971 became a flood as the former "disintermediating" depositors entered a "reintermediating" phase.[24] In a phrase, they put their money back in the savings banks when bond and treasury bills rose (reducing their discount, the equivalent of interest). The year 1971 indicated that if they were indeed losing their ability to attract savings, the loss would be gradual rather than cataclysmic. The deposit growth in 1971, reflecting lower bond market yields and a higher rate of savings as consumers, fearful of the future, eschewed heavy personal spending, was the greatest in the history of the mutual savings banks. New money deposits in mutual savings banks, excluding interest, brought almost $6 billion in funds.[25] The 1971 experience was not without its shadows, however; while the mutual savings banks' deposit growth increased by 115 percent over 1970,[26] the savings and loan associations increased theirs by 165 percent.[27] Although the the commercial bank time and thrift accounts increased by a lower percentage, the share of total savings that the commercial banks held in 1971 was much greater (41 percent against 33 percent) than the share held ten years before.[28] Another shadow on the 1971 performance was cast by the drop in the reserve account ratio —the percentage of assets that is held free and clear of all claims as margin against the losses that might be experienced in mortgage defaults or mortgage sales in advance of maturity. For the first time in many years, the average reserve ratio of all savings banks fell below 8 percent[29] and none would be surprised if, for some unforeseen reason, savings banks had to sell their portfolio of older mortgages carrying interest rates below current market, the losses from book value would wipe out the reserve account entirely. The reason for the shrinking reserve ratio brings up the third major problem: The fact that the margin between the average interest earned on mortgages and the average interest paid to depositors had narrowed perceptibly in the past twenty years.

This narrowing is easily demonstrated. In 1950, the average rate of interest paid on deposits in savings banks was 1.90 percent. By 1971, the rate of interest paid had risen to 5.13 percent.[30] In 1950, the return on mortgages owned by savings banks was 4.24 percent, while the rate in 1971 was 6.20 percent.[31] In other words, the spread between interest earned on mortgages and interest paid to depositors had been 2.34 percent in 1950; by 1971, it had shrunk by more than half to 1.07 percent. It is no wonder that reserve accounts had to be shaved in order to maintain interest payments.

Other steps have been suggested. We have noted the possibility of writing a variable rate mortgage, the interest on which would move up and down in accordance with some general economic indicator, like the interest rate on high-grade corporate bonds. Actually, the Federal Home Loan Bank Board has sanctioned its use. This suggestion was prompted by the observation that the present yield on the savings bank mortgage portfolio is held down by old mortgages with rates that are far below current levels. New mortgages are being made at much higher rates, but the weight of the older mortgages acts as a drag on bank income, sagging bank income drags down interest rates, and lagging interest rates will, in a tightened money market, discourage savings bank deposits, which will cut down the flow of money into mortgages.

While a variable rate mortgage sounds like a reasonable remedy, its weakness, already noted, is the probable resistance of the homeowner to paying higher interest costs than those originally negotiated at the time of the mortgage closing. There would, of course, be little objection to lower interest costs.

To make the proposal more palatable, it has been suggested that the term of the mortgage could be varied with a rising interest cost, so that the total monthly payment on a self-amortizing mortgage would remain the same even after a rise in interest rates. A larger part of the payment would become interest, a smaller part amortization. But the mortgage would last longer, and the total interest paid over its life would become considerably greater. It is also possible that the changes in interest rates are too large to be made up by even an infinite extension of the analytic period. Anyone who has observed the performance of tenant-cooperators in subsidized apartment houses after they have been told that they must pay larger maintenance charges for *any* reason will be dubious of the acceptability of the variable rate mortgage in the only situation in which it would interest the bank—a period of rising interest rates.

In fact, the public sentiment about the interest costs on housing is running in precisely the other direction. Congress has initiated measures that would cut down closing costs, and make mortgagees pay interest on the mortgagors' money held for the payment of insurance premiums and taxes. These are trivial compared with the funds being spent through the Government National Mortgage Association (GNMA), which we will discuss later, to lower the cost of mortgage money by government subsidy, usually expressed by the purchase of mortgages at or near their face value, although they return a below-market interest yield. As the bare costs of land and construction—generally called brick and mortar costs—continue to rise (to say nothing of the cost of maintenance and real estate taxes), the impact of high interest rates on this higher base becomes formidable.

It is possible that if the Congress is prepared to assume a part of the interest cost on all housing and uses GNMA purchases of low interest mortgages at par as the vehicle, almost all mortgages will eventually be held by the government, or passed through the GNMA for resale at a true market price, with the government swallowing the loss without even a hiccup. In that case, cooperation with GNMA in the mortgage field would lead all banks to originate mortgages for sale to GNMA, reducing their own role very considerably. For permanent investment, they might ultimately, one guesses, buy back either their own mortgages or some other bank's mortgages at a market price, having sold it at a high, par price, or they might buy the bonds issued by GNMA. Their depositors would be paid their share of the excess of sale over repurchase price over the years as interest.

The willingness of the Congress to foot the bill varies according to the conditions of the housing industry. When the industry is depressed Congress is willing to consider methods of reducing mortgage interest rates. Other choices besides the GNMA method are tax exemption for interest earned on deposits in institutions like mutual savings banks that invest a preponderance of their funds in residential mortgages; or, as in West Germany, an outright subsidy from government to the saver, augmenting in cash the interest earned, provided that the bank makes mortgages at a below-market interest cost.

Few, if any, mutual savings bankers hope for futures of this kind. The industry position was articulated faithfully by a twenty-man Commission on Financial Structure and Organization appointed by President Nixon. The commission submitted a long report in December 1971, which generally urged that the mutual savings banks be permitted to engage in a wide range of activities beyond their present powers. These would include the making of third-party payments through checking accounts, consumer loans, investments in real estate equity, investment in common stocks—all of these limited to a specific percentage of their assets. Any savings bank that offers third party checking services would be required to join the Federal Reserve System, and ultimately to maintain reserves with the Federal Reserve Bank on the same basis as any similar institution.[32]

We have already noted that each of these powers (except affiliation with the Federal Reserve System) is available in some savings bank states, although no single state permits all of them. New York State, for example, permits savings banks to make long-term educational loans for college students, with or without state subsidy. Massachusetts permits a form of third-party checking accounts.

The basic idea behind the commission report is simple enough—to provide a source of income higher than mortgage money, like consumer loans, in order to sweeten the return on mortgage loans, keep depositors happy, and maintain growth in savings flows. We would, it appears, have *two* kinds of banks advertising that their kind is the only kind a family ever needs. No one can tell whether this encouragement to savers to come home to the savings bank will produce the flow of mortgage money needed or whether the savings banks, once they have found out how to make consumer loans profitably (the commercial banks had to learn the business too), will make fewer and fewer residential mortgages. But no one can doubt that a major change is in the wind for the savings banks. As long as higher-paying Treasury Bills and corporate bonds, or stock market profits, tax-gimmicky equity-cum-depreciation deals, high-yielding corporate and tax-exempt municipal bonds are available to the wealthy, it is fruitless to hope that the families of moderate means will not have heard of them, and will be calmed into inertia by the promise that their day-of-deposit, day-of-withdrawal savings bank 5 percent interest will be compounded daily instead of annually; or that by saving ten dollars per week they will have seventy-three thousand tinier dollars, but dollars, at age seventy-five, *not counting taxes,* of course.

Yet it is equally futile to expect that the housing industry can provide homes for a majority of Americans with mortgage interest pegged at 9 percent in order that savings bank depositors will refrain from voting with their feet to take the money and go elsewhere. Sooner or later the last living survivor of the debacle of 1929–37 will have quietly shuffled off from the scene. No one will be left to place the old emphasis on safety. And unanimously, depositors in mutual savings banks will quiver ever more expectantly for—what is it?—a piece of the action. Unless, of course, the country sinks into another morass like the great depression. This might, of course, happen, helped in part by inactivity in residential mortgages that, in turn, will have been caused by a shortage of mortgage money at a reasonable interest rate. Or perhaps it will be caused by a stagnation reaction from the great overbuilding that would follow the sweetening of mortgage interest rates with large infusions of government money. There really is no easy way; or, at least, if there is one, it isn't easy to find.

CHAPTER 8

THE SAVINGS AND LOAN ASSOCIATIONS

SAVINGS and loan associations are the third largest financial intermediary in the United States, following commercial banks and life insurance companies respectively. But they devote a far larger share of their savings deposits to residential mortgages than does any other type of financial intermediary. In 1973, 85 percent of the assets held by savings and loan associations were invested in residential mortgages,[1] compared to 70.3 percent for mutual savings banks [2] and around 20 percent for insurance companies and commercial banks.[3]

Thus, at the end of 1972, savings and loan associations were by far the largest single factor in mortgage lending for residential purposes, particularly in houses for one-to-four family occupancy. Savings and loan associations held 47.9% of all the mortgages in the United States on properties of one-to-four families. This, furthermore, was the culmination of a significant growth trend. Twenty-two years earlier, in 1950, the savings and loan associations provided only 29 percent of the total outstanding residential mortgage debt.[4]

In the field of multifamily apartment houses, with more than four units, the growth of participation by savings and loan associations was even more dramatic. In 1950, only about 2 percent of the total residential mortgage debt on apartment houses was held by savings and loan associations. Twenty-two years later, in 1972, preliminary figures showed that the savings and loan associations held 27 percent of the outstanding mortgage debt on properties of this type.[5]

Savings and loan associations are deposit-type financial institutions established either with federal or state charters. Until 1955, federally chartered savings and loan associations were forbidden to use language that suggested that they accepted deposits. Instead, they accepted money in return for "shares." In practice, there is no apparent difference between the two descriptions, but savings and loan associations fought for the right to accept *deposits* like mutual savings banks or to sell *shares* like open-ended mutual funds without losing their federal charters. Apparently, savings and loan managers find that the "deposit" language attracts customers.

Savings and loan associations exist in all of the fifty states, in Puerto Rico, and, most particularly, in the District of Columbia, where the savings and loan associations in 1973 controlled total assets of nearly $3.4 billion. That, averaged over the population of the district, would amount to nearly $4500 per person.[6] This is considerably higher than the average throughout the country; in fact, the average savings account at savings and loan associations throughout the country was only slightly over three thousand dollars at the end of 1970.[7] Because the average loan by the savings and loan associations outstanding on the books at the same date was thirteen thousand dollars,[8] it is obvious that more than four depositors were needed to provide each borrower with the money he required.

The first savings and loan associations formed in the nation came to life in the second quarter of the nineteenth century under state laws. Under these laws, associations may be either mutually owned by their depositors, in much the same fashion as mutual savings banks and mutually owned life insurance companies, or stock-owned, in which case the associations are owned, like commercial banks, by investing stockholders who seek to earn an income on the investment they have made. The United States Savings and Loan League reported in 1971 that stock-ownership associations were operating in twenty-one states, including particularly the state of California, which authorized their establishment before 1890, and where nearly 60 percent of the total assets of all stock-owned savings and loan associations are held.[9]

On a nationwide basis, one of every eight associations is a stock-ownership enterprise managed for profit.[10] Since that 12 percent control almost 21 percent of the total assets held by all the savings and loan associations,[11] it is apparent that their average size is larger than the average size of the mutually owned associations. The largest single savings and loan association in 1971—Home Savings and Loan of California—had assets of nearly $2 billion, which, for the sake of comparison, might be set alongside the Bowery Savings Bank of New York, the largest mutual savings bank in the country. The Bowery's total assets at the end of 1972 were $3.4 billion.[12]

The federal government did not pass legislation authorizing federal charters for savings and loan associations until the liquidity crisis of the depression years. In 1933, the Home Owners' Loan Act was passed, providing for the chartering of federal savings and loan associations.[13] The federal Homeowners' Loan Act established the Federal Home Loan Bank System, to which every federally chartered savings and loan association must belong. "Belonging" to the Federal Home Loan Bank System means that an association must buy stock in its regional bank— the amount of stock being the equivalent of 1 percent of the home loans of the savings and loan association. If, at the end of any year, an association's loans have increased, it must buy additional capital stock of the Federal Home Loan Bank System; if, however, the loans diminish, the association must retain the stock it already owns, although the association has some redemption rights.

In 1973, the total capital stock of the Federal Home Loan Bank System amounted to $2.12 billion.[14] Each federal association is required to insure its savings accounts with the Federal Savings and Loan Insurance Corporation (FSLIC), created under the National Housing Act, whose protection is also available on a voluntary basis to state-chartered associations that are not required by federal law to join the Federal Home Loan Bank System. Some states require their state-chartered savings and loan institutions to be insured by the FSLIC. One state, Massachusetts, runs its own insurance system to which savings and loans, mutual savings banks, and cooperative banks must all belong. Incidentally, state-chartered savings and loan associations, mutual savings banks, and life insurance companies may join the Federal Home Loan Bank System, although they are not required to do so. Forty-seven of the 486 mutual savings banks in the United States belonged to the FHLB System at the end of 1972; [15] we will examine the reasons why they found it advantageous to do so later on—together with the reasons why more of them have not.

One significant requirement for chartering a savings and loan association under federal law is that the association must be mutually owned by its members. The affairs of savings and loan associations are controlled by the boards of directors of the individual associations whose elections are subject always to the requirements of federal or state law, and the regulations of the Federal Home Loan Bank and the Federal Savings and Loan Insurance Corporation. Because all federal associations are nonprofit entities, and some state associations are as well, it is interesting to speculate as to the motives that inspire the formation of the associations, and the conditions that foster their continuation and growth.

Some mutual associations were started by local businessmen who were interested in the collateral enterprises that might benefit from population growth or housing development in a particular locale; they started an association because there was no other savings institution nearby that could place funds in residential mortgages, and they would profit from residential construction. Some associations were started because of a general civic interest in the further development of a specific area. Some have been started to help pool financial resources for homeownership among a particular ethnic or racial group. Many associations have been started as the product of a feeling of civic interest, or "boosterism," on behalf of a town or a neighborhood in a city. Once started, those associations that are well managed and grow into full-time, professionally staffed organizations begin to benefit from the life-force of their own. The professional staff runs the organization. While some boards of directors do maintain a vigorous interest in its affairs, in most cases, it is the staff's interest in the continuation of its salary income that provides the *élan vital* of a well-established association.

As the association grows, it generally finds that a spread of between 1 and 1.5 percent between the average interest that it pays to its depositors and the average interest it receives from its mortgage loans is needed to meet its operating costs and to establish additional reserves.

The Federal Home Loan Bank Board has its national headquarters in Washington: Its direct relationships with savings and loan associations are carried out through twelve regional member banks that cover every state in the union. The regional banks of the Federal Home Loan Bank serve as banks for their members, which, as noted, include not only the federally chartered savings and loan associations but some state-chartered savings and loan associations, and some mutual savings banks. Incidentally, in order to become a member of the Federal Home Loan Bank System, an association need not meet the requirements of federal chartering, at least not as to mutual ownership. A stock-owned savings and loan association, operated for profit and chartered by the state in which it is located, may belong to the Federal Home Loan Bank System. Many do: The California stock-ownership associations are an outstanding example. The member organizations maintain accounts in the regional Federal Home Loan Bank, but the Bank does no counter business with the public.

Member associations may keep two kinds of accounts in the regional

Federal Home Loan Bank: demand deposit accounts or time deposit accounts. The demand deposit accounts are precisely the same as demand deposit accounts kept by private citizens in commercial banks; associations can draw out by check in order to meet the day-to-day operating expenses of the associations: payrolls, supplies, withdrawals. The second type is a time deposit account. Into such accounts, which pay interest to the association making the deposit, an association or other member of the Federal Home Loan Bank System places funds that will be held for a period of time. An example of this kind of deposit would be the escrow payments, tax and insurance liabilities on properties under mortgage to an association. The mortgagor makes monthly payments to the savings and loan association from which he borrowed. These payments include an appropriate share of insurance premiums and real property taxes. During the period that this money is in the hands of the regional bank, awaiting the tax and premium payment dates, the regional bank invests it either in federal government obligations or by making loans to members who require cash funds for liquidity or mortgage-lending purposes.

The earnings of the Federal Home Loan Bank System consist of interest earned on the system's advances to its member associations (of which more later), on the investing of funds deposited in regional banks by member associations, and on the investing of funds paid by members for their capital stock. This total income covers the operating costs of that system. Enough is left over to enable the regional banks to pay the member associations dividends on the capital stock that they are required by law to buy and hold. In 1972, the dividends on the capital stock of the regional banks averaged 2.52 percent for the year, corrected for the amount of capital stock outstanding at different dividend periods. This was down from 1970 exactly 1.37 percent (in the language of the money market, 137 basis points, each point being 1/10,000 of the original par value of an instrument), and reflected unusual and continuing efforts of the Bank Board to stimulate mortgage lending by offering to lend associations funds at less than the Bank's own borrowing costs.

Because mutual savings banks earned an average of 5.87 interest on their assets in 1970, while the regional Federal Home Loan Bank stock paid an average of 3.89 percent,[16] the managers of mutual savings banks could calculate that a membership in the Federal Home Loan Bank System would involve them in approximately a 15 percent loss in earnings on the 1 percent of their total loans that would be required to be invested in the capital stock of the regional bank. For many, this was the stated reason for their reluctance to join the Federal Home

Loan Bank System. There may be other reasons as well, which might be examined from the point of view of the history of the system.

The original paid-in capital of the Federal Home Loan Bank System included a $125 million purchase by the United States Treasury, which has long since been repaid. The investment, in 1934, was one of the most effective ever made by the United States government. At the time, savings and loan associations were in desperate condition. Their total deposits were down to $4.5 billion, which represented almost a 30 percent shrinkage from their 1929 level.[17] Furthermore, during the frantic real estate boom of the late 1920s, the savings and loan associations had expanded at a rate too fast to be healthy: Their deposits had increased by almost 70 percent in the five years between 1925 and 1930,[18] a period during which the mutual savings banks experienced a deposit growth of only about 20 percent.[19] The difference in the stability of the two institutions is reflected also in the fact that between 1929 and 1934 the mutual savings banks actually experienced an *increase* in deposits instead of the catastrophic drop experienced by the savings and loan associations.[20] On the asset side, during 1933–34, the value of mortgages owned by the savings and loan associations had shrunk, probably more than the deposits.[21]

When the federal government was finally moved to do something to rescue a situation that seemed likely to precipitate futile and destructive withdrawals by intermediary depositors, it set up two deposit-insuring agencies, one for the commercial banks, essentially, the Federal Deposit Insurance Corporation, and the other for savings and loan associations, the Federal Savings and Loan Insurance Corporation. In the course of the legislation through Congress, the representatives of the mutual savings banks were offered the opportunity to share the law so that their banks could join either of the two insurance plans. They chose to be affiliated with the commercial banks in the FDIC.

The savings and loan associations, lacking any federal control in the 1920s, had developed a somewhat unsavory reputation, an allegation that would be stoutly objected to by many saving and loan executives. The ties between savings and loan associations and developers were nonetheless too close for comfort; loaning standards were inadequate. Even when the associations were entirely ethical, they were so much smaller than the savings banks that they could not afford the same managerial expenses, nor did they get the same choice of mortgage opportunities. The stability of the level of deposits in the mutual savings banks enabled their management to escape the pressure to liquidate their mortgage loans. The instability of the level of deposits in the smaller savings and loan associations presented their management with a liquidity crisis —some were so pressed by their depositors that they failed; others were seriously threatened.

The bare figures of deposit shrinkage do not reveal how much of it in the savings and loan associations represented a total loss of deposits occasioned by the bankruptcy of the depositories, and how much represented withdrawals stimulated by fear or the need for cash on the part of the depositors. Whatever the reason, nobody denied that the savings and loan associations in the 1930s dramatically needed a form of federal regulation that would bring reasonable standards of performance to the industry, build confidence in depositors, and provide a secondary line of liquidity so that calls for money by depositors in one part of the country, or in one association, could be met, with reasonable safety, by a temporary use of the excess liquidity of another part of the country, or another association.

The success of the Treasury investment in the capital stock of the Federal Home Loan Bank was proven by the stabilization of the deposit level in the associations during the second half of the 1930s. The liquidity system provided by the Federal Home Loan Bank, through its ability to borrow money in the money market generally, has been of the utmost importance to the health of the mortgage market. But in the meantime, in the years after the war, the savings and loan associations had grown from the status of a very junior brother of the mutual savings banks— with deposits in 1934 less than half as large as those of the mutual savings banks—to a very senior brother in 1970—with deposits twice as large as the total deposits of the savings banks.[22]

In the first five postwar years, there was little change in the growth rates of these two types of savings institutions; but in the first five years of the 1950s, the savings and loan association deposits grew much faster than savings banks; total deposits in the savings and loans nearly doubled in that period while savings bank deposits increased by 30 percent.[23] By 1954, the deposits in savings and loan associations exceeded those in the mutual savings banks for the first time,[24] and the net gain in assets owned by the associations increased each year, from 1956 to 1963, with the exception of the year 1960 when there was a slight recession in the economy generally, and asset growth was slightly lower than in 1959. The savings banks show a slightly different trend: Their deposit growth increment dropped a year earlier, in 1959 rather than 1960, and did not reach its previous size until 1962.[25]

In 1963, the rate of growth of the savings and loan associations peaked: The added new assets in 1964 and 1965 were smaller than in 1963, but still roughly commensurate with the amount of growth in assets that had been registered in the years just before 1963. By 1966, however, the assets of the savings and loan associations grew by less than $5 billion, due to the money and credit squeeze of that year. When assets leaped again in 1966–67,[26] the gain was a level one, for a new factor had entered into the determination of savings flow. This was the rapidly increasing competition for savings on the part of the commercial banks, which were now permitted to offer rates of interest that were competitive with the savings and loan association and savings bank interest rates. The savings banks, largely concentrated in New York City, near the money market, were particularly vulnerable to the competition of direct market instruments such as federal agency bonds, corporate bonds, and common stock.

The sharp decline in the rate of growth of assets of savings and loan associations in 1966 caused great alarm among those in Congress who were interested in housing. The apparent shortage of mortgage money resulted from an upsurge in the demand for credit due to industrial expansion. The consequent competition for deposits among institutions not involved in the mortgage market and those that were involved in that market threatened to reduce net mortgage flows significantly. The decision to pursue the Vietnam involvement with intense military action placed heavy demands on the national economy, and many members of Congress were afraid that the commitment would restrict funds in the mortgage market. One long-range effect of the 1966 crisis was the passage of the Rate Control Act and of Public Law 89–597, both of which dealt with the status of the Federal Home Loan Bank System: In an effort to provide a supply of money to the mortgage market, Congress broadened the activities of the Federal Home Loan Bank Board, encouraged that board to expand its sale of general obligations, and facilitated the advancing of the proceeds of those sales to the savings and loan associations, not simply for the purpose of providing liquidity to associations that might be caught in local or regional credit squeezes but in order to expand the pool of mortgage money available to the ultimate consumer. Both powers had been available previously, but Congress now moved to strengthen them.

The new laws provided that the Secretary of the Treasury could buy up to $4 billion of the general obligations of the Federal Home Loan Bank System. The previous limit had been $1 billion, never actually reached. The law for the first time made clear in statutory language that the Secretary of the Treasury would be expected to exercise this power not simply to meet liquidity crises in the savings and loan associations and the banking system generally, but also to increase the supply of mortgage money and lower its rate of interest. The power thus given to the secretary is not without a risk of inflating the money supply somewhat: For the secretary, within the legal debt limit, may issue treasury bills to raise money to pay for general obligations of the Federal Home Loan Banking System. In turn, these bills might be acquired by the Federal Reserve Bank through its open market operations, an activity that, as we have seen, expands the reserves of the banking system and greatly broadens the power of the banks to create credit money. Public Law 89–597 made clear the intent of Congress, and its readiness to run a risk of inflation, if necessary, to keep an adequate money supply available to mortgage institutions. The law specifically authorized the Open Market Committee of the Federal Reserve System to buy and sell federal agency issues, including the Federal Home Loan Bank general obligations. The authorization did not command instant acquiescence by the Federal Reserve Board; the board did not undertake these transactions until five years later.

Every purchase of the general obligations of the Federal Home Loan Bank by the Federal Reserve System has the effect of increasing the money supply because it increases the reserve balances of the commercial banking system precisely in the same way as purchasing treasury bills on the open market.

The general obligations of the Federal Home Loan Bank are regarded as very safe by the money market, even though they lack a direct guarantee by the federal government. When the Federal Home Loan Bank goes to the money market to sell such obligations, it first must clear its own timing with the Treasury Department, so that the Treasury will be sure that the market will not be overwhelmed by a simultaneous offering of Treasury and agency securities. The proceeds of a sale of Federal Home Loan Bank general obligations remain in hand until they are advanced to those member institutions who choose to borrow. Under law, the Federal Home Loan Bank System may borrow to the full limit of the secured advances the regional banks make to the members plus the Bank's cash and holdings of federal obligations. The member associations of the system may by law borrow up to 50 percent of their withdrawable deposits to cover withdrawals by depositors, but the regulations of the Federal Home Loan Bank Board will not permit the bank to lend an association for loan expansion more than 25 percent of the withdrawable savings of an association.

All such advances must be collateralized by the mortgages held by the associations. Generally, an association borrowing funds pays a rate

116

roughly equal to the interest paid by the Federal Home Loan Bank to the buyers of its obligations. These obligations are sold in large denominations—twenty-five thousand dollars is currently the minimum size —to discourage savers in thrift institutions from removing their deposits in order to buy the obligations. Any such withdrawal by a depositor in a member association would nullify the point and purpose of the obligation-advance mechanism, because it would reduce the deposits in the savings and loan associations by the sum of the money used to purchase the general obligations. In 1969, determined not to permit the credit crunch to afflict the mortgage market as drastically as it had in 1966, the Federal Home Loan Bank Board sold approximately $4 billion in general obligations,[27] advancing the proceeds to its members. At the end of that year, the obligations stood at a record $8.4 billion.[28]

This system by which the government can generate money in the banking system and funnel it into the mortgage market through the general obligations and advances of the Federal Home Loan Bank would seem to provide a workable, flexible means of assuring that adequate credit for housing purposes would always be available in the mortgage market. Its advantages include the fact that many savings pools—pension and retirement funds, for example—that would not ordinarily invest much of their assets in the ownership of housing mortgages, would be willing to put funds indirectly into mortgages by their purchase of Federal Home Loan Bank obligations. There would seem to be no limit to the extent that this system will work in providing money, but in practice, all is not so easy.

Some of the problems connected with the consolidated obligation system of advances are these:

First, there is the general problem that special credit provisions for extending credit to housing will cause an increase of inflationary pressure throughout the general economy, thanks to the multiplier-effect of housing expenditures on general consumer demand. The public policy question is whether or not housing is so important to the well-being of the people that it needs to be shielded from the effects of anti-inflation efforts. If *some* housing should be shielded, do the savings and loan associations and the Federal Home Loan Bank isolate the housing that needs protection?

Second, and more specifically, we find that savings and loan institutions do not function with great efficiency in taking advantage of the advances offered by the Federal Home Loan Bank. Approximately 50 percent of the associations had no advances outstanding at the end of 1970.[29] Looking more closely at the associations that do take advances from the Federal Home Loan Bank, we find that they tend to be concentrated in California. As a matter of fact, the stockholder-owned savings and loan associations in California held over 40 percent of the outstanding advances at the end of 1970.[30] It seems that the nonprofit savings and loans do not wish to get involved in borrowing money from the Federal Home Loan Bank. Their management is not sufficiently interested in the growth that might result from the borrowing to incur the obligation and risk that accompanies it. Is the system of Federal Home Loan Bank borrowing and advances to associations of special help to some associations without regard for the national housing need?

Third, the savings and loan industry represents only one part of the mortgage depository market, though admittedly the largest part. A system of credit creation, as that offered by the Federal Home Loan Bank System, with the help of the Federal Reserve System and the Treasury, would certainly be more effective if the insurance companies and the mutual savings banks belonged to it. There might also be good reason for including the smaller commercial banks in the Federal Home Loan Bank System so that their mortgage-making potential might be increased, and the major mortgage-making institutions could be handled as a whole.

Fourth, the system includes only an indirect subsidization, and, therefore, it might tend to stimulate unsound loan practices by associations. The interest rate paid to the Federal Home Loan Bank on advances approaches the rate of interest paid by it on its general obligations. If the bank charges less than it pays, the loss is reflected in a drop in the dividend rate that the members of the system receive on the capital stock they are required to hold. In considering whether or not to take an advance, the management of a savings and loan association might look at the mortgages it was assigning to its regional Federal Home Loan Bank as security for the advance, and feel that it was pledging seasoned mortgages on which it has been earning a low income in order to borrow money from the Bank on which it will pay a much higher interest rate. This is good business only if it can lend out its advance at still higher rates. This involves a certain speculative consideration from the point of view of the management, and, more seriously, it threatens to price a part of the home buyers out of the market. To meet this challenge, the Federal Home Loan Bank has instituted for a limited term a special advance at a rate .25 percent lower than its standard advance rate on a short-term basis, starting with a fixed rate of 7.25 percent. An overwhelming majority of the advances now outstanding were of this special type, even though they are, as noted, subject to increase as its standard rate increases. No subsidy supports this concession, which reduces the earnings on the bank capital stock. In 1974, the government allocated $4 billion for further special advances at ½ percent below the government's own borrowing rate on five-year obligations.

This *might* stimulate more associations to take advantage of the advance program on the theory that because they are paying for it they might as well use it. To meet the second obstacle, Congress has authorized and the Federal Home Loan Bank has established the Federal Home Loan Mortgage Corporation to function as a market for mortgages that its member associations might wish to buy and sell. If the sale is at a price that does not involve too large a discount from the face amount of the mortgage held in an association portfolio, this would provide a means by which an association might augment its cash to make new commitments.

We will discuss the Federal Home Loan Mortgage Corporation under the general heading of secondary markets.

Fifth, and socially most important, the whole process of mortgage credit creation avoids the question of how the mortgage interest rates available through the Federal Home Loan Bank System and its members will be low enough to make decent homes available to families of moderate income. Clearly, the government has several alternative methods of procedure, once it decides that the public interest justifies lower interest rates than the market—even the supply-side aided market —can produce: It can offer housing-consumer subsidies to the families needing help. It can provide housing-producer subsidies to the builder— whether the builder is a private or a public organization—that enable the builder to provide low-cost housing to families qualified under law in specific housing developments built under that law.

It can provide subsidies that enable the lender to offer its money at something below its natural cost, provided the homeowners qualify on an income basis. This last is the tenor of a program established by Congress with an authorization of $250 million, of which $85 million was actually appropriated.[31] This program—Housing Opportunity Allowance Program—permits qualified homeowners to reduce their mortgage payments to member associations of the Federal Home Loan Bank System by twenty dollars per month for five years while the member associations receive the difference in the form of subsidy from the Federal Home Loan Bank. Easy to describe, the program has proven so far to be so difficult to administer that on Dec. 31, 1972, the program was terminated.

The savings and loan associations—and the Federal Home Loan Bank Board that was instituted to save them from oblivion in the depression

—are a fascinating ad hoc instrumentality developed to meet a specific problem, and showing remarkable adaptive qualities so that they now are engaged in much more complex operations. They have made a great contribution to the postwar housing boom. Whether or not this contribution will be matched in the future depends on the governmental ability to bridge the present gap between housing demand and housing cost. The management of the constituent members of the system will have to prove themselves adequate to the task. Congress will have to vote adequate funds without continually encouraging construction and land costs to rise still higher. As an imperfect but highly effective institution the Home Loan Bank System demands continuing attention.

CHAPTER 9

THE LIFE INSURANCE
COMPANIES

LIFE INSURANCE companies in the United States held over $200 billion in assets at the end of 1970, making them the second largest financial intermediary for savers in the United States.[1] With approximately 36 percent of their assets invested in mortgages, these companies held approximately $72 billion in real estate mortgages.[2] Unlike the savings and loan associations, however, life insurance companies held a significant part of their mortgages on nonresidential, income-producing property. According to the Institute of Life Insurance, more than one-third of the total assets invested in mortgages was invested in nonresidential mortgages, leaving the companies with something less than $50 billion in residential mortgages.[3] Thus, the life insurance companies rank fourth among the intermediaries in value of the residential mortgages held.

If we were to rank the intermediaries by their fascination, instead of by their real estate mortgages, the life insurance companies would probably rank second—just behind the commercial banks with their uncanny ability to manufacture money by making loans. If, contrariwise, we ranked the intermediaries by their ingenuity, the life insurance companies might well come first. The very fact that the purchase of life insurance has become a means of saving for the individual purchaser demonstrates ingenuity; after all, the purchaser of fire or automobile insurance does not thereby accumulate savings in the hands of the insurance company that he can withdraw at will. Yet any purchaser of ordinary life insurance—to say nothing of the more expensive varieties

—accumulates a cash value that he can withdraw or borrow against. If he chooses to borrow, with the policy pledged as collateral, whether from the insurance company or any other lender, the death benefit of his policy is reduced only by the amount of the loan. All of this means that life insurance companies have been able to collect premiums that are greater than necessary to provide cash sufficient to meet the actual probabilities of death. Purchasers of life insurance have been willing to purchase these guaranteed value policies because the life insurance contract covers an object of lasting value (namely, the life of the insured), and because the pressure of having to make contractual savings under the terms of the policy is sufficiently effective to be worth paying for.

The contractual nature of the relationship between the individual saver and the life insurance company differs from the relationship between the saver and the type of intermediary institution, like a bank or a savings and loan association, in which the saver makes deposits and withdrawals at will over the counter. Because the life insurance companies are the major noncounter intermediaries, they have had an opportunity to exploit the contractual form of saving to cover a host of risks and situations that were not dreamed of when the life insurance business first began in the United States. Thus, the life insurance companies have produced group insurance; health insurance; several types of annuities, including, in some states, variable annuities with emphasis on investments in common stock; and the pension plans of many corporations and professional and business groups, especially those not large enough to justify an independent staff.

Finally, the life insurance companies have attracted the attention of many economists who are interested in the economics of housing and the residential market, men like Raymond J. Saulnier, Jack Guttentag, Saul Klaman, and Morris Beck. The reason for their interest in the mortgages of life insurance companies may well be the fact that each of the major life insurance companies is a national enterprise, making mortgages throughout the nation. Local laws do not restrict lending to a specific state, nor does the policy of a company urge it to concentrate its lending efforts in the local area to which it is tied. The national character of the life insurance companies means, in the words of Guttentag and Beck, that "they have a wide range of investment options, and shift at the margin from one investment to another." [4] This freedom of choice is augmented by the long-term nature of life insurance company liabilities. Unless the nation were to suffer a major health catastrophe, having a profound effect on the death rate, the companies have little fear of a sudden and unexpected need for liquidity. The only exception to this arises from the possibility of numerous surrenders of policies or a growth in policy loans at a time of economic stringency. As to the first of these, cashing in a life insurance policy seems to most policyholders an act of final desperation, taken with greater reluctance than the withdrawal of savings from the bank. As to the borrowing of money from the life insurance company on the security of the policy, this affects the liquidity requirements of the life insurance company only if the loan is made by the insurance company itself. In that case, the interest rate is fixed by the terms of the policy. If this contractual rate is higher than the effective current borrowing rate from banks, the borrower will presumably use his policy to collateralize a loan from a commercial bank at the lower rate. In order, therefore, for the policy loan provision to affect adversely the liquidity of life insurance companies, a recession, with loss of income for policyholders, must coincide with generally high interest rates. This unusual combination of circumstances came about in 1969 and 1970, and in 1974. There had been $11.3 billion in policy loans outstanding at the beginning of 1969; by the end of 1970, these had climbed by approximately 35 percent, and represented a little less than 8 percent of total assets—nearly one-quarter as much as the total of mortgage loans.[5]

A moment's consideration of this statement may be worthwhile. The insurance companies must, of course, make provision to meet the demand for policy loans or cash surrenders of policies with guaranteed values. If the investment officials of life insurance companies had believed that the 1969–70 trend line in policy loans would extend through 1971–72 (there is reason now to believe that the trend did *not* continue), they would have had to consider the need for liquidity in their investment policy for those years. Mortgages, for the reasons we discussed at the very beginning of this book, are less liquid than corporate or governmental bonds, less easily disposed of for cash, because their individual quality varies so widely that no general market for them has existed.

The growth in policy loans would tend to discourage life insurance company investment of the same proportion of incoming funds in mortgages as had been the case in the past. On the other hand, the life insurance companies compete among themselves for the savings dollar and, to a lesser degree, with other intermediaries. Because they compete primarily on the basis of the premium needed per dollar of insurance, each is anxious to earn as much as possible on its investments to gain the competitive advantage of low premiums. The only other bases for successful competition are low costs of operation and favorable mortality experience. If mortgages pay a higher net yield to the lender than corporate bonds, the investment officials of the life insurance companies will naturally lean favorably toward mortgage investment. If bonds produce a greater yield, they will shift toward bonds. If the risks of nonresidential mortgages look insignificant when measured against their high yields (including a participating share of the mortgagor's gross receipts), investment will be made in nonresidential mortgages. Following the withdrawal of life insurance companies from the residential mortgage market, other lenders might find it possible to raise their interest rates on residential mortgage loans. The study of life insurance company investment flows should reveal much information about the American economy, because of the national nature of the insurance company's investment portfolio. That portfolio even reflects international monetary activity and interest rates. In the words of Professor Raymond Vernon of Harvard, "If Germany decided that it had more dollars than were necessary to finance its international business, Germany's measures might affect the interest rate on mortgages in Rahway, New Jersey." [6]

Students of interest rates on mortgage loans tell us that the pattern of changes in mortgage interest rates differs from that of changes in bond interest rates. Generally speaking, mortgage interest rates have historically been far more stable than the interest rates or effective yields on government and corporate bonds. This at least was true until 1961, when the shifts in mortgage yields became much sharper. The reason for the change is still not altogether clear.

More specifically, we should remember that interest rates, in general, were kept very low in the six years following the end of World War II. The dominant fact in the money market during that period was the understanding between the Federal Reserve Board and the United States Treasury under the terms of which the Federal Reserve Board agreed to help the Treasury borrow vast sums of money at a very low rate of interest. If this policy was to succeed with government bonds, the interest rate in general would also have to be kept low, to discourage vast numbers of owners of Treasury bonds from throwing them on the market in order to raise cash with which to buy the higher-yielding securities of private corporations. Thus, the Federal Reserve Board kept the rediscount rate low and used its open market operations to keep up the price of government bonds, an activity that increased the money supply.

During this same period, the Federal Housing Administration's ceiling rate on mortgage interest remained fixed at 4.5 percent,[7] while conventional mortgages yielded somewhere between 4 and 4.25 percent. Because bond yields until 1951 hovered around the 2.5 percent figure,[8] the yield differential between mortgages and bonds ranged from about 1.75 percent to about 2 percent. This had been the historic range of difference that economists took as the reflection of the unfavorable features of mortgages plus servicing costs.

When the Federal Reserve Board terminated its agreement with the Treasury in 1951, corporate bond yields began to rise rapidly. By 1953, bond yields were over 3 percent, but the yield on mortgages remained unchanged at 4.5 percent. Obviously, the differential between mortgage yield and bond yield had dropped; actually, to about 1.5 percent (or one hundred fifty basis points). In 1953, the economy entered a recession, and demand for credit dropped, lowering the yield on bonds to 2.5 percent. Because mortgage interest rates continued to remain stationary, the differential between them and bond interest rates rose at the beginning of 1954 to more than two hundred basis points.[9]

The story becomes more dramatic after 1954. From their low point of 2.5 percent in 1954, corporate bond yields increased to practically 4.5 percent by late 1959. During the same period, mortgage yields increased from about 4.5 percent to about 6 percent, a change of only 1.5 percent. This wider swing in bond interest than in mortgage interest reduced the yield differential to 1.5 percent (or one hundred fifty basis points) once again.[10]

In 1960, the Kennedy Administration took office after promising to "get the nation moving again," a pledge that amounted to a shorthand description of easier money and lower interest rates. The resulting monetary policies kept bond yields from rising from their plateau at about 4 percent, slightly below the 1959 peak. Meanwhile, mortgage yields dropped slowly but steadily throughout the same five years, until the composite yield on conventional mortgages descended from 6 percent to 5.5 percent. By the beginning of 1966, bond rates rose again, and the differential between the mortgage yield and the yield on corporate securities dropped to a postwar low, almost .5 percent below the previous low.[11] Guttentag and Beck briefly theorized at the time that this heralded a permanent disappearance of the traditional differential between bond and mortgage yields.

That point of view was challenged, at least temporarily, by the experience in the mortgage market in the years beginning with 1966 when the military needs in Vietnam were added to a booming economy. Shortly after the beginning of 1966, the mortgage market experienced an unprecedented turnaround; yields jumped one hundred basis points in the one year, almost twice as much as they had dropped in the five years between 1961 and 1966. Because bond yields rose by much less than 1 percent, the net effect was to widen the spread between mortgage and bond yields to two hundred basis points once again.[12] In retrospect, Guttentag and Beck decided that the declining spread of the early 1960s reflected a shift in commercial bank deposit accounts from demand deposit accounts to time accounts, and thus the availability of a larger money supply for mortgage investment.[13] Naturally, this enlarged supply brought down mortgage interest yields over the five years between 1961 and 1965.

When the Indochina war began to heat up the economy in 1966, demands for credit by regular commercial bank customers increased. The commercial banks could afford to lure savings accounts out of the savings intermediaries and into their time departments. Although the commercial banks did continue to make mortgage loans, in 1966 they loaned less in new mortgage loans than they took in as new money from the thrift depositories. Their object in 1966 was to increase their capacity to lend to their commercial customers. Reflecting the high interest that the commercial banks had to pay to attract time deposits, new mortgages in 1966 were written with sharply higher interest rates.[14] Guttentag and Beck pointed out that this development, with its unusual shift in savings from savings intermediaries to commercial banks, may presage far closer and prompter connections in the future between the money market in general and the mortgage market.[15] If mortgages are to act like other money market instruments, the depositories depending primarily on them must be given new strength to overcome the disadvantages inherent in a mortgage. To identify the precise yield for strength, and to provide it by law and regulation, became an important legislative target in the late 1960s and early 1970s.

The life insurance companies themselves began to develop the characteristics of a national market in mortgages as their operations broadened since the end of World War II. Because they are national companies, they have had to develop, or at least to utilize, mechanisms that enable them to scan the entire country in order to find suitably safe investments for that section of their total portfolio that their investment officers wish to place in residential mortgages. In 1961, 96 percent of insurance company residential mortgage loans were classified as having been made by national companies, a category of lender defined by the Federal Home Loan Bank Board as making more than 90 percent of its mortgage loans outside the local area. In contrast, only 11 percent of mortgage companies, 9 percent of commercial banks, 7 percent of mutual savings banks, and no savings and loan associations were defined as national lenders.[16] A measure of the extent to which the national market for mortgages has been dominated by the life insurance companies is provided by looking at the 1960 census data (as reported by Guttentag and Beck). In 1960, 17 percent of the outstanding mortgage loans on one-family residences in the whole nation were held by lenders in a different region from that in which the property was located. All lenders *other* than insurance companies held only 8 percent of their mortgages on one-family houses in regions different from that in which the lender is located.[17] In the case of insurance company mortgages, 56 percent of the mortgages were located in a region different from that of the insurance company.[18] The impact of life insurance mortgage practice distorted the national average.

The reasons for the interest evidenced by life insurance companies in a national market are simple enough: They have a wide range of investment opportunities, unrestricted by laws requiring them to invest in local areas. More significant, perhaps, are the criteria that make a mortgage loan suitable for purchase by a remote insurance company. If a mortgage is to be held by a lender far from the physical location of the indentured property, the lender's first concern is the safety of the debt. Will it surely be repaid? The simplest guarantee of safety on an American mortgage is a government guarantee. Thus, when the life insurance companies started to put large sums of money into residential mortgages after World War II, they turned first to government-insured mortgages.

In 1950, the life insurance companies held a total of $16 billion in residential mortgages in the United States and Canada. Approximately half of these were so-called conventional mortgages, uninsured by any government agency. Approximately one-twelfth were uninsured farm mortgages. The remaining 40-odd percent were insured either by the FHA, the VA, or their Canadian equivalents.[19] Gradually, however, the percentage of insured mortgages held by the life insurance companies began to drop. By 1960, insured mortgages comprised less than 40 percent of the total mortgages held by life insurance companies. Five years later, the insured mortgages amounted to approximately 30 percent of the total mortgage holdings. By 1970, the insured mortgages comprised less than 25 percent of the mortgages held.[20]

Explanations for the shift are easy to find. Government insurance involves onerous paperwork and approvals. In addition, a fee must be paid to the FHA to cover the cost of the insurance. A third disagreeable feature of the insurance from the point of view of the lender is the interest rate ceiling placed on the mortgage by the insuring agency. If this rate is below the market rate for other mortgages, after giving due consideration to the value of the safety factor, lenders will not make these mortgages without discounting them; the practice of discounting is generally disagreeable. It means that lenders actually receive less in cash than the face value of the mortgage debt they are contracting to pay. The result either squeezes the profit of the builder on the sale of a house or the rental of apartments or else it requires a larger down payment by the buyer.

The shift away from FHA mortgages and into conventional mortgages marks life insurance policy in the 1960s. It was accompanied by an even more significant shift in life insurance company housing investment strategy. That was the shift away from equity ownership investment in residential real estate. The large insurance companies, including Metropolitan Life, New York Life, and Prudential Life, had undertaken some equity ownership of large projects in the 1950s, in pursuit of a few pioneering investments that date back to the 1920s. By 1960, it was clear, regrettably, that few such investments would be undertaken in the future. In the late sixties, only the State Mutual Life Insurance Company of Worcester, Massachusetts, had undertaken direct development and ownership of a housing development. It seems highly probable that by 1980 even the last of the life insurance company housing developments will have been sold by its owners. Yet, the implications of this turn of events have been studied only by Louis Winnick in *Rental Housing*,[21] and perhaps even that excellent volume, written in the early 1960s, underestimated the universal implications of the lessons to be learned.

The first truly major equity investment by a life insurance company in rental housing came in the late 1930s, when the Metropolitan Life Insurance Company constructed Parkchester, twelve thousand units in buildings ranging in height from seven to thirteen stories on the vacant site of the former New York Catholic Protectory for Boys in the Bronx. The basic rationale for the investment was simple enough. Because they are contract savings institutions rather than counter-depositories, the life insurance companies can afford to take a somewhat longer view of capital investment than such thrift institutions as mutual savings banks and savings and loan associations. Because all real estate values were greatly reduced by the depression of the 1930s, an institution that could take the long view of its investment policies might rightly conclude that future gains in market value would be a likely outcome of an investment in new construction made at the bottom of the market. Obviously, the standard mortgage offered no opportunity to benefit from the appreciation in value of the underlying property. The dollar amount of the mortgage would remain always the same. A participating mortgage, in which the mortgagee shares either in the gross or net income of a property, or in its resale price, became widely used by insurance companies in the immense commercial development—notably in shopping centers—that followed World War II. But participating mortgages are not widely used in the case of residential property. When Parkchester was built, Metropolitan Life would have found great difficulty in attracting any equity investor to a large housing development, even without insisting on a participating mortgage to drain off part of the ultimate gain.

Believing also that a major investment in new housing construction would boost New York City's employment picture, the management of Metropolitan Life could find no serious alternative to taking the equity position itself. The Metropolitan Life management also believed that owning rental property was not inconsistent with its objectives as a major life insurance company—the largest in the nation. The commitment to better housing would constitute sound public relations and would demonstrate dramatically the role that the insurance industry can play in stimulating employment and production. Finally, Metropolitan Life believed that the management of the property itself would present no major difficulty. After all, Metropolitan Life had been in the mortgage market for years, looking over the shoulders of apartment house owners and operating apartment houses itself after they were acquired in foreclosure procedures. The real estate department of a major life insurance company was certain to include men and women with experience germane to the construction and management of apartment houses.

Parkchester proved to be a very successful development for Metropolitan Life. Because of the condition of the construction business and the labor market at the time it was built, it could be put up quickly and within budget. Its costs compared favorably with the costs of its competition—apartment houses built during the construction boom of the 1920s, approximately ten years earlier. The demand for apartments was so strong that Metropolitan Life was able to select its tenants warily, limiting the number of families it would take from any single preexisting building in an effort to neutralize the adverse effect that the completion of Parkchester might exert on the demand for apartments in existing buildings. The then current state of public conscience with regard to racial integration or equality can only be described as comatose. Few white New Yorkers even considered the possibility that Negro families should be accepted into Parkchester. Not one Negro family moved in.

The development followed the rules that then seemed generally applicable to multifamily housing construction in an urban area not previously used for housing. The development was designed to be so large that it would create its own community, providing its own reasons for attracting people to what was a rather out-of-the-way site, though it was not far from mass transit on the elevated railway. The large scale of the development was deemed to portend low costs in management and maintenance as well as original development per unit. Minimal provision for automobiles was necessary; city people were not supposed to own cars. Stores were located within the individual apartment buildings, instead of being lumped together in one or more shopping centers. The resulting store size was rather difficult to adapt to the supermarket retail operation that developed fifteen or more years after the completion of Parkchester. The site was developed in superblock form, with all except emergency vehicles foreclosed from entering into the vestigial automobile routes within the superblock perimeters. The building configuration permitted the retention of large tracts of open space at ground level. Problems of personal safety from muggers, so important in the sixties and seventies, were inconsequential in the 1930s.

Above all, Metropolitan Life followed the principle of good-as-new maintenance. It was able to enforce its rules on tenants, including meticulous rules on personal behavior such as the ban against doormats outside any apartment, which was intended to simplify the cleaning of the public corridors. Maintenance was held at a very high level during the entire term of Metropolitan Life's ownership.

The remarkable success of the Parkchester investment foreshadowed a number of other life insurance company projects, most of which flowered within the first fifteen years after World War II. They include the Lake Meadows project in Chicago, the Fresh Meadows development in Queens, New York, the Parkmercede development in San Francisco, Manhattan House and Fordham Hill in New York City. The real estate investments of life insurance companies (exclusive of mortgages) stood at less than $1 billion at the end of World War II. By 1960, they had increased more than fourfold. The total continued to rise through 1972,[22] but the figures do not differentiate between multifamily housing ownership and other types of real estate, most of which is presumably nonresidential.

The most dramatic and important of the postwar life insurance company ventures into rental housing ownership was undoubtedly Stuyvesant Town, located on the east side of Manhattan. This 8700-family development was erected not on vacant land, but rather on a large, occupied site on which eleven thousand people had been living in tenement houses constructed before the turn of the century. Stuyvesant Town was thus a slum clearance project as well as a housing project. It predated the federal slum clearance program that was embodied in Title I of the national Housing Act of 1949 and that gave rise to the term urban renewal. The urban renewal program provided federal financial assistance to cover two-thirds of the cost of relocation, demolition, and land acquisition so that a designated renewal area could be turned into a socially desirable development approved by the local government. The same law would require the local government to match the federal government's contribution, fifty cents to the dollar.

The urban renewal program was presaged by a New York State program tailored specifically for the Stuyvesant Town proposal. The state program, embodied in the Redevelopment Companies Law,[23] authorized cities to use a delegated power of eminent domain to acquire a site that was approved for slum clearance. The land would then be conveyed to the developer at a price equal to the city's cost. The new development would be exempt for twenty-five years from all real estate taxes on the land and improvements to the extent that the taxes exceeded the amount of taxes paid on the property before its acquisition by the city for resale. Rents would be subject to control by the municipality, while the owner of the development would be permitted to earn 6 percent per annum on its equity investment, which would not be allowed to exceed 10 percent (originally 20 percent) of development costs. This law, of course, was adopted at a time when mortgage interest rates were below 5 percent.

The law facilitated the construction of Stuyvesant Town and did, in fact, succeed in keeping rents low by virtue of the tax abatement. The construction costs of Stuyvesant Town reflected the unhappy fact that it had been built under economic conditions that differed very much from those that had affected Parkchester. The postwar inflation meant that the cost of construction rose during the construction period, and the dwelling units turned out to be far more expensive to build than Metropolitan Life had anticipated they would be. Operating costs rose too. Meanwhile, public opinion on the race issue had changed more quickly than Metropolitan Life's management had expected, while the management obstinately refused to accept the reality of the change. Although Metropolitan Life tried to do penance for its rigidity on race by constructing Riverton Houses in Harlem, New York City's government denied the rent increases Stuyvesant Town needed to earn 6 percent on its equity investment until black families were admitted as tenants. As operating costs rose over the years, rent increases lagged. Requests for increases have met the united opposition of all elected legislators whose districts included Stuyvesant Town, and the rent issue became politicized. Metropolitan Life claims that it has never earned a satisfactory return on Stuyvesant Town.

The pinch of the inadequate return on Stuyvesant Town came at a time when life insurance companies in general had attractive alternatives to direct investment in rental property. Private developers were moving ahead, stimulated by the promise of useful tax deductions for noncash expenses, notably depreciation. If a life insurance company can earn a handsome yield by lending these developers their mortgage money, why should it bother to carry the burdens of ownership? The demand for capital by private industry and government, including federal agencies, also provided bond investment alternatives that were easier than equity ownership. But the crucial fact seemed to be that the ownership of rental property had stimulated ill will rather than gratitude for the life insurance companies. Every squabble over rent increases was reported in news articles in which the life insurance company appeared the villain, while the tenants appeared to be the victims. As real estate taxes rose to cover part of the increased expenses of municipal government, and payrolls, fuel costs, and contract services rose with them, rents in all developments had to go up. Parkchester's rents were controlled under the rent control statutes of New York State and New York City. Although the laws permit the granting of hardship increases to bring the yield on residential property to a figure that exceeds Metropolitan Life's expected return, operations under the law are cumbersome and stimulate the opposition by the tenants and their legal representatives at every step. In 1968, Metropolitan Life sold Parkchester to private owners who hoped to turn the development into a large condominium. Many of the original tenants were still in Parkchester at the time of the sale. They had remained in the building through an entire life cycle and had reached retirement age, or were now facing it, and showed considerable reluctance about buying their apartments even with credits arranged by the new owners of Parkchester.

The same influences that produced the sale of Parkchester, that are stimulating Metropolitan Life to seek to sell Riverton Houses, and that caused the insurance company to announce in 1973 that it might try to sell Stuyvesant Town upon the expiration of tax abatement in 1974 also caused other insurance companies to divest themselves of their own rental apartment houses. New York Life has sold Fresh Meadows and Lake Meadows. Equitable Life Assurance has sold Fordham Hill. When the Stuyvesant Town tax abatement did expire, the state legislature passed a law which excluded it on a diminishing scale for ten years.

Because life insurance companies seemed to provide uniquely well-financed and well-qualified ownership, motivated to take a long-term interest in the soundness of its properties, their general decision to leave to others the ownership of rental apartment houses has stimulated regret by most students of housing. The problem runs somewhat deeper, however. What others are prepared to take over the ownership of city rental projects, demonstrating a long-term interest that matches the life insurance companies? If rental ownership is bad for Metropolitan Life, why should it be good for anyone else?

The fact seems to be that in an inflationary period, the ownership of family-type residential housing offers a less satisfactory hedge to the investor than other kinds of real estate investments. As price rises come faster, resistance grows to buying all types of merchandise, but rental apartments are in the singular position of requiring tenants to spend more money for exactly the same apartment in which they have been living. When a customer buys something else—a dress or a shirt—at a price higher than before, his eyes may be shielded by two types of blindness. First, the customer may not remember exactly how much the last one cost. Second, the true cost increase may be hidden by a concealed change in quality for the worse, or by a loudly trumpeted minor improvement that costs less than the price increase but may nevertheless succeed in diverting attention. Neither of these blessings is available to the owner of an apartment house. Every tenant has a clear recollection of what his last month's rent was and cannot be made to entertain the belief that he is getting something better than he did before.

As the consumer movement gains strength throughout the United States, the tenant movement, which antedates much of the general consumer activity, gains even more strength. Much tenant activity is directed justifiably against owners who are deriving their profits from the undermaintenance of their properties, but the effects of the movement hit, perhaps harder, those owners with a conscientious desire to preserve their properties for long-term benefits.

Furthermore, the economies that the insurance companies expected to find in large-scale maintenance operations are also proving illusory. While figures are hard to find, it seems likely that apartment house operations were practical before World War II largely because of the gross underpayment of those who worked in the apartment houses—

the janitors, handymen, porters, and cleaners. Their unions have now become much stronger, and their demand for a living wage has been generally successful. The impact of unionization is particularly strong in the larger complexes, and it is making life difficult not only for life insurance companies but for other owners, including both cooperatives and government housing authorities. Increased productivity comes slowly, if at all, in these service areas. Among the large cooperatives that have been constructed, most particularly in New York City, the increased cost of operations has forced increases in carrying charges that have stimulated intramural faction fights among the cooperators, changes in managing agents, and defaults on government-insured or government-financed mortgages. The operating deficits of local housing authorities have threatened their solvency. The federal government has been forced to provide operating subsidies on top of the capital subsidies that alone were foreseen in the original public housing scheme.

It is not surprising, therefore, that the apartment houses being constructed in the United States are predominantly small, averaging fourteen or fifteen units each. Apartment houses are also being developed along specialized lines, catering to young people or to retired people; in the former case, the attractions of social relationships among the tenants may offset the pain caused by rising rents and maintenance costs; in the latter case, special subsidies may be available, but owners are attracted also by the low maintenance costs that accompany an older tenancy. The two forms of mutual ownership—cooperatives and condominiums—appear to be growing in popularity, the latter, particularly, because its flexibility in financing a separate mortgage on each apartment makes it applicable to new construction. One hears of few successful nonprofit owners of community-based housing developments; many have started out and have failed to survive the impact of rising costs, tenant activism, and the problem of succession when the original management has had enough of the brief glory of accomplishment.

One final point has been suggested by the difficulties of the large apartment complex. That is, that the notion of creating a new neighborhood, large enough to be self-sufficient, may no longer be practical on economic grounds as some have suggested that it is not practical on human grounds. If this conclusion follows from the changing cost patterns, then it may also be true that the reconstruction of urban neighborhoods is more difficult than it was even considered to be. It was always considered difficult enough. If many small buildings must be built, perhaps with resident-owner management, to stabilize a central city neighborhood, the cost of governmental or private supervision of mortgages and subsidies rises to a staggering point. One might further conclude from this that the trend of future apartment house development will continue to move inexorably toward the suburbs, where a head-on confrontation on the matter of land use is inevitable. And the crucial issue in apartment house design will be the reduction of maintenance cost, which implies the shifting of maintenance from what might be called a cash basis to an accrual basis. In short, the owner of a small multifamily building will do a large part of the maintenance himself, spurred on by the hope of increasing the value of his property rather than by a weekly wage.

In any case, the disappointments experienced by the life insurance companies in equity ownership serve to focus their activities all the more sharply on the development of a national mortgage market.

The systems developed by the life insurance companies for the making of mortgages nationally depended on the ability to appraise risks satisfactorily. This, in turn, required the development of a national network of mortgage brokers, mortgage correspondents, and mortgage companies, which in many cases originated the loans that the insurance companies took over.

Mortgages made by life insurance companies in areas remote from their headquarters tend to be made in those regions in which there is a sufficient concentration of business to justify the continued existence of a branch office for mortgage originations, or of an independent mortgage broker or mortgage company.

Obviously, the places in the United States most likely to be able to support mortgage operations on a significant scale are the major metropolitan areas. It is not surprising that 80 percent of all first mortgages held by life insurance companies cover properties within metropolitan areas.[24] The percentage of those homes that are conventionally mortgaged is higher than the percentage insured by the FHA; when FHA insurance is involved, there is a somewhat greater likelihood that the insurance companies will be prepared to lend outside of metropolitan areas.[25]

Conditions of safety—and profitability determined by low overhead per loan—also dictate that national market mortgages are made on new structures. One can visualize a tract builder, working outside Phoenix, Arizona, with the prospect of completing one thousand homes per year, approaching the correspondent mortgage company of a major life insurance company. The correspondent—depending on the precise nature of its relationship with the life insurance company—may be able to issue a firm commitment for a mortgage covering all of the houses in the tract, to communicate the offering to the insurance company, or to commit one part of the tract without further communication with the remainder subject to confirmation as to rates and terms. Whatever the result, the number of individual mortgages covered in the single basic transaction makes the existence of the mortgage company possible. It would experience almost as much expense to obtain the commitment on one house as on one thousand houses.

The life insurance company relationship to the mortgage originator offered, therefore, a model of what might be achieved in the dispersal of savings on a very large scale throughout the entire nation. The government, watching how the centralized mortgage companies were able to maintain a flow of capital into faraway housing developments, established in 1970 an instrument for achieving the same thing on a significantly broader basis. If other financial intermediaries, including private and union pension and welfare funds, could be persuaded to invest in mortgages originated nationwide, the money available for mortgages would be greatly expanded. At best, the growing market for mortgages might offer an outlet for investment funds that would be competitive with other borrowers of capital. This has presented a possibility that the flows of funds into the mortgage market might result in lowering the differential return between mortgages and corporate bonds. These have been the basic ideas behind government mortgage policy of recent years.

At the same time, however, the experience of the life insurance companies in the national mortgage market should have raised several warning signals. The danger arises from the fact that the ability to initiate mortgages depends on the existence of an industry of mortgage originators. These originators are, as we have noted, concentrated in the metropolitan areas, particularly in those metropolitan areas in which there has been in the recent past a large volume of mortgage origination. These areas may not in fact be the areas in which mortgage money is needed in the future, resulting in a very significant misallocation of resources to areas that no longer demand the same high level of construction that they have had in the past. The risk-free situation that results from government intervention may overstimulate the misallocation. But such a system would have in it the seeds for self-correction to some extent at least: The builders, unable to sell their houses, could cease being interested in mortgage money, no matter how convenient.

Equally puzzling are the questions of whether or not this system will produce financing for new construction where none has ever existed before—how, in short, it could be used to provide capital for new towns, if a congressional land-use policy recommended them. How would the national mortgage market provide money to fund the very long-term, start-up costs of new towns before the revenues of the developing town would be able to meet debt service on the mortgage? Nor is it evident that the national mortgage market would provide capital funds for housing whose occupants simply cannot afford conventional debt service or, even worse, cannot afford any debt service at all.

CHAPTER 10

THE MORTGAGE BANKERS

MORTGAGE companies are not, in the sense in which we have used the phrase, financial intermediaries. They do not, generally speaking, accept savings from the public and invest them. Instead, they are intermediaries' intermediaries, helping the savings institutions, most particularly the life insurance companies and, increasingly, the federal government itself, to place funds already saved into suitable long-term residential mortgages.

In order to accomplish this function, mortgage companies, or mortgage bankers (as the industry itself prefers to be called), provide three different kinds of help to borrowers and the investing intermediaries. First, they *originate* mortgages, using their own funds or, as we saw in the chapter on the commercial banks, borrowed money. Second, they *service* the mortgages they originate, although a long-term investing intermediary may have bought the mortgages from them and repaid to the mortgage companies the money originally advanced to the borrowers. Third, to suit the convenience of long-term investors, they may *hold* the mortgages they have originated for a period of months after making the loan to the borrower, until the long-term investor finds that acquisition of the mortgage harmonizes with its own cash position and current investment policies.

The data currently available indicates that mortgage companies, or mortgage bankers, make many mortgage loans. In 1971, the Mortgage Bankers Association estimated the total amount of mortgages originated by mortgage bankers at slightly more than $24 billion. Their growth since

1945 has been phenomenal, indicating that they have served a significant purpose in broadening the market in which those intermediaries wishing to invest in mortgages find suitable mortgages to buy. But the most important fact about the mortgage bankers' role in the mortgage market is that every mortgage they make is made in reliance either on the hope or the certainty that they will sell it to a long-term intermediary investor. In the latter case, their certainty is based on a commitment that, as we have seen, is an enforceable undertaking by a long-term investor to a particular mortgage banker to buy from it mortgages meeting its specific standards in an amount not exceeding a specific total.

For the three services they perform, mortgage bankers are compensated separately. For originating mortgages, they are paid fees. In the case of mortgages guaranteed by the FHA or the VA, these fees range between 1 and 2.5 percent of the original face value of the loan, depending on the statutes covering different types of properties as well as on the regulations of the government agencies. To originate mortgages insured under the FHA, a mortgage banker must be approved by the FHA and is subject to audit; the banker may, however, collect the approved origination fee directly from the borrower.

In the case of noninsured (so-called conventional) mortgages, it is rare for a mortgage banker to collect a fee from the borrower for originating a mortgage on a completed structure. The banker generally does receive an origination fee for making a construction mortgage; this fee is usually paid by the borrower to the mortgage banker and is based on the theory that construction mortgages, being riskier, are harder to obtain than mortgages on a completed housing unit that is ready for occupancy.

Federal Housing Administration regulations provide for construction financing only for those special types of housing developments that are intended for residents with limited incomes. Usually, these developments are intended for cooperative ownership, or if not, are owned by limited dividend corporations. In the case of all other FHA-insured properties (except properties in Alaska), the builder must arrange his construction financing without FHA insurance of the construction loan. If the mortgage banker makes the arrangements with a commercial bank—an arrangement that is usually possible only because the permanent financing has already been arranged by the mortgage banker with a long-term investor—he may collect a fee from the borrower.

Alternatively, according to Saul Klaman, whose monograph "The Postwar Rise of Mortgage Companies" [1] is extensively relied on in these remarks, mortgage bankers may make construction mortgages on their own. Klaman, making in 1955 a special study of mortgage bankers (the term is used interchangeably with mortgage companies), found that of the nearly $1.4 billion in mortgage loans held in inventory by mortgage companies at the end of 1955, approximately $260 million, or a little less than one-fifth, were in loans on buildings under construction.[2] Klaman suggests that this probably overstates the amount of direct lending for construction purposes by mortgage companies, because the construction loans are likely to be outstanding over a longer period of time than the loans on completed property; outstanding, that is to say, on the books of the mortgage banker, before the permanent investor takes them over. The process of construction lasts a long time, and while one construction loan may be outstanding on the mortgage banker's books, he may have closed and sold three or four times as large a volume of loans on completed structures. Most of the latter would not remain quietly in the inventory at the year's end.

Some mortgage banking firms specialize not only in providing construction loans but in providing construction loans for the rehabilitation of existing dwellings or apartment houses. The mortgage banking firms in this narrow field finance their construction loans by borrowing from commercial banks, as do all other mortgage banking firms, but in the case of rehabilitation or modernization loans on apartment houses, there is never a fixed commitment by a permanent lender to provide a new, long-term mortgage when the work is completed. On the contrary, the mortgage banker in this field relies entirely on his nose for the market, the talent that enables him to distinguish which renovation plan will be bankable on a permanent basis after completion. This not only implies the ability to judge whether or not a renovated building will command an economic rent in its neighborhood after the new investment has been added to its capital costs. It implies also the ability to judge whether or not a permanent investor—in this case usually a mutual savings bank—will believe this to be the case. Apparently, the rewards that come from being able to exercise this complex judgment are sufficient to justify the organizational overhead, because the mortgage companies that specialize in this line of activity earn no fees from the servicing of the permanent mortgage, which, as noted, generally constitutes an important part of the gross income of mortgage bankers in the postwar housing market.

The renovation mortgage banker makes his money by the spread between the interest he can charge on the construction loan and the interest that he pays on his own borrowings from commercial banks, from which he obtains the money on which his business is based. Obviously, a mortgage banker engaged in this type of construction mortgage financing must be able to convince the commercial bankers of his own credit worthiness. This quality can be established only by a combination of financial net worth and of successful experience in financial renovations that later, without delay, attracted the permanent financing that enabled the mortgage banker to retire his short-term commercial bank obligations.

This type of mortgage banking institution, which exists on the interest spread between the rate that it borrows money from institutions and the rate that it charges on its mortgages, was a not uncommon form of mortgage banking before the FHA insurance system was developed in the depression years of the 1930s. Mortgage banking firms existed in the nineteenth century in the United States, generally making mortgage loans to those who needed to borrow money against the security of existing or proposed real estate development. The mortgage bankers made the mortgage loans, and then sold these to long-term investors who were usually individual persons. Sometimes the mortgages were sold in the form of participations by a number of individual persons. To some extent the need for residential development capital in the older urban centers in the eastern United States was met by the growing mutual savings banks, but there remained real estate situations that were outside the geographic limits in which mutual savings banks were permitted to lend money or else that simply did not meet banking standards. These proposals were put forward by men prepared to pay high interest rates, so high that the mortgage banker could sell the mortgage to investors and retain a fee that approached 5 percent of the face amount for their initial risk. There was, of course, no advance commitment on the part of the ultimate investors that they would buy the loans originated by mortgage bankers. The bankers had to rely on their own sense of the market in order to assure themselves that they would be able to dispose of the mortgages they originated.

DeForest and Veiller, in their classic book on New York City tenement houses,[3] describe the pattern by which many of the tenement houses were built. The builder, usually a fairly successful small contractor, would borrow the money needed to complete the structure from what the authors describe as a lumper, someone who would provide the forty-five or fifty thousand dollars needed to construct a twenty-two-family tenement house, usually deriving a commission or discount on the funds he advanced that ran as high as 15 percent per year. The lumper did not expect to remain with a permanent investment in the building, just as the builder did not expect to own it for any considerable period of time. The builder expected to sell his building to a permanent investor who would either purchase it for cash or make so large a down payment that the balance could be financed by a mutual savings bank mortgage or who would otherwise encumber the building with enough mortgages to individual investors so that the lumper—in effect, a rudimentary mortgage banker providing construction funds—would be taken out. DeForest and Veiller ascribe to the high interest rates and commissions paid the lumper what they took to be the excessive cost of tenement housing in the late nineteenth century.

Some early mortgage bankers did not raise their own permanent financing. They simply originated mortgages that they hoped to sell to investors, making their living on the spread between what builders were willing to pay for their money and the somewhat lower return that investors demanded in return for their cash. Other mortgage bankers regularly sold their own mortgage-backed debentures to the public while at the same time selling some of the mortgages they originated to investing institutions such as insurance companies. Others, described by Klaman as mortgage guarantee bankers, sold guaranteed bonds to investors and mortgages to institutions. In the 1920s, there also developed some firms that operated in the mortgage field without originating mortgages; they acted as brokers between builders and investing institutions. Mortgage brokering continues to the present time.

The major factor that changed the mortgage banking industry in the postwar years has been the institution of mortgage insurance by the United States government under the Federal Housing Administration. Insurance of mortgages opened the whole nation to mortgage investments made by permanent investors; we are already familiar with the fact that the insurance also made possible a very high ratio of loan to housing value.

After World War II, the addition of a housing mortgage insurance program under the Veterans Administration also broadened the market for direct investment in mortgages by permanent investors. The FHA foresaw that a widespread number of independent business organizations could be encouraged to originate government-insured mortgages and that the mortgages originated by them could be sold to permanent investors like life insurance companies at a lower cost than the insurance companies would incur if they endeavored to establish branches throughout the United States.

To encourage the development of the industry, the FHA set requirements for qualifying as an originator, holder, or servicer of government-insured mortgages. The actual requirements were relatively easy to meet. Each mortgage originating company was required to have a net worth of $100,000 unless it was already an institution subject to federal or state regulation. In the latter case, it would be approved by the FHA with a minimum net worth of only twenty-five thousand dollars. As far as the FHA was concerned, there was no limit on the number of branches an approved mortgagee might have within its own state or a contiguous state. Those mortgage banking institutions that were subject to state or federal regulation were naturally subject to whatever limitations placed by those governments on their power to open branches. If, however, an otherwise unregulated but approved mortgagee wants to open branches in a noncontiguous state, its net worth under FHA regulation must be at least $250,000. Those brokerage offices that only arrange mortgages for their principals need have a net value of only five thousand dollars. The FHA classes them not as mortgagees, but as correspondents, and does not permit them to write mortgages or apply for insurance in their own names. FHA-approved mortgagees are subject to annual audits as well as spot checking and must file annual reports with the FHA.

The Mortgage Bankers Association in 1971 described the origination process as follows: "On home loans, the mortgage banker 'originates' mortgages, seeking loans from a variety of sources. He generally uses his own funds in 'closing' the transaction. The origination process means he not only finds an investor for a borrower, but also prepares the loan documents to fit both the borrower's and the investor's requirements. He arranges to evaluate the property with an appraisal. He negotiates loan terms, he submits the loan application and appraisal to his correspondent investor, and he records or documents the transaction in accordance with local laws, in order to protect the borrower. He handles the funding of the loan and settling with the investor after buyer and seller have closed the transaction with him. The origination fee is paid by the borrower." [4]

In addition to the legalization of the origination fee, a further stimulus to the mortgage banking industry was provided by the essential FHA requirement on all of its insured mortgages that they be fully self-amortizing mortgages with very long terms. While the nation as a whole, having seen its predepression housing disappearing in a storm of foreclosure, welcomed the new-style mortgage terms, the change was not so welcome to mortgage lenders. Individual buyers of mortgages wanted short-term, not long-term, loans. And they were frightened by the self-amortizing mortgage in which each monthly payment includes both interest payments and the return of principal.

Institutional investors—including, particularly, the large insurance companies making mortgages on a national basis—carried on this activity on so large a scale that the total volume of returning principal, particularly when added to other investment funds as they flowed into the insurance company from premium receipts of policyholders, enabled them to continue mortgage investments. Nevertheless, the self-amortizing mortgage covering property at a considerable distance from the headquarters of the major investor requires services of a kind not encountered in the case of a nonamortizing short-term mortgage. These services, which mortgage companies provide, and which Klaman found in 1955 to constitute between 33 and 40 percent of mortgage company gross income, are simply gathered together under the head of servicing. We have listed this as the second major source of income for mortgage bankers, while the Government National Mortgage Corporation, in a 1971 release, describes servicing fees as the "prime incentive in mortgage origination." According to the Mortgage Bankers Association in 1971, the origination fee earned for making the mortgage in the first instance does not cover the actual costs of origination, while the servicing portfolio and the fees derived from it provide the entire profit margin of the mortgage banking industry.[5] At any rate, servicing the permanent mortgage by means of an independent mortgage banker rather than establishing branch offices owned by the major investing units has become accepted by the industry as apparently the cheapest and most efficient method of handling the problem.

The servicing of a mortgage portfolio consists of establishing accounts for each of the constituent mortgages, billing the monthly payments of principal, interest, real estate taxes, risk insurance against casualty losses, and FHA mortgage insurance fees. The mortgage banker must remit the proceeds, properly accounted for, to the mortgagee. It must establish, collect, and disburse payments from the borrower for the tax and insurance requirements. Although collected monthly, these tax and insurance payments are usually payable at less frequent intervals. The funds received are by FHA regulation segregated in special escrow accounts until they are paid out as prescribed by the mortgage terms and the requirements of insurance policies and local tax laws. The Veterans Administration does not regulate loans and conventional mortgage operations so explicitly as the FHA does, but according to Klaman, mortgage bankers treat the two insurances similarly, segregating the money received in special accounts that are kept insulated from the daily business of the mortgage banker.[6]

The problems encountered in servicing loans have so far, at least, been sufficiently complex and rooted in local conditions to make local servicing attractive, and yet sufficiently simple to enable the local servicer to handle them at a cost low enough to make his fee profitable. The fee has become standardized at .5 percent of the remaining balance of the principal of a mortgage at the start of the year. It is paid by the lender—the borrower knows nothing directly of what the servicing costs. Obviously, because the only self-amortizing mortgages are involved, the fee collected each year diminishes with the reduction of the outstanding balance. The mortgage banking firm, therefore, has a great incentive to originate new mortgages on which it will have servicing rights. Without the addition of new mortgages, it is faced not simply with a stagnation in income growth but with a steady absolute decline of income volume as the outstanding principal of existing mortgages is reduced. As long as there are institutions prepared to acquire mortgages for permanent investment, and as long as the government is prepared to insure the mortgagee against risk of default, the lure of the servicing fee would appear to be capable of continuing to stimulate the investment of the nation's savings amply in residential mortgages.

Before turning to the third source of mortgage banking income—the holding of mortgages—one might stop to observe that none of these necessary preconditions is intrinsically permanent. The cost of servicing might increase to the point at which it ceases to be profitable, while the major permanent investors might decide to install their own servicing operations rather than to pay higher servicing fees to independent mortgage bankers. Contrarily, institutions might shift their own preferences for investment out of the smaller residential properties best served by independent agencies and into other investments—such as developments large enough to be self-originated and self-serviced—that do not require the service contract. Finally, investor policy might shift away from the direct holding of government-guaranteed mortgages, a trend that is discernible in life insurance investment practices. Federal government policy would, in that event, become crucial to the continuing prosperity and expansion of the mortgage banking industry.

The 1971 policies of the Government National Mortgage Association demonstrate the belief that a thriving mortgage banking industry is essential to a sound housing program and that the growth of servicing portfolios—and their protection—constitute the most significant avenue through which the mortgage banking industry can be assisted. Naturally, any such governmental policy is subject to change if it produces more housing than the market can absorb, or housing in areas where there is insufficient economic demand or significant political opposition or constraint.

In 1971, there were clear signs of increasing bank interest in the mortgage banking industry. In our discussion of Real Estate Investment Trusts we mentioned the acquisition of a major mortgage banking company by a major stock underwriting company. This may presage a growing interest in the earning possibilities of short-term advances from sources outside the commercial banking system. Underwriting firms, particularly those with good connections with pension and other funds, might be able to earn a highly satisfactory return on money used on a revolving basis to finance the temporary holding of mortgages by mortgage bankers. This temporary holding of mortgages is called warehousing, meaning, usually, that the mortgage documents and long-term commitments are held in the vaults of the institution making the temporary loans.

Another development has been the increasing interest by the commercial banks in the acquisition of mortgage banks, a type of transaction that would be possible only if approved under federal laws covering the legitimate activities of national bank holding companies. Commercial banks would seem to be wondering why, if they are providing the funds with which mortgage bankers operate, they should not also be entitled to participate in the profitable part of the business: the servicing of permanently sold mortgages. The tie-in between mortgage bankers and commercial banks would also seem to offer a relatively fixed, captive market: The wholly owned mortgage bank would be required to finance its operation with the funds of its parent bank. At least, there would seem to be a presumption to this effect.

In the meantime, however, the commitment from the long-term investing institution, tied to the servicing contract on the mortgage, remains the essential element in the mortgage banking business. The normal, advance commitment is the type most attractive to the mortgage banker, because it offers the mortgage banker a firm contract of sale for the mortgages it originates in accordance with the lender's standards up to a stated maximum. Delivery must be made as soon after the mortgage closing as is practicable from the point of view of the originating mortgage banker. The period usually runs from sixty to one hundred eighty days, depending upon the speed of processing a group of loans that were handled together.

As a shortage of mortgage funds available for permanent investors developed in the course of the late 1960s, forward commitments became more readily available. Under such a commitment, the permanent investor agrees with its correspondent to purchase a stipulated amount of mortgage investments, each of which would meet the investor's standards. The investor, however, at its sole option, reserves the right to acquire and pay for the mortgages at any time up to about two years after closing. This forces the mortgage banker to be prepared to warehouse mortgages for a two-year period, making his own financial arrangements to do so and, of course, paying interest on the borrowed funds.

The third type of commitment, the standby commitment, is issued by an investor who wishes to keep a mortgage banker actively in the market, but is not truly prepared to bid to purchase the mortgages within any specific time limit. Therefore, the standing commitment promises only that, subject to familiar general terms and conditions, the permanent investor will buy a stipulated number of mortgages, but only at a price so low—with such a deep discount from face value—that the mortgage banker can scarcely be expected to demand fulfillment of the commitment. Such a standby commitment enables a mortgage banker to qualify for commercial bank credit sufficient to warehouse the mortgages covered by the commitment. During the warehousing period, the mortgage banker tries to find another, more enthusiastic long-term investor willing to take them, paying a price nearer to their face value (less, of course, any amortization received by the mortgage banker during warehousing).

All of the commitments include the proviso that the mortgage banker will have the right to service the mortgages originated by it, and that the permanent investor will pay the agreed fee to the mortgage banker —.5 percent on individual residences per year, less on larger projects. Without some sort of arrangement like this—giving the mortgage banker the inducement of servicing in order to lure him into mortgage origination, and providing a take-out strong enough to justify commercial bank temporary credit—the mortgage banking industry could not exist in its present form. Without a mortgage banking industry, a nationwide mortgage market would be an impossibility. This explains why the government has tried so hard to supplement the life insurance companies in their role of major purchaser of mortgages from mortgage bankers. Without a clear picture of the industry, it becomes difficult to understand the two agencies that have been devised to provide a continuing market for mortgages—the Federal National Mortgage Association, otherwise known as Fanny Mae; and the Government National Mortgage

Association, otherwise known as Ginny Mae. These agencies, working in tandem, have sought to find new pools of money that might be tapped for the ultimate acquisition of mortgages, just as the life insurance companies tapped the saving impulses of life insurance policyholders and thereby developed, through the mortgage bankers, a national mortgage market.

CHAPTER 11

THE STATE AGENCIES

IN THE MIDDLE of the 1920s, Governor Alfred Smith of New York State urged the legislature of that state to pass what he called a Permanent Housing Program for the people of the state. The word permanent was intended, by implicit contrast, to refer to the tax exemption that New York City, with the state's permission, had offered for a limited period of time to all builders of residential structures. The tax exemption had been intended to make new housing construction competitive with prewar development despite the vast increase in its cost. The tax exemption program was about to come to an end in 1926; yet it was clear that private builders could not possibly build new housing at prices that working-class families could afford to meet.[1] Smith's program was based on the notion that housing should be a public utility industry. He intended to stimulate the formation of companies that would be given extraordinary powers and that, under strict regulation, would be allowed to earn a limited return on their equity investment in housing developments. To keep the rents low, they would be given the benefit of land condemnation, freedom from all state taxes, substantial reduction of normal real estate taxes over a long period of years, and low interest rate mortgages advanced by the state to such projects, which would be open only to families whose income did not exceed a stipulated multiple of their rent.

Smith's plan was adopted with the exception of government mortgages. These had, not surprisingly, stimulated the opposition of the financial institutions that were already in the mortgage market. Government entry into the mortgage field was quickly described as unfair competition, and socialistic besides.

By 1955, however, events had changed the significance of government mortgages. In the middle fifties, the federally subsidized public housing program was effective in providing housing for low-income families, but the high cost of urban construction and maintenance had continued to rise in the post-World War II economy faster than the median wage. Subsidies were needed to produce housing for those whose incomes were too high to qualify them for public housing, but who still could not afford what was being produced by private enterprise. Meanwhile, the federal income tax rates had risen so high that the tax exemption extended by the federal government to interest earned by the owners of municipal bonds encouraged high-income taxpayers to buy those bonds at yields 1.5 to 2 percent lower than those of high-quality corporate bonds.

The New York State legislature once more took up the Smith proposal and found that the prospect of saving rent by utilizing the federal tax concession for municipal bonds had bleached out the socialistic stigma that it had suffered from years before. A Limited Profit Housing Company Bill passed the state legislature in 1955,[2] and offered regulated housing companies not only the privileges that were established in the 1920s but the additional privilege of borrowing 90 percent of their development costs from the state or city government. This enactment, known colloquially as the Mitchell-Lama Law, has been in effect for nearly twenty years. It stimulated what has become a widespread national movement to raise mortgage money for special housing programs by the sale of earmarked local government bonds.

It was, of course, true that public housing has been financed by the sale of municipal housing authority bonds, but these were secured as to interest and principal by an annual contributions contract with the federal government. New York's entry into housing mortgage finance without federal government guarantees was a new movement. The state's ability to sell bonds would no longer depend on a guarantee by the federal government, but rather on the state's own credit—which might be pledged to repay the borrowings in part or in whole—and on the fiscal sagacity with which the government mortgages might be made.

The New York program offered each housing company the choice of two sources of mortgage money—the state or the city. Both governments were to provide mortgage money to the housing companies by borrowing from the public; in short, by selling bonds. Under relevant provisions of law in the State of New York, the voters must approve by referendum, held at the time of a general election, the sale of any bonds that bear a repayment pledge of the full faith and credit of the State of New York. Aside from the requirement for a referendum, the state (unlike the federal government) is free of any specific statutory limit as to the total amount of bonds that may be outstanding at any time.

The City of New York has a different problem. Under state law, the city is allowed to borrow for all purposes up to 10 percent of the equalized assessed valuation of its taxable real estate. To determine the equalized value, the taxable value must first be adjusted by a formula relating it to market values—the State Equalization Board performs this calculation for all of the cities, towns, and villages of the state. For housing purposes, state law permits New York City to borrow another 2 percent of the assessed value of its taxable real estate (without application of the equalization formula). In 1955, when the Limited Profit Housing Company Law first was passed, the statutory Housing Debt Limit permitted New York City to borrow approximately $600 million for housing purposes. These housing funds could be loaned not only to private corporations building housing but also to the New York City Housing Authority, which would build public housing with it, even though this public housing would lack the benefit either of federal or of state annual subsidy payments, and would, therefore, cater to a higher-income tenancy.

Looking first at the problems of the city, it quickly appears that the $600 million at 1955 prices would finance no more than thirty thousand apartments, scarcely enough to make a dent in the need for so-called middle-income housing in the city, where there are approximately 3.2 million dwelling units. The law, however, makes the ceiling flexible. It provides that if a housing company meets all of its obligations on its city mortgage for one year, it may be considered a self-liquidating enterprise. In that case, the sum of its mortgage ceases to be a charge against the city debt limit, and the city may sell additional bonds up to the amount of debt that this self-liquidation, in effect, releases. Thus, the city need merely maintain its mortgages on a fiscally sound basis, and it will be able to use its debt-incurring, housing power as a revolving fund. An infinite amount of housing might theoretically be built under such an arrangement, which would be useful also in any other state with similar laws.

In fact, the greatest difficulty faced by the City of New York has been its inability to enforce the terms of the mortgage loans that it has extended to housing companies.

Two significant trends pushed the city into its awkward corner. First, inflation forced the costs of construction and operations up so fast—and local taxes with them—that rents had to rise beyond, in some cases far beyond, the levels foreseen when the buildings were started or when their occupants first moved in. Second, a rise in interest rates multiplied the effect of both construction and operating costs on the rents.

Under the pressure of these rising costs, city housing officials discovered that their mortgagors, the families living in the limited profit, housing company projects, were constituents as well as debtors. This first discovery led to a second: Rent increases to enforce the requirements of the underlying mortgage would be extraordinarily unpopular with the very citizens whom the program was designed to help. Within a few years, New York City found that a majority of the housing companies—many of which were cooperatively owned by their tenants—were in default on their mortgage commitments, or that their contractual mortgage interest rates were too low to cover the city's cost of borrowing. Their occupants were paying less rent than necessary to meet the operating costs, taxes, and debt service. Once city officials had made their discoveries about the connection between rents and votes, they naturally hesitated to institute foreclosures or any of the other dramatic devices (like removing the boards of directors) with which the law arms them to meet defaults.

For its part, the state government, too, encountered difficulty in making direct mortgages to housing companies. The difficulty arose from the state constitutional provision requiring the assent of the voters to each flotation of bonds bearing a pledge of the state's credit. Because these bond issues did not provide revolving funds, the state was faced with two unattractive choices. It could ask for approval of an initial financing large enough to take care of foreseeable, long-term requirements; or it could ask for authorization of less frightening sums, in the expectation of asking for them repeatedly, year after year. The first method might well alarm the voters so badly that the first authorization request would be defeated in the referendum. The second would not firmly sustain a continuing program of state borrowing and lending. Sooner, more likely than later, the voters would turn down a referendum. In that event, prospective developers might find themselves high and dry, having acquired land and paid for preliminary architectural drawings only to find their projects unfunded. To resuscitate a lapsed program would be difficult. It would involve inflating the confidence of prospective sponsors to the point at which they would invest their own money in acquiring land options or making plans for future developments.

Faced with these alternatives, in 1959, the Rockefeller Administration in the State of New York began to design an independent authority that, with state support but without state fiscal backing, would sell bonds to the public to raise money that the state housing officials might then advance to housing companies.

The agency would have to be close enough to the state so that its interest payments to the purchasers of bonds would qualify for tax exemption under federal statutes, and close enough also so that the bond buyers would feel protected, not only by the soundness of the underlying mortgages that the agency would make but also by a sense that even if the mortgages turned sour the State of New York would come galloping to the aid of the bondholders, bringing general revenue tax money in sufficient quantity to make good the deficit. At the same time, the agency had to be sufficiently far from state government so that the constitutional provision that the voters must ratify direct state borrowing would not be deemed violated.

The first effort of the state legislature to design such an agency was a failure. The agency was to be called the New York State Limited Profit Housing Mortgage Corporation,[3] and it failed because it was a little too far from being a state agency to impress prospective bond underwriters with the probable readiness of the state to come to the aid of their customers. On the second try, the legislature approved a provision that more or less miraculously spanned the unspannable chasm.[4] To begin with, it was to be called the New York State Housing Finance Agency (the new name made no discernible contribution to its success, but it is, at least, briefer). The Housing Finance Agency was to be required by law to maintain for the benefit of its lenders, under each of the separate bond resolutions that it might pass, a so-called reserve fund. This fund must contain at least enough money to meet debt service in full for one year of all issues of bonds outstanding under the bond resolution before the Housing Finance Agency may make delivery of any bonds. Money may be removed from the reserve fund only to pay interest and amortization on the bonds issued under the resolution appropriate to the specific reserve fund. On December 1 of any year, the chairman of the Housing Finance Agency may notify the governor and the director of the budget of any deficiency in the reserve fund and the size of the deficiency. The state legislature is obliged to pay into the reserve fund whatever sum is needed to bring the fund back to its required size. However, the obligation of the legislature is not absolute, because it is subject to appropriation by the legislature itself. This provision means to the bond buyers that the State of New York is morally obligated to see that they lose no money from defaults, but it also means to the constitutional lawyers that the people, who retain the right to elect the legislators, have not been deprived of a final review of the assumption of the agency's indebtedness by the taxpayers. In fact, at no time in the twelve-year history of the Housing Finance Agency has any appropriation been required by the legislature. The mortgage payments have been met when due, and none is in default. The good record, contrasting with the many defaults in city housing companies, may depend on the exercise of judgment and prudence by the Housing Finance Agency: Builders have said that its investments are strongly market-directed. The city officials, contrariwise, claim to be social pioneers in selecting sites and in pressing for the inclusion of a large percentage of low-income and welfare families in the limited profit, housing company projects. Or the good record may reflect the separation of the state agency from direct control by elected officials. They can point to this separation when their constituent mortgage defaulters come crying for help in staving off rent increases necessary to pay mortgage installments as operating costs rise.

New York City has recently moved in the same direction as the state. The state legislature has given it the power to establish its own mortgage finance agency, in this case called the Housing Development Corporation.[5] The corporation has the right to sell its own bonds, without invoking the full faith and credit of the City of New York, and to lend the proceeds to regulated housing companies that are to undertake new housing construction or rehabilitation. The corporation is also permitted to participate in first mortgages with other nongovernmental lending institutions.

Because New York City does not guarantee the principal and interest of the bonds, and because the taxing powers of the city are limited, except as may be required in order to meet its own obligations, the basic security for the bonds would ordinarily be the housing mortgages themselves. In the light of the city's disastrous record in collecting its mortgage payments, this would probably be insufficient to assure the sale of the bonds to private investors. The legislation establishing the corporation, therefore, permits the corporation to replenish any deficit in its reserve fund or funds by invading the financial payments that the state government makes to the city for any purpose whatever, even including education. In short, if the housing companies cannot meet, or refuse to meet, their mortgage payments, the schoolchildren of the entire city may suffer. Aside from the financial security that this procedure offers to the prospective bond purchasers, it also will tend, one suspects, to stiffen the spines of the board of directors of the Housing Development Corporation. At least four of the board members will be private citizens—two appointed by the mayor, two by the governor—not seeking election and presumably not susceptible to the desire to be loved, which is a fatal flaw for mortgage bankers, bookmakers, and college professors, *inter alios.*

The New York City Housing Development Corporation represented the first attempt to involve a city agency in the mortgage market as an independent entity, but before it had even floated its first issue, seventeen states other than New York, had established their own finance agencies.[6] Each was based on the same principle as the New York Housing Finance Agency, the principle of using the tax exemption of municipal bond interest to lower the cost of the mortgage. Because the states other than New York started later in the 1960s, when housing costs were much higher, they relied from the beginning, as New York State was later to rely, on combining with this partial indirect subsidy the direct mortgage payment subsidies offered by the federal government through the FHA.

The state mortgage agencies that followed New York, however, lacked New York's experience in the management of subsidized or partially subsidized housing programs. Since the midtwenties, the State of New York has had an official agency charged with the supervision of those parts of the permanent housing program that Governor Smith had been able to enact. The problems that arise in government financing of privately owned housing had already become familiar to the public officials involved; these problems do not arise in quite the same form as they do for a savings banker making a mortgage on a purely private piece of property. In that case, for example, the banker does not care whether or not the builder makes a very large profit in the course of constructing the apartment house on which he seeks a mortgage. Nor does the savings banker much care what the original cost of land to the builder may have been. As we have seen, the savings banker is concerned primarily with the realizable value of the completed building. Does the mortgage provide a reasonable margin for safety in the event of foreclosure? Will the apartment house attract a rent roll that will cover all of the operating expenses with enough left over to cover debt service, again with a margin for contingencies?

Government, as a mortgage banker, must ask different questions. Officials must anticipate the criticism of those who hear that government money has been loaned to private persons at an artificially low cost, as a result of which the recipients may make money for themselves.

In fact, under the New York State constitution, loans of public money to private people are generally forbidden. The housing mortgages may be made only because the constitution provides that the construction of housing for persons of low income is a "public purpose." All housing agencies in other states require similar definitions of public purpose, either by their constitution or by the highest court in the state, before the agency may make loans. In some states, housing generally, without limitation as to the income of its residents, is considered to be a public purpose.

The definition of purpose must always be sustained by the way in which the agency does business. New York State housing officials found themselves perforce adopting so-called safeguards to protect the state, and ultimately their own reputations, from charges of corrupt practice. They have developed procedures for calculating the value of land contributed by a sponsor to the development that the agency is funding; procedures for allocating allowable rates of profit and office-and-field overhead in construction; specifications for room sizes, project design, and materials that are more highly restrictive than the applicable local building codes and zoning regulations. The New York State Division of Housing and Community Renewal supervised the projects when they were directly financed by mortgage loans from the state. The same agency continues to perform in an identical function even though the mortgage function has been assumed by the State Housing Finance Agency. Upon completion of a financed project, the division continues to supervise the operations of the building or buildings, auditing its books, approving major expenditures, and exerting control over rents and income levels of entrance and continued occupancy. All of these operations far exceed the work performed by any normal mortgagee in the private market; all of them are imposed by the political and legislative need to ensure that the people's money be used in fulfillment of a public purpose in a manner that will keep the state's character unspotted. They are all safeguards that, looked at from the developer's side, might be characterized as bureaucratic red tape. Nevertheless, the State Housing Finance Agency provides a regularized governmental body through which federal subsidies might be channeled with a minimum of direct federal participation in housing management.

Although close supervision by a government agency is expensive, its cost should be set down under several different headings. First, obviously, comes the cost to the state of operating the necessary bureaus and staffs. In New York State, this is met by a direct charge against each housing company: A rate of .5 percent of the outstanding mortgage amount is included in the debt service to cover the cost of the continuing supervision. In addition, there are fees to be paid for the initial review of the plans and application for funding. The Housing Finance Agency, despite the fact that the New York State Division of Housing performs many of its supervisory functions, nevertheless must pay for its own offices and personnel, its extensive legal and accounting services. These are met by a onetime charge against the mortgage sum advanced to a housing company. These same costs, incidentally, are met in different ways by other states. Michigan, for example, receives reimbursement for its finance expenditures through a single 3.5 percent discount on the original mortgage amount. On a mortgage with a face amount of $1 million, it actually advances only $962,500 to the housing company. Massachusetts discounts its mortgages by only 1 percent, but makes separate charges for site inspection and other special identifiable services.[7]

The second set of costs involved in the governmental supervision of its direct mortgages may be even more serious than the direct set, although they may be more difficult to identify. These are the costs to the developer—whether it is a nonprofit entity, a profit-motivated builder, or even a public body—that result from the delays and uncertainties incidental to government supervision. Such delays include more than the review process in the lending agency, or in the effort to plan a coordinated housing program, however important coordinated planning may be to the ultimate value of the state's investment. The delays include the process of approval by local governing bodies of the local tax exemption and abatement that is frequently a necessary adjunct to state financing, particularly when the state financing is intended to take advantage of the debt service subsidies offered in the FHA 236 program.

As an ironic consequence of the expense engendered by the government mortgage administration, New York State learned that government regulation of the mortgage process had become so complex, in effect, that a new government agency was needed to circumvent it. This agency, the New York State Urban Development Corporation, possesses the power to float its own bonds, backed by a provision similar to that which succeeded for the Housing Finance Agency. Financial independence enabled the Urban Development Corporation to develop its own construction standards, freeing it from the necessity of review by the State Division of Housing. The Urban Development Corporation's powers extended beyond the ability to sell its own bonds. It also was initially granted—subject to constant and ultimately successful threats of legislative rescission—the right to proceed without regard to local zoning and construction ordinances, a right later revoked. Some of the other states, watching New York and finding themselves challenged by the complexities of their own regulations, also granted to their own mortgage agencies some of the Urban Development Corporation's power of acting not merely as the mortgagee for some other developer but as the developer itself. In either case, the basic financing method—tax exempt bonds to raise mortgage money—remains the same.

In its first ten years of operation, the New York State Housing Finance Agency provided the mortgage funds for more than fifty-five thousand apartment units throughout the state. In other states, housing agencies were still barely getting under way. Only four states other than New York had sold any notes or bonds by April 1, 1972, and the total number of units scheduled to be constructed with those funds amounted to about sixteen thousand. By the end of 1971, the New York State Housing Finance Agency had issued commitments to provide mortgage funds of almost $1.3 billion. Many of these commitments had already been fully funded, and the agency had raised more than $1.1 billion through the sale of its obligations.[8]

Unquestionably, the use of municipal bonds as a funding vehicle has played a significant role in the construction of housing in New York State. Its importance in the future, and in other states, is not quite so clear. A first question concerns the future of federal government policy toward the tax exemption of interest received on local government bonds. A second question concerns the ultimate size of the market for such securities, and the identification of the sources from which the money to buy them comes. Finally, there is the question connected to both the others, as to the interest rate that must, in the future, be paid on local government securities in order to make them marketable as the other two questions change the objective facts of life.

As to the first of these three major policy questions, there has been increasing pressure in Congress, expressed as well in party platforms, to reexamine all of the so-called tax loopholes, those arrangements that offer the taxpayer certain deductions from his gross income that do not, in fact, represent cash outlays. Among these are depletion allowances that permit deductions for the gradual diminution of reserves of raw materials that cannot be duplicated, such as the using up of the rock in a quarry or the oil from an oil field. Depreciation allowances for buildings are also questioned, particularly when it seems to be a fact that many buildings are worth more years after they were built than they had been worth immediately upon completion. In the case of subsidized housing, the difference between the depreciated value and the market value is treated as a capital gain—an important tax concession to stimulate ownership of this type of housing. Under present law, there is no limit to the amount of tax exempt bonds that an individual may own. If some wealthy bachelor decided to invest all of his $10 million in municipal bonds, he would enjoy (let us hope) an income of more than $500,000 per year without paying any more than a minimum income tax; while a taxpayer who went to work, without so heavy a nest egg in his lunch box, and earned fifty thousand dollars a year, one-tenth of the bondholder's income, would pay twenty thousand dollars in normal income taxes.

On a more profound level, the tax exemption offered to holders of municipal bonds can be attacked equally strenuously. First of all, this exemption amounts to a subsidy from the federal government to local government; but as a subsidy, it violates the basic rules of subsidies. Its size is unknown. There is no way of calculating how much income the federal government actually gives up by offering the tax exemption, and, therefore, the people's representatives are unable to measure the benefits of the subsidy against its cost. A second objection often made involves the blindness of the subsidy. Because all municipal bonds receive the same indeterminate subsidy—amounting to the difference between the rate of interest at which they would sell without the tax exemption and with the tax exemption—the federal government has no opportunity to review the programs that it subsidizes. Third, because the subsidy is based on the ownership of bonds, a large part of the burden of paying it is thrust disproportionately on those who do not earn enough or own enough assets to benefit from the tax exemption. In effect, the cost of the subsidy is paid for by higher income taxes generally, while the tax exempt feature of the bonds enables some taxpayers in high brackets to minimize their share and pass the burden on to others, generally with lower income.

To each of these objections, there is an answer; even, perhaps, a refutation. To the first objection, the lack of precision about the cost of the subsidy, it could be argued that no one ever knows the true cost of a subsidy because no one knows how much activity would have taken place without the subsidy. Therefore, one cannot truly calculate how much of the subsidy cost is recouped by taxes on incomes generated by the subsidy. In the case of ship-building subsidies, for example, government figures reveal precisely how many dollars are given to those who build approved ocean-going ships in American yards. But nobody knows whether or not all of these ships might be built outside the United States if the subsidies did not exist. Therefore, one can only guess at how much governmental revenue is generated by the income tax on the wages of the shipyard workers and to what extent the subsidy is offset by all of the other economic activity that is generated, directly or indirectly, by the shipyard activity. The difficulty of estimating the cost of income tax exemption differs only in degree from that of estimating the cost of any other federal subsidy program.

Even in the case of subsidies that appear to be more precisely measurable, local tax exemption may be involved, as in the case of public housing projects, in which the federal subsidy appears to be readily calculable. At a closer look, the precise cost of the local tax exemption is impossible to determine because it involves a guess as to what might be done with the land involved if public housing were not put on it. At a still closer look, even the federal subsidy is incapable of precise computation. Although the federal subsidy to public housing consists of annual cash contributions that can readily be totaled, the contributions on capital account are equal to the annual debt service that the local housing authority has incurred on its bonds in order to raise the money needed to build a specific project. Those bonds, being local obligations, offer tax-free interest to their purchasers. We have thus come full cycle to confront the fact that the federal government does not know precisely how much public housing costs, any more than local government knows. Nor does either the government or the beneficiary know the precise value of the benefits received. What is the social value of public housing? Can it be computed at all so that the legislature might be able to make an informed judgment as to whether or not the cost of it is justified by the results?

As to the criticism that the subsidies of tax exemption are bad policy because they are blind, we have already noted that blindness may be a virtue rather than a defect in public policy. If the federal government were to abrogate its present tax exemption and replace it with a cash contribution to any local government that seeks to borrow money—the size of the cash contribution, representing the difference between the present cost of local government borrowing and the future, nontax-exempt cost —the Congress of the United States sooner or later would find itself in the position of appropriating the necessary funds and making provision for collecting the taxes needed to raise those funds. At that point, again sooner or later, questions will be raised as to the size of the appropriations and the size of the taxes needed to support them. Someone will bring in horror stories of frivolous capital investments by local governments, and a properly run Congress will be forced, ultimately, to evaluate the projects on which it is spending money, no longer blindly, but open-eyed. Many congressional subsidy programs have been governed by the principle that no state may have more than 15 percent of the total appropriation. Would that principle remain in a conscious program of appropriations to replace tax exemption? Local government capital needs are not necessarily arithmetically proportional to population: High-density population creates important needs for public investment, as in mass transit and pollution control, of which states with smaller populations have no need. In 1971, all local and state governments sold $24 billion in bonds; New York State alone sold $4.8 billion of that total—20 percent. Should individual states be limited to 15 percent of the national total in tax exemption replacement subsidies? This would be crippling to many serious New York State programs. Should there be no comparative limit on the amount of subsidies paid to any state? This will seem hardly fair to the senators from a sparsely populated state that has few governmental capital requirements. Of course, that smaller state has paid its share of the cost of tax exemption in the past—but it paid that share blindly. Unmasking the participation, a subject for dispute and perhaps accommodation, has been added to the already overlong agenda of the Congress.

We come to the third objection, which is that the tax exemption is regressive because it raises money through a process that is valuable only to the wealthy. This, no doubt, is true, although it is only one part of the complex taxing system of the United States. A general demand for reform of the tax system comes readily to the lips of all of us; specific proposals for constructive change appear more rarely. They must contend with the consequent effect of tax changes on the productive and distributive systems of the country. These may be astonishing. In the early 1960s, the Internal Revenue Service sought to stiffen its requirements for deducting entertainment expenditures that were classed as business costs. The effect of this policy was felt as much by the entertainment and restaurant industry—and its workers—as by the wealthy taxpayers. Obviously, this practical problem does not vitiate the injustice of a regressive tax system, but it should have the effect of generally slowing the agitation for reform until a reasonable substitute for specific measures can be worked out.

A few points might be made in addition. As an escape from taxpaying, the municipal bond represents a relatively minor avenue, as compared with the shift of ordinary income into capital gains, the depletion allowance, and the use of depreciation accruals. Just as these more significant tax devices have their economic justification, so has tax exemption. It does not represent sheer gain to the taxpayer; on the contrary, it forces him to arbitrage the tax exemption feature against the lower interest rate; he accepts the diminution of ordinary income in order to benefit from a subsequent tax benefit. It must be balanced against alternative investments, such as the purchase of stock or convertible bonds. In this respect, it may have a healthy, dampening effect on stock market inflation by offering an alternative to many investors who would not otherwise be interested in fixed-price securities. As the income tax rate rises in the middle brackets, the spectrum of taxpayers benefiting from tax exemption grows much wider; it is questionable whether or not some of these market strengths would survive any transformation of the tax exemption privilege. Without the attraction of tax exemption, a smaller pool of capital funds might remain for investment in municipal securities, inelastic in size no matter how attractive the interest rate. Most students of this market feel that any effort to limit the ability of an individual taxpayer to invest in municipals to any stated figure would be discouraging to the bond buyers as a group. They would regard this intrusion as merely the first step in a long process to deprive their bonds, and possible further purchases, of the value imputed by tax abatement.

The market for local government bonds grew at a very rapid rate during the 1960s. The total state and local debt outstanding (including both short- and long-term debt) swelled from $68 billion to $154 billion in the twelve years from 1960 to 1971.[9] The character of the holders of this debt changed markedly. Individual and family owners increased their holdings by only 35 percent, far less than the growth of the total market. Commercial banks, in contrast, increased their holdings from $17 billion to $78 billion, more than 435 percent. Fire and casualty insurance companies more than doubled their holdings.[10] In both cases, changed tax treatment accounted for the change in emphasis, but the actual growth rate from year to year reflects the condition in the money market. The year to year gains in periods of monetary tightness are sharply reflected by the commercial bank totals. Obviously, the future size of the municipal bond market depends on the flow of savings and on the general tax structure. The future taxes that might be levied on those financial intermediaries that, like the mutual savings banks, do not now buy tax exempt bonds, might greatly increase their purchase of tax exempt bonds by those intermediaries.

The implications for housing mortgages of these shifts in savings patterns are significant, even though the direct housing portion (not including the local housing authority bonds) of the total local and state government debt can scarcely amount to more than 1 percent. Other capital needs of local government show no current signs of diminishing (although the reluctance of local taxpayers to authorize new issues is readily noticeable). If the pool of savings does not grow in proportion to local government needs, the spread between taxable interest on corporate bonds and the nontaxable interest of local government bonds will narrow.

A comparison of the interest rates on high quality corporate bonds with those of high quality state and local government bonds—and of a sample portfolio of the latter, with a wide range of quality—would reveal constant fluctuations, the analysis of which lies primarily in the field of public finance. With some exceptions, it can be stated as a rough guess that buyers will be interested in purchasing corporate bonds if their yield, after deducting normal corporate income taxes, is as much as 1 percent less than local government bonds of similar quality. In other words, investors feel rather safer with good corporate bonds.

There is one major exception to this. Local government bonds that, like local housing authority bonds, are guaranteed by the federal government as to principal and interest (in effect, at least, by the annual contributions contract between the federal government and the local authority), sell quite readily even though their yield is approximately eighty basis points less than the yield on nonfederally guaranteed local government bonds.

This may suggest that some money might be saved by local government housing agencies—and thus by the residents in the housing projects they finance—if the Housing Finance Agency bonds could be guaranteed by an agency of the federal government, like the Government National Mortgage Association. So far, these guarantees have been offered only on bonds secured by FHA-insured mortgages; these possess no miraculous tax exemptions.

There is, however, a real question as to how broad the market is for the higher-quality, lower-yield United States guaranteed bonds. Many buyers of local government bonds—institutional buyers as well as household buyers—seek a balanced portfolio that will provide maximum yield consistent with a prudent dispersal. Offering a government guarantee of all housing bonds might merely narrow the spread between such guaranteed bonds and the nonguaranteed bonds. Contrariwise, there is reason to believe that in the long run those housing agencies that run their affairs in the most businesslike way will be able to sell bonds at the lowest rate of interest. The rating of local government obligations by bond-rating houses has had a significant effect on the differential rates of interest paid by different governments at different times.

Despite these cautionary words, it is also true that the fluctuations among bonds holding the same rating at different times has been much greater than the differences among bonds with different ratings at the same time. A survey of the possibility of local government financing of housing (other than federally guaranteed public housing) indicates that this method does provide the possibility of financing a considerable— though not precisely ascertainable—quantity of housing at an interest rate lower than needed to market taxable mortgages. It seems equally clear that these local government obligations must be sold in the same general money market in which all savings seek placement, and in which the price of money fluctuates under an almost incalculable number of pressures and demands. Tax exemption is interpreted by that market merely as one characteristic to be evaluated in fixing the price of the obligation; the quantity of the offerings, the quality of the individual obligor, and the state of expectations as to future legislation—all play an important role in setting the price.

Finally, we must not forget that the proceeds of local government bonds are largely used to improve the utility and social packages of housing. It is fruitless to discuss improved housing for low-income families without recognizing the vast public investment that will be needed either to improve the facilities in existing low-income neighborhoods or to construct new neighborhoods in which many low-income families can satisfactorily move.

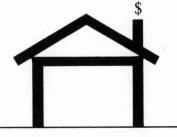

PART THREE

Governmental Institutions and the Future of Policy

CHAPTER 12

THE FEDERAL
HOUSING ADMINISTRATION

OUR DISCUSSION of the several types of institutions that offer money to the mortgage market included frequent references to the Federal Housing Administration. We used, with presumptuous familiarity, the term FHA-insured mortgages. The history of the FHA, and the explanation of its role in speeding the flow of mortgage money, has been reserved until now, however. It properly belongs here at the commencement of an examination of federal institutions in the mortgage market.

Although the FHA was established primarily to warm the willingness of financial institutions to make mortgages by reducing, if not abolishing altogether, a lender's normal risks, the FHA has served the federal government's housing policies in other ways as well. Originally, its ambit was limited to insuring modest loans for the modernization of occupied homes and to financing new one-family homes. Subsequently, the FHA has been used to ease the financing and hasten the construction of larger apartment houses; to facilitate the renewal of deteriorated urban areas; to support cooperative ownership of multiple dwellings; to assist the development of vacant land and to prepare for new subdivisions and new towns; to help construct special facilities like nursing homes; and finally, to reduce the effective cost of housing for special categories of citizens by providing a channel through which government subsidies could be made available for the reduction of effective mortgage interest rates.

These several functions—the risk-reducing function on one side and a variety of implicit social purposes on the other—make somewhat unusual and uneasy bedfellows. The FHA-insuring organization that was established to remove risks necessarily included people whose nerves were alerted whenever unusual and questionable circumstances surrounded an underwriting proposal. Their professional success at the FHA was generally measured by the low number of claims filed by mortgagees whose mortgages they had approved for insurance.

Administrators of social housing programs, in contrast, measure their success by a different and vaguer criterion. They aim to increase the number of people who are satisfactorily housed by the social programs, people who might otherwise not be satisfactorily housed at all. The incompatibility of the two goals becomes clearly visible when the social objectives of housing require a drastic change in the living patterns of American cities and suburbs. Such a change strikes mortgage insurers as highly risky and unusual, just as a change in building materials alerts fire underwriters to possible new risks.

In the 1930s and 1940s, FHA insurers characteristically considered that racial integration in apartment houses or in neighborhoods was newfangled, untried, and possibly dangerous. They objected to attempting it in any mortgaged property that they were asked to cover. Increasingly, at least since 1960, the social objectives of the federal administration have included a serious measure of racial integration in housing. In consequence, the chief housing administrators have struggled to make their own employees, the FHA insurance underwriters, change their views of the actuarial danger of racially mixed housing and neighborhoods.

Similarly, the commingling of families with substantially different incomes—so-called economic integration—has become something of a social goal in housing. Once again, the FHA became the main vehicle on which this program was to be carried. Rent supplements—direct payments made on the accounts of lower-income families in a given apartment house—could be made under law only in the case of apartment houses whose mortgages were insured by the FHA under specific sections of the National Housing Act. Once again, there might be a feeling on the part of the insurers that this commingling of socioeconomic classes would upset the building and its occupants. Clearly, the insurers might as easily be right as wrong in their stress on the fiscal soundness of an insured development: An apartment house that cannot meet its mortgage payments is probably in trouble on a number of other counts as well. The issue is not whether the insuring mentality is inappropriate to the financing of housing developments but whether the insuring agency is the most appropriate vehicle through which to pass the execution of social housing objectives.

In any case, the historic logic of using the FHA for this purpose was irresistible. The FHA was the largest, least controversial housing agency of the federal government. In addition, it operated at a profit, as we shall see. If efficiency experts set themselves the task of realigning the functions of the government in housing, so that subsidization of privately owned housing would be separated from the FHA, production of housing for the low-income families of the nation would slow down, pending the rearrangement of an organization chart.

The Federal Housing Administration came into existence as a result of the passage of the National Housing Act in 1934. Like many other major new programs of government, this act resulted from the coalescence of a number of different interest groups about a goal that each of them shared fractionally. Among the supporters of the act were all the construction interests—employers, materials men, and labor. The bill would put them back to work constructing and repairing housing at a time when millions of construction workers were idle, and the materials-manufacturing businesses were operating at a fraction of maximum output.

The financial interests—commercial banks, mutual savings banks, and savings and loan associations—supported the legislation because it would stimulate the flow of money through normal, existing financial intermediaries. The act would not permit the entry of government into direct financing, involve government ownership of housing, or make any threatening gestures toward private ownership of land and improvements.

The socially progressive interests of the nation—those concerned with better housing for families of low income predominantly—accepted the act because it provided for some improvement in housing conditions and some economic movement. Although it did not go nearly so far in the direction of public ownership of urban housing or of subsidization as they might have wished, the act did not foreclose the possibility of accomplishing these goals at a later date.

The National Housing Act of 1934 [1] established the Federal Housing Administration as a government enterprise the sole function of which was to insure two types of risks experienced by lenders. The first, and by some odds the simplest to activate, was the risk to which a lender is exposed when it makes a loan for the improvement of an existing home. The FHA permitted the existing private intermediaries to solicit and originate such improvement loans, and guaranteed to repay the lender any loss suffered up to 20 percent of the amount of the loan in the event that the loan was unpaid. The limitation of the insurance to no more than 20 percent of the loan meant that the lender bore 80 percent of the risk, a distribution that enabled the FHA to insure the loans without specific collateral. Because the FHA provided the guarantee, it insisted as a *quid pro quo* that the terms of the loan be more generous to the lender than the banks might otherwise have been inclined to be. FHA interest rates were set lower, and repayment terms covered a longer period than would have been the case with conventional, uninsured loans.

While the improvement-loan program of FHA was simple, the insurance of mortgages on residential buildings, both new and existing, was more complex. In 1934, the law authorized a mutual mortgage insurance pool to be established by the FHA, and provided Treasury funds with which to start the pool. The original regulations were easily articulated. The FHA would insure first mortgages on new and existing homes, charging a premium that may not be less than .25 percent of the outstanding balance of the mortgage, nor more than 1 percent. The commissioner of the FHA would determine how big a premium was needed at any time, a responsibility that has since been assigned to the Secretary of the Department of Housing and Urban Development.

Originally, the law provided that the FHA could insure a mortgage equal to 80 percent of the appraised value of the home (by definition, a home could contain from one to four residences). Subsequent amendments to the law have increased the loan-to-value ratio until, in the case of families displaced by public action, it currently may equal 100 percent of the appraised value of the house, plus the closing costs.

The law established a dollar limit on the amount of mortgage that would be insured, irrespective of the value of the building. This limit has also been repeatedly increased over the years as construction costs have risen along with the rise in the loan-to-value ratio. By 1972, the dollar limit for insuring a mortgage on a one-family home reached thirty-three thousand dollars.

The National Housing Act of 1934 required the term of the mortgage not to exceed thirty-five years in the case of a new building mortgage approved prior to construction, or three-quarters of the remaining economic life of the building, as estimated by the commissioner, in the case of an existing or renovated building.

The law also provided that the form of the mortgage was to be fully self-amortizing, consisting of equal payments (usually monthly) partly made up of interest and partly made up of amortization. Naturally, as in the case of other level-payment mortgages, the owner-mortgagor of a home on which the FHA has insured the mortgage pays far more interest than principal in the early years of the mortgage life. His equity in the building builds up very slowly. This type of mortgage would surely not have been acceptable to lenders in 1934, when the economy lay in what seemed to be permanent ruins. Even those home buyers who had jobs were all too likely to lose them with little or no warning. In the event of such a commonplace catastrophe, only a sizable owner's equity would likely cushion the bank against a loss on foreclosure, but the FHA insurance worked.

As economic activity gradually recovered from the prostration of 1934, and the level of employment first stabilized and then began to ascend, the money supply expanded and prices rose. With the exception of the sharp recession of 1937, the rise in prices continued generally for a period of more than twenty years. So, of course, did the earnings of the population in general. Despite the fears of the banks that level-payment mortgages would build insufficient equity into the FHA-type mortgage, the rising price levels of the houses themselves created a dramatic increase. No matter how much the value of the house increased, of course, the mortgage was limited always to outstanding balance in dollars. As a result, the default rate in the home mortgage insurance program was very low and the mortgagee's loss on foreclosure, even lower. If this was true of the FHA mortgage insurance program, it became almost equally true of the Veterans Administration mortgage insurance program,[2] which was passed for the benefit of World War II servicemen and, subsequently, extended to Korean and Vietnam veterans.

The VA program offered even higher loan-to-value ratios than the FHA program and also permitted the Veterans Administration to make direct mortgage loans in cases in which qualified veterans were unable to find banking institutions that would make mortgages even with the VA guarantee.

In the early days of the mutual mortgage pool, fear of the possible insuring losses prodded FHA officials to develop a series of standards for the housing that they would approve. The first standard was the imposition of a maximum interest rate.

The establishment of interest ceilings on mortgages insured by FHA has given rise to a persistent argument over the program. Certainly, it seems fair that because the government has exposed itself to what is usually the mortgagee's risk it should demand in exchange that the mortgagee charge a lower rate of interest than would otherwise be the case. The social purpose, after all, was not merely that of stimulating the repair and construction of homes in order to put people back to work during a business depression. It was, as well, to improve the housing supply for those who could least afford it. A group of legislators continues to believe in the interest ceilings of the FHA, and Representatives Wright Patman and Leonor K. Sullivan have forcefully explained this point in the course of a report on mortgage interest rates issued by a joint presidential-congressional commission in 1969.[3]

Yet it can as cogently be argued that the interest ceilings imposed by legislation on mortgages insured by the FHA have less and less effect on the mortgage market as time passes. The FHA's low record of loss proves the safety of its formula. If the FHA insuring losses are low, then presumably mortgage lenders can more often dare to forego insurance, while the interest ceiling placed on the FHA-insured mortgages offers them an incentive to do so. When mortgagees insist on FHA insurance as a condition for making a mortgage loan in the face of possible higher interest on noninsured mortgages, they insist that the borrower accept a discount from the face amount of the mortgage. By charging interest on a sum larger than the amount actually loaned, and by recapturing through the amortization of the mortgage the full face amount rather than the discounted amount, the lender earns as much as it would even if there had been no FHA ceiling. The process of discounting a mortgage is hardly more complicated than that of discounting a color television set, but the phraseology strikes many who are unfamiliar with the business as more mysterious.

Everyone seems to understand clearly (if a bit skeptically) an advertisement in which a television dealer announces, "Prices slashed, 30 percent off." The advertisement is instantly read to mean that the dealer will sell his color sets for seventy cents per dollar of the so-called list price at which he claims to sell them ordinarily. It needs little specialized wisdom to understand the dealer's reason for discounting: He simply can't sell enough of them at the so-called list price to cover his overhead and make a profit. A mortgage borrower is simply selling to a mortgage lender his promise to pay a certain sum of money in a certain number of years at a certain rate of interest. If the number of years and the rate of interest are fixed, in the case in question by the FHA, and the buyer of the mortgage-promise does not wish to buy on those terms, the only remaining variable with which the borrower can hope to tempt the lender is the basic sum of money; the borrower will promise to pay back, with interest, a greater sum than he actually borrows. Instead of advertising that bankers will buy standard FHA mortgages provided they can get them at 10 percent off, the mortgage industry reports that new FHA mortgages are being made at a ten point discount.

The meaning is precisely the same. In a fictitious, but on the whole plausible, case, with the FHA rate fixed at 6 percent, while the free market interest rate for mortgages is 7 percent, established as we have seen by the ebb and flow of money supply and investment opportunity (and by a mysterious x factor that stands for nothing more specific than the way bankers feel about mortgages at a particular time), a bank might discount new mortgages by ten points. It would accept a borrower's promise to pay back thirty thousand dollars and actually give the borrower a check for twenty-seven thousand dollars. The borrower would pay 6 percent interest on the basic price, thirty thousand dollars, even though he received only 90 percent of the money. In effect, on his first payment (assuming monthly payments), the borrower would pay one hundred fifty dollars in interest—thirty thousand dollars times 6 percent divided by twelve, the number of months in a year. If one takes the trouble to calculate the effective yield produced by a monthly payment of one hundred fifty dollars in interest on a loan of twenty-seven thousand dollars, the real amount loaned, one finds that the actual interest rate earned by the bank is not 6 percent but 6.66 percent. To this should be added the current value of a part of the three thousand dollars extra that the lender will make by virtue of the fact that it has given the borrower twenty-seven thousand dollars, but will receive thirty thousand dollars in amortization. This is more of a guess than a precise calculation, because no one knows exactly how long a mortgage will be allowed to remain in effect by the borrower, even if its contract term is stipulated as, say, thirty-five years. The owner may sell or refinance at any time (although the mortgage instrument may provide for a penalty for prepayment).

If the owner prepaid his discounted mortgage at the end of the first year, the bank would receive a three thousand dollar, one-year bonus on its initial outlay of twenty-seven thousand dollars. This is 11.11 percent of the original amount, which when added to the contract interest would provide a return of not less than 17.77 percent. Actually, its percentage yield would be slightly higher on an annual basis because the whole twenty-seven thousand dollars was outstanding for only one month, not for entire year, but one need not bother with trifles. In the more likely circumstance that the original mortgage borrower kept the mortgage on his house for seven years (a figure that the industry reports as about the average for noninsured mortgages), the annual bonus would no longer be three thousand dollars, but rather thirty thousand dollars divided by seven, the number of years over which it would be earned. This comes to approximately $428 per year. A yield of $428 per year on an investment of twenty-seven thousand dollars is a 1.58 percent yield. We should properly perform some mumbo-jumbo to reduce to its current worth the value of 1.58 percent that is not earned with each payment of the mortgage but only at maturity, seven years away. But forgetting it for the moment, it is apparent that the return on a 6 percent mortgage discounted by ten points and remaining in effect for seven years is approximately 8.25 percent (6.67 percent in current interest, and 1.58 percent in what might be called presumptive approximate amortization of the discount).

Discounts cause difficulty not only because they require the borrower to pay a higher rate of interest than he expects to, or perhaps even knows about, but because they reduce the amount of cash made available for purchasing a house. If the FHA places a loan value of thirty thousand dollars on a house that the builder prices at thirty-three thousand dollars, a nondiscounted mortgage will require the purchaser to put up only three thousand dollars in cash (plus closing costs and the costs of all the other elements that are part of the human process of moving into a new house). If the mortgage is discounted by ten points, the unhappy buyer would now have to locate three thousand dollars extra in cash while making precisely the same mortgage payments he would have made on the non-discounted mortgage. Many buyers cannot produce the cash, while the FHA forbids second mortgages. The result, then, of the discount is a loss of the sale of the house, or a reduction by the builder or seller of its sales price.

A third possibility can be found, but it is expensive and requires the use of tax money. Government can provide the funds to buy FHA mortgages from lenders at artificially high prices on condition that the lenders require only a correspondingly small discount by the original borrower. Government then resells the mortgage at a realistic and much greater discount, which means, of course, that the government absorbs a loss by selling at a lower price than that at which it bought. This, as we shall see in the dicussion of the Government National Mortgage Association, has become a program of the federal government.

In addition to fixing a ceiling on mortgage interest rates in what must be regarded as a slightly successful, largely futile attempt to control them, the FHA exerted a mighty effort to standardize housing specifications throughout the United States. This was an essential part of the process of writing insurance profitably on mortgages covering housing units in every part of the country. While many cities and states had previously adopted their own housing codes, many others had no codes, and many of the rural districts in which FHA-insured mortgages were written had neither codes nor any serious building inspection system. In many of the cities with codes, the FHA underwriters believed that standards were not high enough to provide the mortgage insurance underwriter with adequate protection from default. Thus, it happens that some housing units must meet a double standard by which the FHA may be more restrictive in some categories while the local building requirements may be more restrictive in others. There are some localities—New York City is an outstanding example—in which state housing codes (such as New York State's Multiple Dwelling Law) impose more restrictive standards in some respects than either the building laws of the City of New York or the FHA minimum property requirements. The city's building inspectors are required by law to inspect for compliance with the state as well as the city laws, but the FHA must put its own inspectors into the field to make sure that the building meets FHA requirements for mortgage insurance.

The development of the FHA standards has been a long, complicated, and not altogether satisfactory process. The first effort at establishing standards resulted in a handbook of minimum requirements issued in 1935, one year after the passage of the original National Housing Act. Five years later, multiple dwellings were covered in a special publication. After the war, two new publications appeared, one covering one-family housing, the other covering housing with three or more units. Geographical differences were noted to cover the obvious climate differences in the several regions of the country, and this, in turn, meant that instead of a single set of national standards some fifty different sets were developed. For builders who operated across regional lines, these differences represented something of a hardship as well as a source of constant irritation. Ultimately, in 1958, the FHA issued a new set of standards applicable to all one- and two-family buildings. This was followed in 1964 by a single national standard for multifamily housing.

Unfortunately, the single standard did not eliminate all of the difficulties. There remained the problem of rehabilitated older structures, particularly in cities that had a substantial backlog of deteriorated multiple dwellings built to standards predating the FHA's. No distinction was made in the property standards between old and new buildings, with the result that FHA insurance, essential in many urban localities to make rehabilitation mortgages possible, simultaneously required costly structural changes that were far in excess of those required under local laws. Special property standards with respect to rehabilitation of older buildings were in the process of being worked out in 1973.

The last half of the 1960s, with the emphasis on social change implicit in the great society programs of the Johnson Administration, brought new problems to the FHA. The previous efforts of the federal government to provide housing for low-income families had depended on public ownership of housing developments. The low-rent program depended on the establishment of local government agencies, called housing authorities, that were empowered by state law to sell their own debt obligations. The National Housing Act of 1937[4] stimulated the formation of these local bodies and enabled the federal housing agency to enter into annual contribution contracts with them. These contracts, in effect, offered the buyers of related housing authority obligations a federal guarantee of repayment. Each year, the national government would pay to the fiscal agent of the local housing authority whatever funds became necessary to meet the debt service requirement of the authority's obligations. Thanks to these annual contributions, the residents in local housing authority projects were required to pay no more rent than that needed to cover the operating costs of the projects. As civil rights, black liberation from the ghetto, and social equality became important public concerns of the 1960s, the public housing formula came increasingly under attack, not only as in the past from the right but from the left as well. The opposition of progressives was stimulated by the growing black occupancy in public housing, so that the institution failed to provide the balanced racial mixture for which the times seemed to call. In the search for racial balance, emphasis shifted to the placement of low-income families in new, privately owned developments erected with FHA mortgage insurance. The projects that emerged were financed with bank mortgages bearing rates far below the market. Government subsidization made them possible.

In the first program, the so-called 221(d)3 program, the interest rate was fixed at 3.5 percent, and the bank that originated the mortgage was able to sell it immediately at par to an official agency.[5] The second program, including FHA 235 and FHA 236, provided for government mortgage subsidy payments that would bridge the gap between an effective annual debt service of 1 percent (which the residents actually pay) and the 6 percent contract rate that the mortgage lender must receive.[6] As market interest rates rose above 6 percent, mortgagees were permitted to sell these mortgages at par also to official agencies. They, in turn, sold the mortgages at market discounts.

The pressure on FHA-insuring offices to approve these special insurance programs with social objectives may have tended to open the FHA to a related pressure, the pressure to approve the insurance of high-risk mortgages in urban settings under nonsubsidized FHA programs. Builders who would buy up older buildings and remodel them in a very sketchy way could make the plea to the local FHA office that the government was saving the cost of subsidization by approving mortgage insurance on the properties. Because the federal government in 1970 and 1971 was placing great emphasis on the brute number of housing starts, some FHA employees were able to convince themselves that in bending property standards (and accepting a private fee to cover the risk involved), they were actually helping to support the national economy and the administration's housing goals. In Detroit and in Nassau County, New York, major scandals broke out in the wake of this pressure. Buyers of homes found themselves saddled with mortgages that required debt service they could not meet. Buildings started to deteriorate rapidly, thanks to inadequate reconditioning. Investigation revealed that the buildings had been greatly overappraised by officials who had been paid to make mistakes.[7]

The scandals, which were erroneously ascribed to the subsidized programs by the press, astonished no one who had been following the course of administration housing policy. All the emphasis in federal housing policy had been on the achievement of new quantitative records in housing production. The builders wanted to build. The bankers wanted to make mortgages. The public wanted to move into the new houses. The FHA, which insured the banks against loss and made it possible for the banks to sell their new mortgages at par to specialized agencies of the government, was the vital connecting rod of the housing engine. As long as the local FHA appraiser approved the mortgage for insurance, the program ran and everyone smiled. Only a dogged believer in human innocence could have expected *all* FHA officials to survive the pressures without succumbing to the temptation to make everyone, including themselves, happy even when they should not have been.

Despite such occasional lapses, which have had the effect of raising the claims for insurance benefits, the FHA has been a consistently profitable operation for the United States government. Initially, it was funded and its operating expenses were paid by the United States Treasury through the Reconstruction Finance Corporation. By fiscal year 1938, however, the FHA was already earning enough from its premium income to meet part of its own operating costs. By 1940, it was fully self-supporting.[8] Despite the intervention of the war years, during which little housing business was transacted, by 1954 the FHA had repaid with interest all the original advances made to it by the Treasury.[9]

Its growth in the postwar years has continued at an accelerating pace, although the line of growth on a graph is rather jagged, reflecting both the general state of the economy and the fluctuating share of the total mortgage loans that the FHA insures in any year. From its founding in

1937 to 1971, the FHA had received $5 billion in premiums, fees, and interest earned on its invested surplus.[10] That surplus, incidentally, is invested in Treasury obligations, mortgage participation certificates issued by the Government National Mortgage Association, and debentures of the FHA itself. Debentures—interest-bearing unsecured bonds— are issued by the FHA to its insured mortgagees in payment of claims. Offsetting the $5 billion in gross income, the FHA has incurred slightly more than $1.5 billion in operating expenses from its inception through fiscal 1971.[11] This leaves approximately $3.5 billion from which the FHA met its net losses on defaulted insured mortgages and established a reserve of $1.7 billion [12] to cover possible future losses.

The term net losses is used to describe the financial results of ship-wrecked mortgages. When a claim for insurance is made by a mortgagee because one of its insured mortgages has gone sour, the FHA investigates, and after paying off the loss of the insured mortgagee with debentures, the FHA takes over the mortgage. Ultimately, the mortgaged property will probably be resold subject to the foreclosure laws of the state in which it is located (rental property may be operated by the FHA for a period of time). All of the net proceeds received by the FHA from the operation or sale of the acquired properties reduce its actual losses below the amount of the original claim. In the two biggest FHA accounts —the mutual and the general insurance accounts—the net losses on the payment of claims and the disposal of properties covered by defaulted mortgages came to approximately $1.2 billion in the 37 years between 1934 and 1971.[13] The figure is certainly understated because it does not, by definition, include the final figures of losses on properties that have been acquired as a result of insurance claims but have not yet been disposed of.

If one assumes that the FHA will suffer considerably greater losses in disposing of its present inventory of defaulted property, and even if one assumes that many properties in its newer, subsidized programs will go into default because their residents' incomes will not rise as fast as the operating expenses of the buildings they are living in, the FHA remains a remarkably profitable enterprise. Starting with no funds in 1934 (and, of course, paying no taxes on its profits), it has become one of the world's largest insuring organizations.

Clearly, these splendid financial results reveal a most important fact about the risks against which the FHA insured its customer-mortgages: The risks were smaller than they seemed. The high loan-to-value ratio of housing mortgages, the slow buildup of the owner's equity, the low down payments, the long-term mortgage, and the deliberate effort to cater to an economic segment of the population that clustered around or perhaps slightly below the midpoint—none of these traditionally worrisome characteristics of the FHA insured mortgages turned out to be as risky as mortgagees had expected them to be. There were defaults, as we have seen, but the defaults in neither the one-family nor the multifamily home/mortgage funds reached 4 percent of the total number of units in force in any one year.[14] As noted earlier, the operating expenses of the FHA over the years since its establishment consumed about 30 percent of its gross income ($1.5 billion of $5 billion). The .5 percent premium that the FHA charges produces a net premium of approximately .33 percent after subtracting the operating costs. If we assumed that every default resulted in a total loss to the FHA of the amount insured, the .33 percent effective premium after subtracting operating costs would cover a 2 percent annual loss rate if it were collected for a six-year period on the average of all mortgages. If the premium is collected for a longer period, the FHA's margin grows. Reasoning inversely, we can see that if the average mortgage remains outstanding for six years, 16.66 percent of all FHA mortgages would be paid off each year. In fact, from the FHA actuarial tables, we can find that only in one year, 1945, did the retirement percentage climb to nearly so high a figure in the one-family home fund. It never approached so high a figure in the multifamily fund. In 1970, retirements in both types of housing were running at less than 6 percent a year, meaning that the typical mortgage produced premium income for a sixteen-year period.[15]

There must be good reasons for the financial success of the government mortgage insurance program, but they can only be guessed at. The primary reason would seem to be the general wage and income inflation of the postwar years, an inflation that meant that the fixed costs of the mortgage consumed a diminishing part of the family earnings. Naturally, operating costs and real estate taxes rose with the general inflation, but in the one-family-home segment of the FHA market, those householders who did a substantial part of their maintenance themselves did not pay themselves in cash at the current labor rate. This minimized the increase in operating costs. It is too early yet to tell whether or not the more rapid inflation of the 1971–73 period will more adversely affect the cost of operating multiple dwellings. As the population in the older FHA buildings—both one family and multifamily—grows older, the family income may no longer rise as operating costs rise. All of these factors suggest that the success of mortgage insurance under the FHA may have resulted from factors that were applicable to a specific period in time, and that it might be unwise to apply the FHA formula indiscriminately to new construction at another period.

Private industry seems to feel differently, however. Private mortgage insurance has become widespread in competition with the FHA. In 1957, a privately owned insurance company—Mortgage Guaranty Insurance Corporation—began operations; state laws have been amended in several states to provide insurance protection for mortgagees in a fashion similar to that of the FHA. Such companies had been in business before and during the depression, but their reserves were inadequate to make good on the policies they had written when the severe economic difficulties of the 1930s hit the housing market.

Only New York City has established its own mortgage-insuring entity. In this case, the public corporation will insure a small part of the institutional mortgages on multiple dwellings in specific sections of the city. The insurance is intended to stimulate banks to renew expiring mortgages by offering the city a participation in the risk; the city will insure a larger part of a newly expanded mortgage, seeking to encourage rehabilitation by that commitment.

The New York insurance plan frankly envisions the city as accepting more hazardous risks than those that the FHA will accept. Of course, the private plans tend to move in the opposite direction: They will charge lower premiums than the FHA and accept only the lower risks. The spread of private plans might have a seriously adverse effect on the FHA, unbalancing its portfolio of mortgage insurance contracts by removing many of the good risks and leaving the shaky ones.

If the private insuring entities take these relatively safe loans from the FHA, the high-risk city loans will remain in the portfolio under the new category of social purpose mortgages. In such an event, Congress would find the FHA turned into a subsidization unit of the government instead of a profit-making entity. This would offer the advantage of clarity, but it would also deprive the government of a source of imputed revenue from housing (*imputed,* because the net earnings of the FHA go into its own reserve funds rather than into the United States Treasury). A measure of the size of the FHA's gross earnings (before calculating the losses) can be seen in the fact that all of the annual contributions actually paid by the federal government to all of the local housing authorities all over the United States up to June 30, 1971, had reached $3.8 billion.[16] This is only a few hundred million dollars more than the gross income of the FHA before calculating the net loss on defaults. While nothing in law or tradition forces the annual contributions for low-rent housing to bear any relationship whatsoever to the FHA's net income before defaults, it does not seem quite right that the government's mortgage insurance program should take all of the bad cases and none of the good. Without the FHA, the national mortgage market would not exist; the investment of funds in mortgages would be much more difficult indeed; and this confrontation would make much more difficult the formulation of a subsidization program for remedying the worst of housing shortcomings in the nation.

CHAPTER 13

THE FEDERAL NATIONAL
MORTGAGE ASSOCIATION

THE Federal National Mortgage Association (FNMA) presents a certain difficulty in discussion because its name, like that of the Holy Roman Empire, does not precisely describe its character. The Holy Roman Empire, as every schoolchild allegedly knows, was neither Holy, nor Roman, nor an Empire. The Federal National Mortgage Association is now neither Federal, nor an Association. It is no longer federal because it is now entirely privately owned, just like the Chase Manhattan Bank; it is not an association because, in fact, it is a corporation. It is, however, national because it is intended to perform a public service for the government as well as to earn a profit for its stockholders; and it does deal in mortgages on a national scale. Its current president, Oakley Hunter, has explained that the association achieved private status on September 1, 1968, and thereupon entered a transitional phase that was finally completed on May 21, 1970.[1] By the end of 1971, the Federal National Mortgage Association held assets valued at over $17 billion,[2] which made it by that measure the fifth largest corporation in the United States.

Most people who have occasion to discuss the Federal National Mortgage Association refer to it jocularly as Fannie Mae, a name loosely based on its initials. Fannie Mae was a depression baby. She was born on February 10, 1938. Her mother was the United States government, while the doctor who officiated at her birth was the Federal Housing Administration. At birth, all of the paid-in capital and surplus of Fannie Mae was provided by the Reconstruction Finance Corporation (RFC). This government agency had been established under President Hoover during the early stages of the great depression. Its purpose had been to provide refinancing for business organizations and banks that were threatened with liquidation; the hope behind it was that if essentially sound enterprises could be relieved of the severe economic pressures resulting from a drop in business, their revival would, in turn, stimulate new activities that would increase employment and stiffen economic demand.

The Reconstruction Finance Corporation became involved in residential mortgage lending, although this was not its original purpose, because of the disastrous drop in activity in the home-building industry that reduced housing starts throughout the United States to fewer than 100,000 in 1931. As in the case of most government economic intervention during the depression, help for the ailing home construction industry involved two allied but distinguishable goals: to relieve immediate hardship and to find a better future method. The Roosevelt Administration's first objective in housing construction was to rescue already built and occupied housing from the threat of foreclosure and liquidation as a result of the loss of earnings by the owners. This the government sought to accomplish by establishing the Home Owners Loan Corporation (HOLC). That agency offered the mortgagees whose assets were frozen in mortgages that yielded nothing the option of trading their mortgages for tax-free debentures issued by the Home Owners Loan Corporation; the corporation would simultaneously take back from the owners of homes with one-to-four dwelling units a new type of long-term mortgage that provided for total self-amortization through monthly payments of equal size. In the course of this refinancing, the corporation also advanced sufficient cash to pay off delinquent taxes and special assessments. By this procedure, the HOLC tried to quiet the panic in the breasts of banks and insurance companies that already held portfolios of shaky home mortgages. This program succeeded so well that when it was abolished, in 1954—twenty-one years later—the HOLC returned to the Treasury $14 million in profits over and above all of its initial government investment and after all operating costs.[3]

The second phase of the depression program then involved the stimulation of new housing construction. Taking the self-amortizing mortgage developed by the HOLC, the government adopted it as the cornerstone of the National Housing Act of 1934. This act established the Federal Housing Administration, which was empowered to insure the lender of mortgage money under a new self-amortizing mortgage, not exceeding a stipulated value per dwelling unit, against loss due to the failure of the borrower to meet the terms of the mortgage. The FHA has remained a major constituent of federal housing structure and policy ever since. Its basic concern—the insurability of the risk in housing mortgage finance—enabled it to return to the Treasury substantial profits over the years. While some people refer to the FHA as an agency that dispensed subsidies that made possible the development of the suburban population shift in the postwar years, the fact that the FHA's insurance operations were profitable to the government seems to indicate that they involved no real subsidy from the United States government. They did, however, mean that the FHA has tended to measure by the test of marketability the worthiness of specific housing programs. This has both advantages and drawbacks. We have mentioned the drawbacks.

The advantage of the market psychology, however, is equally important. It inserts a measure of economic realism into a process of capital allocation that, free from the consequences of imprudent risk, might persistently allocate funds to the construction of housing in areas, or of a type, that would not find buyers. The fear of unwise investment may sometimes, or even often, prevent the construction of housing that is *not* desired by anyone and that promotes a socially undesirable misapplication of capital funds that might well have been better used elsewhere.

In any case, the FHA insurance commitment, which was very effective in the years following World War II, failed in its early years to show much practical promise of its future strength. As noted before, the self-amortizing feature of the FHA mortgage threatened the mortgagee with the nagging problem of reinvestment of small increments of returned capital. In addition, the procedures of the FHA itself were strange to the bankers; the 1930s were not a period in American history characterized by good feeling between the bankers and the government. Bankers may have been suspicious that the FHA was a scheme to put further controls on their operation. Still another possible reason for the slow acceptance of the FHA-insured mortgage has a more rational economic base, which accounts for the interest taken by the Reconstruction Finance Corporation in this aspect of the residential mortgage market and hence, incidentally, for the development and growth of the Federal National Mortgage Association—Fanny Mae.

Bankers were afraid to touch FHA mortgages previously because they feared their very long term. A specific loan might be sound, the interest rate might be thoroughly acceptable to the banker at the time of the origination of the loan, and the suspicion of the government itself might lie dormant in the mortgage officer's chest, but his uneasiness about the FHA mortgage persists because of its long term which is combined with almost complete illiquidity. Only an approved FHA mortgagee could acquire an FHA mortgage from the originating mortgagee, and even if a possible buyer could be found arrangements had to be made to service the mortgage. Servicing—the process of collecting the mortgage payments and the installment deposits to cover future tax payments and insurance premiums—is the process described in the chapter on mortgage banking. How could the mortgagee of an FHA mortgage with years to run sell that mortgage to an approved buyer if that buyer resided in an area far removed from the location of the mortgaged property? How could such a mortgagee remain aware of changes in local tax rates, requiring changes in advance payments from the mortgagor? How could a distant mortgagee decide whether or not insurance proceeds had actually been used to repair the damages to a property financed with an FHA-insured mortgage?

In order to meet this fundamental question of nontransferability, or illiquidity, the Federal National Mortgage Association was established to provide a so-called secondary market for mortgages. This phrase— secondary market—is, like the phrase money market, not intended to describe a specific marketplace—like the floor of the New York Stock Exchange—but rather an institution or a network of institutions that are generally engaged in the business of buying and selling mortgages. The National Housing Act of 1934 authorized private persons to establish mortgage associations that would be authorized to borrow money from the public and use it to trade in FHA-insured mortgages. No private persons appeared on the scene who were financially able to establish any such mortgage association, even though the Reconstruction Finance Corporation offered to help with the financing. The official history of FNMA recounts that several applications for such charters were filed, but that none was ever issued.[4]

When private industry failed, even with proferred government assistance, to establish an organization able to purchase FHA-insured mortgages and, on occasion, to resell them to other qualified mortgagees, the government's natural response was to establish such an association. In 1935, the Reconstruction Finance Corporation accordingly set up the RFC Mortgage Association, which was originally authorized to make mortgage loans on new construction when such loans were unavailable from private sources. Because of the stickiness of the FHA mortgages generally, however, the RFC Mortgage Company's program was stretched to permit it to buy FHA-insured mortgages from their originators. From 1935 until 1948, when the RFC Mortgage Company was dissolved, that agency purchased more than $250 million of FHA-insured mortgages from the banking institutions that had originated them.[5]

This figure, although in total it may be impressive, was clearly inadequate to provide the liquidity that the banking system needed by 1938 if it was to lend money on FHA-insured mortgages on a scale commensurate with the immense needs of a prostrate mortgage banking industry suffering from a relative shortage of funds. Accordingly, the Federal National Mortgage Association, devoted solely to the purchase and sale of FHA-insured mortgages, was established in 1938. The Reconstruction Finance Corporation provided the original $11 million in capital and paid-in surplus, a figure that was subsequently increased to $20 million in capital in 1948.[6] When the FNMA was first established, Congress permitted it to borrow twenty times its capital and paid-in surplus, which came to $220 million. In 1948, this figure was increased to forty times its paid-in capital and surplus, plus forty times its earned surplus—a minimum of $840 million.[7] The narrative becomes considerably more complicated later on, as the success of the FNMA in providing a secondary mortgage market impelled Congress to assign to it two other functions. In 1968 these were separated from the FNMA, and will be discussed in greater detail in the chapter on their present locale, the Government National Mortgage Association, which came into existence for the very purpose of removing these functions from the FNMA so that it could confine itself entirely to the responsibility of providing a secondary market for mortgages.

The importance of such a market to the whole process of initiating new residential mortgages can scarcely be exaggerated. Those mortgage originators who control their own capital funds—like mutual savings banks and insurance companies—are presumably somewhat readier to invest their funds in residential mortgages provided that they know that a regular market exists in which the mortgages can be sold. Such a market becomes vitally important in meeting the collateral demands of savings bank depositors at times of credit stringency and high competitive interest rates. The originators without vast resources in their own capital funds—the mortgage bankers—are able to originate mortgages primarily for the purpose of earning income through the servicing function. They are able to embark upon a program of mortgage origination *only* in the knowledge that a market exists in which the originated mortgage can readily be disposed. The commercial banks, which usually provide the funds for the mortgage activities of mortgage bankers, will do so only if they are convinced that the mortgage they have financed will quickly be sold in a continuing market and their advances repaid. Thus, commercial banks may, if necessary, discount some of their prime customers' loans with the Federal Reserve System; any corporate or government bonds that they hold may quickly be liquidated in markets. The normal customer's note runs for only ninety days. Mortgages alone lack liquidity; a secondary market might provide it.

Yet it is not difficult to find the reasons why such a national market did not grow up by itself. Most important, of course, is the very local nature of the collateral value behind a mortgage; as a debt, it is secured only by the value of a specific piece of property located within specific boundaries. The credit-worthiness of the obligor on a mortgage is almost impossible to determine by anyone who lacks what navigational charts sometimes describe as local knowledge. Furthermore, the laws governing mortgages vary from state to state, so that even if a bank in, say, Vermont had surplus deposits that it would like to invest in good out-of-state mortgages or yield higher than that carried in corporate bonds, its investment committee would have great difficulty in evaluating the possible recovery and the cost of a foreclosure on, say, a tract of homes in faraway Oregon. In this sense, the evaluation of the risk in out-of-state mortgages differs only in degree of difficulty from the evaluation of the risks in banknotes issued by commercial banks. Such banknotes have entirely gone out of circulation. While they were part of the general money supply of the United States, the uncertainty as to their true value was constant.

A national mortgage market could not become possible until a way had been discovered to standardize the local differences in mortgage instruments and to reduce the mortgage risks. The FHA, subsequently supplemented by the VA mortgage insurance program that insured mortgages on homes for veterans after World War II, provided an answer that applied to FHA- or VA-insured mortgages.

Once the paid-in capital funds for the FNMA had been supplied in 1938, and its borrowing limits were established by law as a multiple of its capital, the FNMA was ready to buy FHA mortgages from their owners. It provided itself with funds adequate to do its job by borrowing from the United States Treasury. During the initial period of its operations, which lasted from its inception until 1954—when the FNMA's functions were more rigorously defined than they had been previously —the FNMA twice augmented its Treasury borrowing by borrowing money directly from the public. At the same time, its ability to borrow, based on a congressionally-approved multiple of its outstanding common stock, grew steadily because it required approved mortgage sellers to buy its common stock as a condition of their selling mortgages to it. The precise amount of common stock that the FNMA required its mortgage sellers to buy was defined as a percentage of the unpaid balance of the mortgages they sell or propose to sell to the FNMA, and varies from .5 to 3 percent, depending on the state of the money market as interpreted by the federal housing official in charge of the agency of which the FNMA was a subsidiary. In effect, this means that if the XYZ Mortgage Company wanted to sell FNMA $3 million of mortgages, its stock requirement could range between fifteen thousand and ninety thousand dollars. When the FNMA's administrators wanted to increase the flow of money into the mortgage market, feeling that housing construction was too slow, they decreased the required stock purchase, making it easier for possible mortgage originators to become approved mortgage sellers to the FNMA.

Between 1954 and 1968, the FNMA sold more than $160 million in preferred stock to the Treasury Department from which it borrowed most of the funds it required in order to purchase mortgages.[8] The income from the mortgages it purchased and held served to pay the interest on these borrowed funds; sales from its mortgage portfolios helped to repay the principal borrowed. Later, sales to the public of FNMA's own debentures and notes gave it the money to reduce the government loans. A standby credit from the Treasury Department still provides FNMA with its ultimate reserve liquidity. Because this borrowing is limited to a statutory multiple of the outstanding capital stock, FNMA's ability to borrow is increased, at the present time, by $600,000 every time a prospective seller purchases fifteen thousand dollars in FNMA stock (the current debt-to-stock ratio is forty times). Dividends are paid regularly on the common stock. They were also regularly paid on the Treasury-held preferred stock until this stock was retired in 1968 with part of the proceeds of a $250 million issue of debentures sold to the public. The sale took place when the FNMA was changed from a government-controlled enterprise, in which none of the common stock had voting rights, into a private business corporation, in which all the common stock had voting rights. The government, through the Secretary of the Department of Housing and Urban Development, has retained the right to name one-third of the membership of the board of directors.

At all times from the beginning of FNMA's existence, the prospective sellers had the right to sell the stock they had been required to buy in order to deal with the FNMA. Because the stock was readily salable, although not eligible for listing on the New York Stock Exchange during the period in which it lacked voting powers, FNMA common stock has been quoted on the over-the-counter market for years.

A company that is able to borrow money at relatively low rates and use it to acquire mortgages that pay relatively high rates should be able to make money on the fiscal spread between the money it borrows and the money it lends. Its stock-in-trade depends on the existence of an adequate supply of mortgages whose owners wish to sell them to FNMA, or who intend to sell them to FNMA after they have, in fact, originated them. The mortgage bankers in this latter group are anxious not merely to sell mortgages but to obtain advance commitments from FNMA that they can rely on to sell mortgages to FNMA *if* they later originate these mortgages and *if* they can find no other buyer who is willing to pay more money for them.

FNMA charges prospective sellers a commitment fee for its promise to purchase specific mortgages if they were delivered to FNMA within a stipulated period of time. The commitment period has varied from time to time over the life of FNMA. In most cases, the prospective mortgage seller who receives a commitment from FNMA to buy a stipulated amount of mortgages, and who pays a fee for this commitment, is not actually obligated to sell the mortgages when they are actually delivered. The commitment fee binds FNMA to buy the mortgage, but does not bind the originator to sell it. The commitment fees collected provide the FNMA with a significant source of income in addition to the income earned on the mortgages themselves (there is always a reverse possibility that, as in the credit pinch of 1970 and 1973–1974 the interest paid by FNMA on its borrowings will be more expensive than the interest received on its mortgages). At such times the cost of FNMA common stock drops along with that of all other banks.

Practically from its beginning in 1938, FNMA has had little trouble in finding sellers who were prepared to offer mortgages to it. In its very first year of operation, $37 million in mortgages were acquired, representing approximately ten thousand separate housing mortgages.[9] They were valued at approximately four thousand dollars each, at a time when that small figure represented the cost of a fully standard new house. The FNMA's rules prevented it from buying mortgages on any house unless, as we have seen, it was guaranteed by the Federal Housing Administration; the regulations established by the Reconstruction Finance Corporation limited eligible mortgages still further. FNMA could not buy mortgages on any housing that had been started before January 1, 1936, or that, though started later, was insured by the FHA before January 1, 1937. In 1939, purchases nearly tripled—to $92 million—and they would presumably have continued to rise except for the shift to a wartime economy.[10] The restriction of credit and the rationing of materials brought new mortgage purchases practically to a standstill along with new construction. During the war years, FNMA was a net seller of mortgages from its portfolio by a very wide margin.[11] As interest rates were low during the war, the mortgages were attractive to investors.

The postwar housing and construction boom required a vast mobilization of resources. We have seen how the savings needed for that mobilization were gathered in the different types of intermediaries.

A special imbalance in the location of savings and the demand for mortgages resulted from the shifts in population that were characteristic of the period. Some shifts, like the move from central city to suburb in the same region, were probably not hampered by a local shortage of mortgage funds. But other relocations of population accompanied the growth of new industries in new areas of the country, such as the California migration that was linked to the development there of the aerospace industry. The local need for capital for use in commercial and industrial expansion was already tapping local fiscal resources to their limits. In these long-range shifts, housing capital frequently ran short.

The volume of mortgages bought *by* FNMA rose sharply beginning in 1949, and one may theorize that this trend was not unconnected with the capital shortage in developing areas. In 1950, purchases of mortgages *from* the FNMA spurted remarkably,[12] possibly reflecting an imbalance between the demand for mortgage money in some parts of the country and a surplus of money available for investment in the savings institutions in other parts of the country that were not feeling the effects of industrial and population expansion and that may, in fact, have been suffering from the 1949 recession in business activity. In 1950, FNMA purchased almost $1 billion in mortgages and sold almost $300 million. This approximate three-to-one ratio contrasts sharply with the last prewar year, 1939, when purchases of mortgages by FNMA totaled $92 million, while the sales were only $345,000. It also contrasts with later experience. In 1952 and 1953, purchases amounted to a little over $1.1 billion, but sales dropped to less than a one-to-ten ratio, standing only at $100 million.[13]

The reasons for this downward turn are easy to find. It is explained by the sharp rise in interest rates in the economy as a whole, following the dissolution of the arrangement by which the Federal Reserve Board had been keeping government interest rates down in an effort to minimize the Treasury cost of the debt incurred during World War II. As interest rates rose, the attractiveness of existing mortgages made at lower rates vanished. This major cause was complicated by the Korean war and the credit restrictions that followed it. As interest rates rose, it was clear that the old FNMA system of buying and selling FHA mortgages over the counter at par would no longer work. People holding mortgages made at the old, low rate would, of course, be delighted to sell them at par. But no one would buy them at par when he could earn more interest in other investments. As interest rates in the conventional market rose higher than the interest rate ceilings permitted by the FHA, it was clear that mortgages at FHA rates could only be sold at a discount from their face value.

Nevertheless, FHA interest rates on new mortgages were not allowed by the government to rise in step with the conventional market. To begin with, there are political difficulties in the way of such a rise. Many influential congressmen feel that the imposition of ceilings is a fair restriction on the earnings of bankers who are presumably benefiting from a government guarantee against risk. Others feel that the ceilings do tend to limit the rise of mortgage interest rates at times of mortgage stringency. Still others would argue that none of these advantages fully compensates for the difficulty in borrowing mortgage money at fixed, low rates when comparable investments permit a more remunerative yield. To all of these various arguments, the FNMA system offered a compromise reconciliation: The system maintained the FHA ceilings for whatever their value, but encouraged a flow of mortgage funds by offering to purchase the mortgage at or near par even though the market price would be considerably below that same par value. The FNMA would simply be able to keep on buying mortgages by borrowing more money with which to pay for them.

The existence of FNMA as an enterprise that could purchase insured mortgages at a price below their market value made possible the evolution of a system of indirect subsidization of interest rates—a subsidy, in effect, is provided when FNMA treats a mortgage with an unrealistic interest rate as though it offered a market yield. By buying the obligation at a higher price than anyone else in the market would pay, the government, in effect, is paying a subsidy to the borrower. Without it, he would, of course, have to pay a higher rate of interest in order to obtain a loan.

By 1954, it had become perfectly clear to the home-building industry and to Congress that FNMA was becoming something more than merely a government agency buying and selling mortgages. It was actually providing a form of special assistance to certain types of mortgages that Congress believed to be in the public interest. The federal government had since 1937 provided direct subsidies for publicly owned housing projects whose occupancy was restricted to families and then single persons of low income. The government had no program for the partial subsidization of housing for those whose incomes were too high for public housing and yet not high enough to be able to carry costs of new housing without assistance. FNMA became the vehicle through which special assistance in the form of partial capital subsidization would be given by the federal government to families above the public housing income level.

A third function for FNMA, appearing by the early 1950s, is referred to as the management and liquidating function. This merely meant that FNMA—an agency within the Housing and Home Finance Administration of the government with unique direct governmental access to the housing capital market—became a suitable vehicle for managing and disposing of housing belonging to the government. This housing might have been acquired through foreclosures of FHA- or VA-insured mortgages that had gone into default, or through the liquidation of housing developments that had belonged to the government in the first instance. An example of this type of development would be housing built during the war by the government to facilitate population movements linked to armament production.

In 1954, Congress recodified all of the legislation pertaining to FNMA under Title III of the National Housing Act.[14] The primary purpose was to establish and separate the three major functions then being performed by FNMA—the secondary mortgage market function, the special assistance function, and the management and liquidation function. The act, called the Charter Act, permitted the Treasury to buy and hold preferred stock in FNMA while the public would be able to hold common stock; neither class voted, as we have seen. The Charter Act looked forward to a time when all of the Treasury stock would be retired and the secondary market function of FNMA would be separated from the special assistance and management and liquidation functions. At that point, FNMA would become a private, profit-making corporation, trading in mortgages at market rates while the special assistance and management and liquidation functions would be carried on by a government association—the Government National Mortgage Association.

Subsequent to 1954, but long before 1968 when the separation actually took place, Congress developed programs of special assistance for mortgaging housing developments for residents of limited income. One of these, the FHA 221 (d) 3 program, offered the mortgagor the possibility of obtaining a 3 percent mortgage at a time when the market rate was over 6 percent. Clearly, no financial institution was able to lend at a 3 percent yield and keep its depositors happy when competitive agencies were lending at much higher yields and were, therefore, able to pay their depositors higher interest rates. FNMA became the vehicle that made these mortgages possible. With FHA guarantees in hand, FNMA made the special below-market rate mortgages directly to the builder. Other programs authorized by Congress to rehabilitate slum areas and to provide special low-rate mortgages for other socially desirable housing purposes also became practical through the medium of direct placement with FNMA.

These programs grew during the decade of the 1960s as building costs increased and interest rates stiffened. In 1966, purchases of mortgages by FNMA reached an all-time high, $2 billion, two hundred times greater than sales of mortgages. In 1968, purchases rose to $3.5 billion, almost one thousand times greater than sales.[15] With the government straining to finance the Vietnam war, and the private capital market straining to provide the credit for factory and inventory expansion to supply military and civilian needs, the administration recognized that any governmental deficits would simply increase the money supply because, ultimately, the Federal Reserve Bank would fund them, increasing bank reserves. Against this background, a study of Treasury accountancy recommended that mortgages acquired by FNMA on a below-market basis must be considered as cash expenditures chargeable entirely against the current federal budget.

This was a most serious matter. FNMA's whole portfolio became a charge against the federal government's debt limit—instead of the much smaller sum that would represent FNMA's actual loss if it sold its below-market interest rate mortgages at whatever discount might be necessary to move them off its hands.

The ruling that established this principle made imperative the separation of FNMA from the federal government. The government had to find a way to get rid of its below-market interest rate mortgages as quickly as possible, charging the discount as a current loss, but saving the federal budget from the charge of the total face value of the mortgages. The FNMA—now a private corporation—would buy an FHA-insured below-market interest rate mortgage at a discounted market price and would then either hold it for income or sell it to other private investors. Simultaneously, this new, privately owned FNMA would maintain a vast secondary mortgage market, buying and selling FHA-insured (and ultimately, noninsured) mortgages at market prices.

After getting away from the purchase of specially assisted FHA mortgages at artificial prices, the Federal National Mortgage Association had to find a market mechanism that would determine which mortgage would be bought and at what prices. It found the solution by turning to one of the oldest forms of commercial transactions: the auction. It allowed prospective mortgage sellers to compete with each other by submitting at biweekly intervals the prices at which they would agree to sell to FNMA new FHA mortgages. Then FNMA would decide how large a dollar amount of the mortgages it would accept, paying the prices that the mortgage sellers were asking. The successful bidders—those asking the lowest prices—would receive a commitment from FNMA, on the strength of which they could actually raise the short-term money necessary to originate the mortgage.

Summed up so simply, the process sounds as clear as a pane of glass, but the practical working out of the terms of the auction is not so simple. Because mortgage bankers are spread across the country, an auction involving their physical presence in a single location was out of the question on the grounds of cost. FNMA first tried mail auctions, but during the postal strike of 1970 it was forced to experiment with a telephone auction. To the surprise, no doubt, of more conservative spirits in the agency who might have been afraid that telephone bids would be subject to misunderstandings, or claimed misunderstandings, the telephone system worked out so well that it has become the standard auction system. A windowless room at FNMA headquarters in Washington constitutes the auction chamber. The telephones are answered by a staff of part-time employees, all of them retired from their permanent jobs. Each operator works with a pad of printed forms on which are entered the name and identification number of the caller, together with the information as to the mortgages offered and the price at which they are for sale to FNMA.

In order to submit an offering, the bidder must be a qualified seller-servicer under FNMA's rules. This means that the prospective seller must have signed a contract under which it will agree to service mortgages that have been acquired by FNMA. This means, for example, that it has met minimal financial standards and has not become delinquent on payments that it has already collected and is required to pass on to FNMA.

The seller-servicer must also have qualified to sell mortgages by having met its past obligation to FNMA as a seller, meaning that it must own a minimum amount of FNMA stock (at this time .5 percent of the face value of mortgages at the time sold), and must have paid the commitment fee that it must pay to FNMA. The commitment fee, when fully earned by FNMA (this will be explained in a moment), amounts to a further .5 percent of the face value of the mortgages being sold.

The commitment fee that FNMA collects from its seller-servicers can be understood only when one realizes that—despite everything already discussed in the preceding paragraphs—the sellers are not really selling mortgages to FNMA at the auction. Instead, they are, in effect, buying options to sell mortgages to FNMA at a later time. Their bid, however, represents the option price, but not the cost of the option: The so-called commitment fee is the cost of the option. The bid that is submitted is the price at which the seller wants to be able to sell its mortgages to FNMA at a future time. The time of ultimate sale is also excluded from the auction procedure, because FNMA regulations currently specify that all one-family-home mortgage commitments run for the same period: six months.

Thus, if seller-servicer number 007 (to pick a familiar, fictitious number) calls during the auction hours, 10 A.M. to 3 P.M. Washington, D.C., time, and tells the telephone operator that it wishes to sell $1.5 million in FHA one-family-home mortgages at ninety-five, it means that it is actually buying from Fanny Mae an option—irrevocable on the part of FNMA—that empowers the seller-servicer to send to FNMA $1.5 million in mortgages within six months. Upon receipt, FNMA will send its check to the mortgage banker for $1,425,000 ($1.5 million times 95 percent), provided that the mortgages are in fact bona fide FHA-insured, one-family-home mortgages. For the right to demand this sum of money from FNMA, the seller-servicer must pay, in advance, a fee of $7500—.5 percent of the face value of the $1.5 million—and must buy stock equal to $7500. The stock, of course, may later be sold.

At the time it bids at the telephone auction, seller-servicer number 007 probably does not own the mortgages that it wants FNMA to commit itself to buy. Most probably it intends to make these mortgage loans within the next six months, borrowing most of the funds that it will need from local commercial banks. If its bid is successful, seller-servicer number 007 receives a card in the mail that commits FNMA to buy the mortgages up to a total of $1,425,000, provided that they are delivered within six months. Taking the FHA commitment card to its banker, seller-servicer 007 is able to open a line of credit against which it can draw cash as needed to close mortgages as they are prepared. The commitment from FNMA assures the commercial bank advancing the money that its obligation will be repaid within a six-month period; the bank is, therefore, making a loan secured not only by the mortgage banker's credit (which probably would not justify so large a loan) and by the FHA-insured mortgages (all of which are long-term) but by FNMA's commitment that is recognized as an unimpeachable credit and that by its terms is to be liquidated within six months.

After it has received its commitment card and proceeded to make some of the mortgages it was considering at the time of its bid, seller-servicer number 007 may find that the XYZ Life Insurance Company decides it wants to buy mortgages that will yield it approximately 7 percent. In that case, seller-servicer 007, who has experience in dealing with the XYZ Insurance Company, will prefer to sell its completed mortgages to it. Among the considerations are a higher price than the price at which the FNMA is committed to under the bid previously submitted by 007. Perhaps equally compelling is the long-term servicing relationship. When seller-servicer 007 sells a mortgage to the XYZ Insurance Company, the seller has a contractual relationship to service the mortgage during its life. Under the FNMA bid procedure, the seller-servicer is committed on its part to servicing the mortgages it sells to FNMA, but the possibility remains that the FNMA will sell the mortgages to some other permanent investor at a future time, and that the future buyer may wish to make its own arrangements for servicing. FNMA permits buyers of mortgages to cancel the previously arranged servicing contract with the mortgage originator upon the payment of a one year's fee (in effect, a one year's notice of cancellation). Of course, FNMA may cancel without such notice if the servicer is delinquent in its handling of the funds received from the mortgagor.

If, and this is increasingly what happened at the end of 1971 and in 1974, no life insurance company was interested in buying the mortgages that seller-servicer 007 originated as a result of its FNMA commitment, 007 would ultimately sell the mortgage at the agreed price to FNMA, taking from the money paid to it by FNMA the permitted 1 percent origination fee. The balance would be used, in all probability, to repay the bank borrowing that originally funded the mortgages.

If the seller-servicer does not finally sell the mortgages to FNMA on which it paid a commitment fee, it is entitled to regain the commitment fee. The return of the fee is based on a sliding scale that allows the seller-servicer a larger return if it cancels its commitment early than if it allows the commitment to remain outstanding. Obviously, the FNMA must calculate its own fiscal needs by measuring its cash resources against its outstanding commitments. The earlier a seller-servicer cancels an outstanding commitment, the greater the amount of money that FNMA can commit at its next auction. Because it hopes to encourage mortgage bankers to place their mortgages ultimately with private investors, FNMA offers to return the commitment fee in return for the cancellation of its obligation.

FNMA does not announce in advance of each biweekly auction how large a supply of mortgages it will commit itself to buy. The actual purchases are determined after the bids are tabulated; the tabulation, which is done by computer, arranges the bids in order of the current yield to FNMA of the mortgages offered by the seller-servicers. Because all of them are current FHA home mortgages bearing the maximum FHA rate, the yield is easy to calculate as a function of the FHA contract interest rate and the price at which the mortgages are offered. Those seller-servicers who compete in the telephone bidding are, under current regulations, permitted to tender a maximum of $3 million in mortgages at each auction. There is nothing to prevent, or even discourage, a mortgage banker from establishing affiliated companies and submitting bids on $3 million blocks under the name of each company. Each company, of course, would have to qualify under FHA rules as an approved originator and have entered into an FNMA seller-servicer contract.

After the bids have been tabulated, FNMA decides how many of the proposals for commitments it will accept. This decision will reflect the condition of FNMA's own portfolio, its sense of the interest trend in the mortgage market, judging by reports on mortgage transactions elsewhere than in the FHA sector, by movements in the money market, and by its own current average net interest cost, reflecting the level of its own borrowings and the latest interest rate that it must pay for money. These calculations are not unlike the calculations of the Open Market Committee of the Federal Reserve Bank. Although its motive is to make a profit on the spread between the cost of its borrowing and the yield on its mortgage portfolio, it is interested also in discouraging wide swings in the mortgage interest rate and tries to balance its natural desire for profitably high yields on mortgages with the discouraging effect of such yields on the ultimate customers for homes.

By the end of 1972, FNMA moved cautiously to develop an auction procedure for non-FHA insured mortgages. It had already announced terms on which it would buy mortgages made by private non-FHA insurers and had developed a standard mortgage form. A secondary market for noninsured mortgages would be a mammoth undertaking because, as we have seen, uninsured mortgages constitute the majority of all American mortgages.

CHAPTER 14

THE GOVERNMENT NATIONAL
MORTGAGE ASSOCIATION

WHEN in 1970 the Federal National Mortgage Association took flight from the coop of the national government and became a full-fledged private corporation whose capital stock was soon listed on the New York Stock Exchange,[1] it left behind in the hands of the government several onerous fiscal responsibilities in the mortgage field. These responsibilities were essential to the national housing program enacted by Congress, but they were either unprofitable by definition or else they required such a vast amount of risk capital that they could not be arranged under purely private auspices.

The first of these responsibilities was called, in the Charter Act, special assistance. Special assistance is described as being of two general types. First, there is a special assistance that is offered to classes of citizens who cannot afford to live in apartments or one-family houses *if* the mortgage that financed the housing construction carries a full market rate of interest. In the case of such citizens—under the specific authorization of Congress—the government must make up the difference between the interest rate, authorized by law, that the resident can afford to pay and the contractual rate of the actual mortgage. Obviously, these payments are a simple and straightforward loss to whoever makes them, and only the government will make them. And then only because Congress believes that the resulting housing values are in the best long-range interest of the nation as a whole.

Because this activity represents an inevitable loss—paying out more money each year than it takes in—it could not follow Fannie Mae into the world of private finance. While subsidy payments to mortgagees in fulfillment of this governmental objective could have been made in any one of a number of forms, the form actually chosen by Congress was to establish a new secondary market mortgage-holding organization— the Government National Mortgage Association (GNMA). Deriving its funds directly from the Treasury, as authorized, GNMA developed a system for providing subsidies in the special assistance program without establishing on the books of the government a long-term liability for the mortgage. We shall examine this method presently.

The need for a second type of special assistance function occurs when the mortgage money market temporarily tightens up; in this case, the assistance is not a form of continuing subsidization but a mere replacement of capital so that the originating mortgages can replenish the funds that it has committed to a mortgage or series of mortgages. This, in very general terms, is the same kind of liquidity that the Federal National Mortgage Association—Fannie Mae—provides in its issuance of advance commitments and its other secondary market operations. The Government National Mortgage Association's activity in this kind of special assistance is limited to a firm commitment to purchase from an originating mortgagee at a stipulated price, provided that this is the same price at which the originating mortgagee actually initiated the mortgage.

In 1971, at the time when this plan was first announced by the Government National Mortgage Association, the Department of Housing and Urban Development was trying to keep the mortgage interest rate from exceeding the FHA contract ceiling of 7 percent. By providing for a fixed price at which the originator could turn over its mortgages to GNMA (on the condition that this was the same price at which the mortgage itself was originated), GNMA held the discount to a stipulated number of points. Obviously, the mortgagee could not make any profit other than an origination fee by selling the mortgage for the same amount of money that it disbursed when it made the loan. By making the sale, the originating mortgagee even lost the right to service the loan, the source of most of the earnings of mortgage companies. Obviously, the originating mortgage banker would prefer to be a successful bidder for an FNMA commitment, meaning that it might not only make some profit on the sale itself but that, in addition, it would be able to retain its servicing rights. The GNMA commitment was important to the mortgage market for two reasons: It provided a safe outlet for mortgages that could not, for one reason or another, be sold successfully to FNMA, mortgages on existing as well as on new houses; and it placed a suggested ceiling on the actual interest rates by placing a floor under the price of the discounted mortgage.

In 1971, when GNMA announced this special assistance program, the association expected that its mortgage volume under the plan would run at about $15 billion per year. GNMA proposed to raise this money by selling the mortgages either to FNMA or to other, general investors. But Fannie Mae, the Federal National Mortgage Association, a publicly held corporation, was now dependent for its own supply of funds on the private money market. It needed those funds to buy from the mortgage bankers who originated the FHA loans that did not require special assistance and, later, to buy from commercial banks and others non-FHA- or non-VA-insured mortgages. Thus, the amount of money that might be available from FNMA for GNMA's nonsubsidized assistance function was necessarily quite limited. GNMA, therefore, had to get its funds from the United States Treasury, where, in fact, it enjoys a practically unlimited line of credit. However, although GNMA's credit at the Treasury loan window is impeccable, the Treasury itself cannot lend money to GNMA without authorization from Congress, because the money loaned by the Treasury to the GNMA must be considered a budgeted federal expense in the year in which the advance takes place.

The reason for this is fairly obvious. The Treasury can create money for GNMA in only two ways, each of which has the effect of increasing the total money supply of the nation as against what it would otherwise have been.

Thus, if authorized by Congress, the Treasury offers a credit of $5 billion to GNMA, and GNMA issues checks to mortgagees for $5 billion worth of mortgages; these checks will ultimately be presented for payment into the Federal Reserve Bank accounts of the mortgagees or their bankers. The Treasury must make the credits available either by reducing its possible annual tax surplus—the existence of which is highly implausible in the American economy—or by borrowing, which, if it is not simply to absorb savings already available for mortgage investment, will most probably require the indirect support of the Federal Reserve System in the expansion of the total money supply. If a limit were not placed on this kind of so-called deficit funding, the increase in the money supply would be adverse to price stability, including the stability of housing costs.

The second type of special assistance provided by the GNMA affects only those mortgages that are intended to fulfill specific social functions that, in the opinion of Congress, justify federal subsidization. For the most part, these include mortgage loans that are to be extended for the benefit, first, of people who by reason of age or other special disability cannot be expected to pay for the financing of homes—including apartments in buildings financed by a single undivided mortgage. The special assistance for what might be called special housing programs began in 1954 and has covered as many as fourteen different programs.[2] Since the separation of Fannie Mae from Ginnie Mae, the special programs have narrowed down to a smaller number, but their ambit has become considerably wider. Special low-cost mortgages are still provided for homeowners and, indirectly, for renters who have suffered from specific disadvantages; but the congressional interest has broadened to include Americans who suffer from no specific disability but who, nevertheless, lack the income to provide themselves with new standard housing without subsidization in the form of lower-than-market interest rates.

These include disaster housing, urban renewal mortgages, housing in Guam, such basic below-market interest rate mortgage housing as the 221 (d) 3 program, and now, more recently, so-called 235 (J) Housing, and FHA 235 and 236 housing, generally. These last two programs are carried out by cooperation between the GNMA and the FNMA under a scheme that has been called the tandem plan.

Until the Nixon Administration announced its intent to end the 235 and 236 programs, they played so large a part in the national housing production—nearly one-third in 1971—that they deserve careful explanation. On June 30, 1970, GNMA had borrowed $3.1 billion from the Treasury, with which it was carrying an inventory of slightly over $5.0 billion in FHA- and VA-insured mortgages.[3] By June 30, 1971, the Treasury loan had grown to $3.5 billion, and the portfolio of insured mortgages stood at $5.2 billion.[4]

Because, by definition, the special assistance program involves the purchase by GNMA of mortgages that cannot be readily sold in the private market—either because of their riskiness or because their contract rate of interest provides a below-market return on the face value—the purpose of the Government National Mortgage Association is to lose money. It loses money in an effort to encourage private investments made in areas of the housing market in which they could not otherwise be made profitably. GNMA's losses on special assistance functions turn out to be the least expensive way in which the government can provide a stimulus to the use of the people's savings in this type of housing.

The FHA 236 program involves subsidization by the Department of Housing and Urban Development of a special FHA-insured mortgage written with a standard 6 percent interest rate. The proceeds of the mortgage must be used to build approved housing developments that will be lived in only by families whose income falls below the median income of the area in which the housing is to be located. In any case, the families must spend at least 25 percent of their income as rent—a calculation made after deducting from their income some sources of funds, such as the earnings of children under eighteen. Because mortgage interest rates near 1971 have generally been higher than 6 percent—meaning that savings institutions would not place their money in 6 percent mortgages when more remunerative opportunities were available elsewhere—no bank would originate a 6 percent FHA 236 mortgage unless it knew it could immediately dispose of that mortgage at par, pocketing for its troubles a small fee for originating the mortgage. If the Government National Mortgage Association purchased and held such a mortgage, written at a below-market interest rate, the entire mortgage would be chargeable to the government's operating expenditures in 1971. Therefore, the tandem plan provides for the sale of the mortgage by the Government National Mortgage Association at a discount.

Naturally, the 6 percent mortgage required by FHA 236 does not provide enough of a subsidy to bring the cost of housing down to a level at which families whose incomes are below the median can afford to live. Thus, the FHA 236 program involves not merely the taking of a capital loss on the sale of the mortgage bearing a below-market interest rate but, additionally, annual subsidies paid to the housing borrower. These have the effect of reducing the effective cost of the mortgage from 6 percent interest per year, plus amortization, to 1 percent per year for interest and amortization combined.

In 1972, the Government National Mortgage Association reported to Congress that it lost $119.4 million in its handling of mortgages, without making provision for its own expenses. Of this sum, $84.5 million was the loss suffered from the tandem plan purchase at par, and sale at a discount of FHA 235 and 236 mortgages primarily, while $34.9 million resulted from the purchase and sale of the 221 (d) 3 mortgages written with a below-market interest rate.[5] The Government National Mortgage Association looked forward to an increasingly successful operation of its special assistance function, meaning that it expected to lose even more money in the future. It told Congress that in 1973 it expected to lose $248 million, after providing for its own operating expenses, an increase of approximately $100 million over 1972's losses.[6] GNMA requested Congress to make appropriations of funds to cover its deficits, pointing out that the only alternative available to it was to borrow enough from the Treasury to replenish its depleted capital. If the GNMA had to increase its borrowings from the Treasury to cover its losses (in addition to the borrowings necessary to provide it with capital with which to buy and hold mortgages in inventory), its losses would be all the greater, requiring Congress to appropriate even more money at a later date to discharge the interest due on the deficit financing. Of course, as noted earlier, this is a small part of the government expense involved in these special assistance programs that, in effect, are the price paid to induce savers to invest their money in housing for moderate-income families at an interest rate so low that the families are able to afford it. Because these subsidies are distributed by the Department of Housing and Urban Development rather than by the Government National Mortgage Association, the total involved must be sought elsewhere. Secretary Romney's representative told a congressional committee that when the FHA 235 and 236 programs reached their full flowering, the total cost to the United States government might reach $100 billion. Alongside this, the GNMA losses in buying retail and selling wholesale—buying at artificially high prices and selling at market prices—are dwarfed into insignificance.

The principal justification for GNMA's losses has been its ability to sell the mortgages purchased by it at par so that funds may be channeled into the mortgage system. The so-called tandem plan, which we have discussed in the preceding paragraphs, uses the Federal National Mortgage Association as the medium through which private savings move into the mortgages that the government seeks especially to assist. Fannie Mae's understanding with GNMA encourages it to purchase mortgages at discounts slightly shallower than would be demanded by a purely private institution; for, although FNMA is actually a privately owned institution, it operates under what amounts to a special government license, and the manageable losses that it may incur in holding mortgages with an effective yield below the general market level (or the level at which it borrows funds from the general public) are offset by the advantages accruing to it from its more or less unique position with reference to the United States government.

As we have seen, FNMA raises funds from investors by selling its own obligations—including both debt and shares of stock. It also, from time to time, raises capital to buy more mortgages by selling mortgages from its own portfolio. GNMA, on the other hand, not only sells its own obligations to the Treasury of the United States and receives direct appropriations from Congress but it also is active in the housing market by making possible the sale of debt by mortgage holders to other investors. Thus, the GNMA not only is now prepared to sell mortgages directly to those who might wish to acquire mortgages but it is also prepared to make possible the retention of mortgages by mortgage originators, by enabling those originators to raise money through the sale of their own obligations. The obligations are secured by the pledge of mortgages that have been insured by FHA. This may recall the guaranteed mortgage bonds to which we referred in our discussion of commercial banks. Those were guaranteed by mortgage bankers; GNMA's guaranteed mortgage bonds are guaranteed by the United States government.

The obligations of mortgage originators can, in theory, be of two different kinds. One type of obligation would provide that the originator issue a general bond with a definite term and that, in accordance with the indenture of the bond, a group of mortgages be held as collateral. The bond would require the payment of regular interest payments in accordance with its terms. At the maturity of the bond issue, the issuer would pay the full face value of the obligation, unless the bond provided for a call before maturity. While this is the common form of a bond secured by specific property, or as a general obligation of the debtor—both cases in which the security for the obligation is of a continuing, presumably long-term value—the form is not so well adapted to bonds secured by mortgages because mortgages are subject to reduction by amortization and may be prepaid in full by their obligor at any time. If, say, the XYZ Mortgage Banking Company (a name that we trust is fictitious) holds $3 million in mortgages and wishes to raise money with which to acquire more mortgages—either by origination or by purchase from some other originator—it can, in theory, sell bonds secured by its pool of mortgages. To sell the bonds, it must offer the purchaser a promise to pay interest at a specific rate—say 8 percent per annum for twenty years. Presumably, this would be slightly less than the average interest rate on the pool of mortgages that is backing up the bonds. Alternatively, the dollar value of the bonds sold by XYZ would have to be somewhat less than the face value of the mortgages held by XYZ, so the interest actually earned would be sufficient, at least in the first year, to cover the interest to be paid to the bond buyers, after XYZ pays its own expenses. But as the face value of the bonds is reduced by their normal amortization, the actual cash interest received each year by XYZ declines.

In order for XYZ to sell bonds providing for a continuing flow of interest equal to the original interest that it promised to pay its bond buyers, it must have secured its bonds with such a large pool of mortgages that it will be able to reinvest the amortization it receives in new mortgages that will earn interest at the same rate, at least, as the mortgages with which it started out. Three million dollars—the fictitious figure we described as held by the XYZ Mortgage Banking Company in mortgages—would provide an amortization flow of $100,000 per year, if we assume that they are to be thirty-year, level amortization mortgages. If these mortgages are subject to monthly payments, XYZ will receive eight thousand dollars per month in amortization payments. It is hardly possible that the officials of XYZ, however eagle-eyed they might be, will be able to discover an eight thousand dollar mortgage investment each month, month after month, and yet this is precisely the sum they would be required to find if there were not to be a lapse in the earning of interest.

This gap—which would probably stretch for longer than a month while XYZ waits for a suitable reinvestment opportunity—would discourage XYZ from issuing bonds of this type and would, in fact, impose a credit risk on the bond buyer that the FHA insurance of the mortgages themselves would not completely meet. If the mortgage market interest rate shifted downward while the bonds were outstanding, XYZ would be committed to pay out interest not actually earned. The guarantee by GNMA of the bond of this type would involve GNMA itself in a credit risk for which it would not be prepared.

Accordingly, GNMA has limited its guarantee of this type of FHA-insured-mortgage-backed bond to the very largest of the mortgage banking enterprises in the country. These are the Federal National Mortgage Association—which we have already discussed and which is one of the largest private corporations in the country—and the Federal Home Loan Mortgage Corporation (FHLMC), a subsidiary of the Federal Home Loan Bank that buys noninsured mortgages primarily from the savings and loan associations that are members of the Federal Home Loan Bank System.

Even for very large mortgage holding institutions, the problems involved in maintaining level-interest-rate payments on borrowings are serious. The Federal Home Loan Mortgage Corporation permits the institutions that sell mortgages to it to maintain their servicing. This means that each month each seller collects a payment from the owner of the mortgaged property including interest on the balance outstanding, amortization of that balance, and tax and insurance escrow payments. The originator-seller-servicer of the mortgage that has been sold to

FHLMC must subtract from the payment received from the mortgagor the escrow payments and its own servicing fee and remit the balance to FHLMC. FHLMC must be able to distinguish which part of the money is interest and which part is repayment of principal expended by it when it purchased the mortgage. The accountants of FHLMC must be able to work out a bookkeeping system that will adequately reflect the interest due and actually collected, and the balance of principal outstanding after each payment so that FHLMC will be able to ascertain whether or not it is earning the interest on the money that it borrowed in order to purchase the mortgage. It must also be clear as to how much money is available to it with which to make necessary repayments of those borrowings, or to make new purchases of mortgages.

If one imagines that the average size of a single home mortgage is twenty thousand dollars and the average size of a bond-type security issue is $250 million—both reasonable figures—it is a simple matter of arithmetic to calculate that the mortgage pool backing up such a bond issue contains more than 12,500 separate mortgages. Even though FHLMC would seek to categorize the mortgages used to back a bond issue, each individual mortgage will have its own history, involving late payments, defaults, prepayments, foreclosures, fires, and claims for reimbursement from the FHA or casualty insurers. In order to maintain the integrity of a bond issue of a fixed amount, such as $250 million, the borrower whose bonds are to be guaranteed by GNMA must have developed an accounting system of spectacular efficiency and must be able to draw on a reserve of mortgages great enough to replace those paid off, defaulted, or canceled for one or another of the suggested reasons.

If GNMA were limited in its bond guarantees to the mortgage purchasers large enough to meet these qualifications, it would not be providing a secondary money market for mortgage originators spread throughout the country. Taking our fictitious XYZ Mortgage Banking Company as a prototype of such an originator of FHA-insured mortgages in its part of the country, we can recapitulate the several options open to it for the replenishment of its capital after making a group of mortgage loans. It could sell the mortgages either to a purely private purchaser eligible to acquire and hold FHA-insured mortgages, such as a life insurance company, or to the FNMA or the GNMA. The other alternative would be to sell its own obligations, backed by the insured mortgages and insured by GNMA. Because XYZ lacks the broad base on which to issue a bond-type security that promises its buyer a fixed income to maturity, it must necessarily turn to the other type of mortgage-backed security that the GNMA will guarantee to its purchaser: the pass-through type of security.

This note, or certificate of obligation, of XYZ, guaranteed as to principal and interest by the GNMA, differs from the bond-type note in that it does not promise repayment at maturity. Instead, XYZ, the obligor, commits itself to pay out not only the interest but also the principal repayments that it receives from the mortgagors during the life of the mortgages. Thus, the burden of reinvestment falls on the shoulders of the buyers of GNMA-guaranteed obligations rather than on the shoulders of XYZ itself. The interest rates paid on such obligations are determined by the market; obviously, XYZ will not avail itself of its right to sell such obligations with a GNMA guarantee unless it can sell them at a rate of interest lower than the interest rate that it will earn on mortgages. If XYZ were to pay more on its GNMA-guaranteed obligations than it earned on the mortgages underlying them, it would clearly prefer to replenish its capital by selling its mortgages to FNMA, GNMA, or to the private market directly.

Within two years after the development of the notion of the GNMA-guaranteed pass-through type of security, or by July 1, 1971, more than $2.5 billion of such securities had been sold.[7] For the most part, these securities have been purchased by financial intermediaries like mutual savings banks, insurance companies, and savings and loan associations who find them a convenient, easy-to-operate substitute for more direct participation in the mortgage market. Because new issues are coming out regularly, and because certificates can readily be bought and sold by securities dealers, the reinvestment problem that holders face when principal payments are passed through is not so great as it would be for the small originator of the securities. On the other hand, the widespread purchase and holding of these securities by financial intermediaries would seem to dilute their traditional usefulness as originators of mortgages. Increasingly, the structure of the mortgage market would appear to depend upon FHA or VA insurance that underlies the GNMA guarantee of the securities bought largely by the intermediaries. In the final analysis, this would seem to place an extraordinary burden of responsibility on the shoulders of FHA underwriters. As a result of their approval of a mortgage commitment, the element of risk is entirely removed from the mortgage process. Because all of the forces in the market are, as we have noted, mobilized to increase housing production, the absence of restraint might easily result in overbuilding or slipshod evaluation of risks in areas where restraint would be salutary. No one benefits from mortgage foreclosure for nonpayment, least of all the family-in-possession, which frequently finds that its savings, or its potential savings, have been wiped out in a process in which all of the more sophisticated actors have been insured against risk.

According to officials of GNMA, the funds invested by thrift institutions in the guaranteed pass-through securities would not otherwise have been invested in housing. The officials have, furthermore, claimed that of the more than $2 billion worth of these securities sold by June 30, 1971, $400 million had been purchased by money managers who would not normally be in the mortgage market at all: pension funds, trustees, welfare funds, and others.[8]

In addition to the special assistance function, of which the GNMA-guarantee program is a part, GNMA also handles the liquidation functions of the government in all of its housing programs. This means that GNMA must take over the management and ownership of housing that the federal government owns but no longer needs, or housing that was acquired by the FHA or any other mortgage-insuring agency because of default, and that cannot be sold on the market without special attention. These programs do not directly affect the mortgage market, but the GNMA as a whole—at least under the conditions prevailing in 1971—has had a striking effect on traditional institutions in this market, and on their way of conducting their affairs.

CHAPTER 15

POLICIES AND PROSPECTS

WE STARTED our examination of the process by which resources are allocated to housing with the question of why the supply of resources remains in many ways inadequate. Having now followed the process of resource allocation through the private and public institutions that constitute the mortgage market, we can return to the preliminary question.

The first, and in many ways the most pertinent, fact to recognize about the condition of American housing is its general excellence. The allocation of resources has been, on the whole, satisfactory; its major trouble is its shocking unevenness. The quality of housing does not slowly diminish as one goes down the income scale; the differences between the housing available to different income groups among the population do not resemble the notes on a piano keyboard, separated from each other by half or full tones. On the contrary, we have exceedingly high quantitative allocations for the homes of the rather small group of very wealthy families; adequate allocations, at a level that would be called luxurious elsewhere in the world, for the middle groups in the population; and, by and large, grossly inadequate resource allocations to provide and maintain homes for poor families and single persons at the low end of the scale.

Gone are the days when the president of the United States could talk with some accuracy about one-third of the nation being ill-housed. The total percentage of the population that lives today in houses lacking some or all plumbing facilities (the simplest and most objective measurement despite its failure to distinguish the housing units in which some or all of the plumbing doesn't work) was down to about 8 percent, according to the 1970 census.[1] According to the 1960 census, the figure had been twice as high: 16 percent of all housing units had lacked some or all plumbing.[2] Another significant statistical indicator —the persons-per-room ratio—also dropped. Specialists in family life agree, generally, that a housing unit is overcrowded when its total number of rooms is smaller than the number of people occupying it; when, in short, the ratio of persons per room exceeds 1.00. Between 1960 and 1970, the Bureau of the Census reported a drop of more than 11 million housing units with a person-per-room ratio of 1.01 or higher.[3] In 1970, about 15 percent of the dwelling units in the United States remained overcrowded by this standard; in 1960, the overcrowded units had exceeded 20 percent of the total.

It has become very chic to decry the typical American house as ticky-tacky, wasteful of land resources, vulgar, and unwisely planned to depend upon the automobile. The second of these criticisms may indeed be valid: Americans have the habit of thinking their land resources are limitless, and were brought up to believe that a man isn't a man until he owns land. The criticism of automotive dependence may also be valid. Yet one would have to have great faith in one's superiority to the desires of his fellow citizens to insist that their homes should be designed to be independent of automobile access; the people want their cars.

These general criticisms of American housing are important, nevertheless, because they refocus attention on the significance not only of the shelter package of housing but of the utility and the social packages as well. The general sense of disappointment over public housing achievements—a disappointment that may well be exaggerated in the light of many positive accomplishments—should remind the advocate of better housing for low-income families that successful housing is not provided by shelter alone. The utility package suggests the imperative need for adequate municipal services and for vast expenditures on transportation, sewage disposal, and solid waste handling (to name only a few categories) if the shelter aspect of housing is to remain of lasting social value. Obviously, the capital requirements of these utilitarian investments will to some extent compete with the capital requirements of housing. To the extent that they would engage national resources that would otherwise go to consumer products, they will compete with the wishes of those in the population who are satisfied with their own current housing package, but who desire a higher level of personal expenditure, no matter who preaches to them on the folly of worldly goods. Even in a state that permits no organized political opposition, the concentration of productive effort on capital goods and capital formation is likely to stir conflict. There are limits to the useful concentration of activity on the general good, although no one can precisely locate them in advance, and they surely have not been reached in the United States. When the limits are passed, production falls.

The social package requires two major constituents that can be provided only through large expenditures: jobs and schools. Yet neither can be provided by expenditure alone. The major American cities were once primarily centers of manufacturing and transportation, activities that have either drastically changed in character or that have been decentralized elsewhere. New and expanded service industries, such as higher education and health, will inadequately take their place as employment generators. Furthermore, the service industries generally will be established only with far more public than private effort. We have consistently noted the desirability of blindness in the formulation of public policy, yet the future promises us that blindness will become less and less useful; matters will not take care of themselves. Some people view with complacency the decline of industrialization and urge that work itself is merely a recent phenomenon of western society with which the social order can readily dispense.

They offer no substitute activity that can inspire the same balance—shaky as it may be—between discipline and self-gratification as that provided by work. Nor do they convincingly suggest how a degree (but not an overwhelming degree) of social order is to be maintained without the balance that work provides. To plan housing as shelter, or even housing as shelter-cum-utilities, without offering both work and educational opportunities that are taken seriously by the students is not to solve the housing problem but simply to engage in vast public works that are nearly as fruitless as the building of pyramids.

Finally, one returns to the description of American housing as ticky-tacky. It is instructive in this connection to look at the vaunted housing developments of continental Europe and the British Isles. While the European town has been far more effectively planned than the American in preserving open space, common facilities, and independence from the automobile, the individual houses are truly ticky-tacky by American standards. Rooms are small, storage space limited, cooking and bathing facilities inadequate. The structural standards, including such matters as the size of timbers and the electrical capacity of the wiring, do not meet most American codes. Equally significant, they would be rejected as second-rate by most American families.

Yet none of this offers any grounds for complacency on either side of the ocean. Europeans, having discovered motor cars, are now buying them in large numbers. Town plans that depended on excluding cars must be revised to take them into account. The notion of the one-family house has recrossed the Atlantic, eastbound, and the country that most Americans heard described as having achieved great housing goals—Sweden—now hears from many of its people that it has overbuilt the large cooperative development, and should concentrate now on the same-row or terrace houses or free-standing villas that some call ticky-tacky in America.

Americans, on the other side of the sea, should be noting portents of a continuing rise in housing costs relative to the increase in family income. In the twelve years from 1955 to 1967, the Bureau of Labor Statistics' index of shelter costs (an average of rental cost as well as the costs of homeownership) rose slightly more than 26 percent,[4] while the total disposable personal income in the United States almost doubled. In the four years between 1968 and 1971, the shelter index has advanced by almost as high a percentage as the total disposable personal income in the United States.[5] If both indices continue to move at their present velocity, housing costs will rise faster than personal income. Obviously, personal income is unequally distributed, and the rates of increase among the several segments of the population are very different, but surely those with lower incomes who reside in the highest housing cost areas—the central cities—will find the pinch even worse than it is today. It is also ominous that the level of contract rents paid, according to the Bureau of Labor Statistics, is not rising as fast as the costs of housing maintenance, including mortgage interest. This foreshadows the deterioration of rental accommodations.

In the case of a specific subsector of American housing, the new one-family house insured by the FHA, the trend is clear. In 1965, the median family moving into such a new house paid 24.7 percent of its income after taxes for housing. This figure was precisely the same as it had been since 1960, five years earlier. In 1971, the median family moving into a similar new house, with its mortgage insured by the FHA, paid 26.8 percent of its after-tax income for housing. The increase is almost 10 percent—meaning that housing was consuming 10 percent more of the income. If one picked 1970 instead of 1971 for the comparison, the rise would have been still sharper because of the high interest rates that prevailed in 1970. The housing income ratio in 1971 was 27.5 percent, and as interest rates rise, the ratio will rise with them.[6] Undoubtedly, the dramatic interest rise in 1973–1974 will force housing costs even higher.

The connection between interest rates and housing costs affects not only the new housing constructed and financed for the first time in a high interest rate period. It affects apartment houses, which are generally not financed by self-amortizing mortgages, and which face frequent refinancing problems. Each time the mortgage is refinanced, its effective interest rate will be the rate current at the time of refinancing. High interest rates also affect the resale and refinancing of existing houses, which, as we have noted, is a vitally important part of family mobility, a quality essential to the marketing of a large output of new homes.

Ever since the dissolution of the accord between the Treasury and the Federal Reserve Bank in 1952, an accord in which the Federal Reserve Board had made low interest rates, and cheap carrying costs of the national debt, the primary object of national monetary policy, interest rates have been moving up. The curve is a jagged one, but the general trend is very clearly upward. Even if the Federal Reserve System continued to direct its policy primarily to keep interest rates down, the growth of the world economy would make its success dubious. In the period from 1945 to 1951, the United States so overshadowed the rest of the world in economic power that low interest rates in this country would not send funds elsewhere in search of investment: Foreign investment opportunities were relatively unattractive. In that period, the excess money supply that had accumulated during the war, when rationing prevented the spending of income, remained in excess of current needs; interest rates were naturally low. Although there were vast pent-up demands for private and public improvements, the rate at which they could be undertaken was limited by the time involved in making plans, training work forces, and gaining approvals from authorities.

Now, nearly thirty years later, a vast demand has developed world-wide for consumer goods and a higher standard of living, bringing with it a demand for capital projects to make increased consumer goods production possible. Only the basic maldistribution of physical assets and organizing experiences explains the gap in effective capital utilization between the already industrialized nations and those parts of the world (like Africa and central Asia) that only a few years ago seemed to be forever asleep. These populations, too, are demanding more food, better homes. There is only one moderating force, whose full effect cannot yet be seen: the force of environmental conservation, which may slow down the rate at which men will allow each other to deplete the natural storehouse of resources. On the other hand, conservation may result in higher production because the achievement of its goals may involve vast quantities of labor and energy.

In any case, the upward trend in interest rates suggests that the availability of resources is limited, the demand enormous. If, as these hypotheses suggest, it is impossible to control the interest rate in general, what steps should be taken to protect housing in the United States from the effect of high interest, to plan policies that will increase the quality of housing for low-income families, to maintain the housing stockpile in good condition, and to provide the flexibility that will enable housing production to follow the shifting demography of the United States, the changes in urban life, racial distribution, family size and composition, the patterns of industrial and service employment that may emerge over the next half-century?

The policies should involve at least three major objectives. First, the objective of limiting the resources needed or used in the provision of housing so that less capital (or proportionately less capital) will be required to build future housing than is the case at the present time. Second, the objective of facilitating the flow of money into the mortgage market, by strengthening the capacity of intermediaries that customarily make mortgages, and preserving or enhancing the attractions of mortgage lending in comparison with alternative investments for such institutions. Third, the objective of providing appropriate and effective assistance, which will attain a significant measure of public support, to the families of modest or low incomes so that they can pay for the housing created or modernized.

Objective No. I—
The Limitation of Resources

To diminish the demand for resources for housing, three separate offensives are required. First, economy in the use of land must be achieved. Second, economy in the structure becomes essential. Third, economy must be attained in the operations and maintenance of the completed housing unit.

Starting with land, we find that American practice and law has been extremely profligate in its use of land. Because the federal government was produced as what might be called a secondary federation of sovereign states, control over land use remains in local hands. The state legislatures have been reluctant to impose their judgment on the local municipalities for the obvious reason that the state legislatures are made up of locally elected representatives. No issue could be less popular in the local municipalities than a weakening of their control over land use. Rezoning not only raises the specter of invasion by low-income families but also poses a financial threat: The arrival of new bodies brings demands for new services while they pay less money in local taxes than the services cost.

The guiding principle of land use should not be sentimental. Its purpose should not be to punish those who have found a satisfactory living environment in the suburbs. Rather, land use should be based on the economic notion that housing must accompany industrial and commercial job development. Zoning, which makes industry possible but eliminates any chance of providing housing for those who might work in the factories, has been challenged on constitutional grounds; such a challenge may prevail when a municipality has welcomed the industrial tax revenue. But if a municipality has not admitted industry, procedural mistakes alone offer the basis for a successful legal appeal to force the opening of zoning that excludes both housing and employment opportunities.

The British new towns are the culmination of the national government's effort to provide new industry together with new housing in an attractive, more or less self-contained setting on what had been grossly underutilized land. In order to override all local land use controls, the separate government corporations, each of which is responsible for one new town, have the power to acquire land by condemnation, make their own rules about land use, and exert whatever charms they need to seduce industry to pick their new town site for future development. The profits that accrue from the increase in land value that inevitably follows successful new town development reverts to the national government because it provided the initial financing.

Obviously, the land use problems of the United States are very different from those of the British Isles, and the total population density in the United States is far lower. Many states and many municipalities already in existence are exercising all the charms they can find to bring industry to them. The urban housing problem will not be solved until these expanding industrial facilities are able to employ the current central city populations. Those who are unable to find work that fits their training, or lack of it, or who are unprepared for the experience of working, by virtue of having experienced only the most brutal, transitory, and disorganized work, must be given realistic new training if they are to live successfully in new housing. If American society cannot provide this, it had better reconcile itself to the continuing decay of its older cities, with growing permanent slums to guarantee their uselessness.

The British new towns offer only a negative example here. They are generally providing housing only for those who have already been accepted for employment by the new, local industries. Just as in the United States, an unskilled nonworking underclass is left behind in the center of the older cities, while the possible job base diminishes around them.

A program of minimizing land cost in connection with housing development might well involve federal government intervention and control of the industrial development of existing municipalities. The community development sections of the National Housing Act offer assistance, but the current emphasis on revenue sharing with large elements of local self-determination has undercut what might be a fruitful use of the government carrot to accomplish important needs. Towns and cities wishing to use federal grants-in-aid for such community development costs as schools, sewers, and public safety facilities should be required to accept government standards on land use zoning. Row housing, two- and three-family housing, and apartment houses with low profiles should be welcomed as a condition of community development, particularly for aged or single persons. Grants should be made contingent on the establishment of training programs in overpopulated urban centers geared specifically to the type of industry moving into the municipality benefiting from the grant. A target quota for trained new arrivals might be established for any industry benefiting from the community development grants that make industrial relocation possible. The expanding municipality should be encouraged by the federal government to acquire the land for housing just as it acquires the land for industrial development. Land for housing purposes would have to be made available at a price that is reasonable. Housing cannot afford to carry a land cost that reflects the cost of industrial development or municipal expansion. A program of encouraging industrial and community development, only if housing opportunities are made available to untrained workers who are to be prepared at government expense, will, of course, engender serious opposition. Perhaps a special commission would be required to formulate policies and see to their adoption. But it is the only serious hope for engaging the present urban slum dweller in a new future.

In the older urban centers, reduction in population offers an opportunity to find cheaper land, already served with many of the contents of the utility package. Modernizing the social package to include industry and workable schools presents more of a problem. As new industrial development takes place outside the older cities, the depopulation trend that is already occurring will accelerate. In some sections of the older cities, land already has a negative value. If no one wants to own or live in an abandoned house, and no one offers to demolish it in order to make use of the underlying land for any purpose whatsoever, the land value is demonstrably negative. Owning it imposes a financial burden that only nonowning relieves.

Increasingly, the old cities are being relegated to the role of service centers, but this change does not indicate that the external dependencies of service centers will provide the employment and the tax base that the cities need to pay for the services they must give their inhabitants. The last best hope for the cities is that they will contain educational and health institutions for populations recruited from outside their borders; that they will offer entertainment, cultural activities, and spectator sports (even these are drifting away); and that they will institute foci for government service centers and back-office activities (even though the federal government, following industry's lead, has been decentralizing its functions to smaller towns). The cities will also provide service assistance to support business and government headquarters activities.

This shift of function will cost vast sums of money, both in the new centers and in the adaptation of the old cities to newer functions. It may seem futile to distinguish between the housing and the other costs of these changes, but the distinction is essential for political justice. It is hard enough to get the federal government to provide transfer payments to cover merely the shelter package needed by low-income families. When the costs of utility and social packages are added (although in part these would be paid for by local municipalities in the case of building types occupied by other citizens) the political difficulty in obtaining adequate funding is greatly increased.

Although we referred to European housing as being structurally less generous and ample than new American homes, and have suggested that many Americans would not accept housing built to the standards of current European and Soviet production, it does not follow that American taste is necessarily right. Although American housing has been criticized as being ticky-tacky, this may be precisely the wrong conclusion. American housing may indeed be overbuilt, embodying structural safety factors that exceed the necessary (even admitting that a depressing fraction of American housing is built on hillside sites or flood plains where it is unsafe no matter how strongly it happens to be built). American housing may also include too large a share of frills and surplus amenities: powder rooms, picture windows, and meaningless individualizing decor.

Without anyone saying so out loud, a very significant fraction of American housing is moving toward a simpler and less expensive norm. The growth of mobile housing, which is intended to be moved only once—from its source to a site that will be its lifelong resting place— indicates that many Americans are settling for a simpler model. In 1965, mobile home factory shipments accounted for 216,000 units out of almost 1.5 million [7] total housing starts. Thus, mobile homes provided approximately 14 percent of all new housing starts. Seven years later, in 1972, over 575,000 mobile homes were shipped from the factory. This represented approximately 24 percent of the total number (2.3 million) of housing starts in that year.[8] In short, the market share of mobile homes rose by about 50 percent in a six-year period. In part, this may represent a special situation—the production of a large number of homes in the southern states where the warmer climate makes mobile homes less problematic than they may be in the northern states. The mobile homes are characterized by a framing and construction system that would fail to meet most local codes for in-place construction.

The increase in the market share of mobile homes is not the only indicator of a change in housing standards. In the same seven years, 1965 to 1972, the median lot size of FHA-insured one-family homes dropped by about 20 percent, from 9300 square feet to 7200 square feet.[9] The percentage of such homes with full basements dropped from 21 to 12 percent, while the percentage of such homes that were built on a slab at ground level, with no basement at all, rose from 48 to 61 percent. Nevertheless, the evidence is spotty. At the same time that the lot size shrank and the basements turned into ground slabs, the incidence of central air conditioning increased dramatically, from 6 percent of new FHA-insured one-family homes in 1965, to 32 percent in 1971.[10] This, again, may emphasize primarily the relatively faster development of housing in the South and the West, which seems to mean primarily the Southwest. The number of new one-family houses sold (not limited to FHA-insured houses) actually dropped in the Northeast and North Central States, where air conditioning is less important, between 1965 and 1971. Over the same period, sales of one-family houses in the South and West rose by approximately 30 percent and 40 percent, respectively.

The room count of one-family homes insured by the FHA also

changed over the same period, probably in response to changes in family composition. Three bedroom units lost in popularity, while four bedroom units gained, as did two bedroom units, though less dramatically. Naturally, the greater the number of rooms, the greater the number of bathrooms. Despite the fact that the average room count of FHA-insured one-family homes rose by about 5 percent between 1965 and 1971 (5.7 rooms to 6 rooms), the average total improved floor area rose by only 3 percent (1228 square feet to 1268 square feet).[11] The average square footage figure of improved floor areas runs far higher than the square footage of the average British home.

Under the pressure of costs that rise faster than income, some reassessment of housing specifications would seem to be required, but there has been none. In Britain, all housing standards have been reassessed and assembled under the general heading of the Parker-Morris Standards. Yet the life-styles in America have changed drastically since many current room-size standards, for example, were set down more than thirty years ago. The assumptions about kitchen space, for example, on which the Committee on the Hygiene of Housing of the American Public Health Association based recommendations that later became embodied in law or department regulations, are no longer generally valid. Because housing costs can be closely correlated with square footage (provided that some extraordinary items like elevators are left out of the calculation), a review of the standards should be mandated. Is there anything wrong with double-decker bunks, for example, in a bedroom shared by two young sons? Does the kitchen of the modern home require a table on which the housewife can roll her pie dough with a rolling pin?

One major obstacle to any serious revaluation downward of housing standards is that ancient bugaboo of American life, the brilliant contrast between the assumptions of an egalitarian society and the facts of a grossly nonegalitarian distribution of capital and income. One way in which to facilitate the review of housing standards for the relatively low-income family is to do something about the excessive elaboration of housing quality for the wealthy. Not only are new homes of the wealthy displayed for all the rest of the population to wonder at, not only does the display undermine any attempt to diminish housing standards generally, but the income tax laws, in effect, subsidize it.

The Internal Revenue Code permits any taxpayer to deduct from gross income almost all forms of interest paid without any limit as to a fixed dollar amount or a ratio of total income. This practice has been drawing heavy fire from a number of housing commentators, notably

Henry Aaron, who, writing for the Brookings Institution, has concluded that rental tenants are unfairly treated in comparison with homeowners who are, in his view, subsidized by the income deductibility of home mortgage interest and local real estate taxes.[12] Whether or not one accepts his figures, which perhaps inadequately evaluate the indirect tax benefits of tenants, and argues as well that homeownership is a socially desirable state of affairs deserving of tax encouragement, it is clearly inequitable that there is no limit whatsoever on the deductibility of mortgage interest. Elaborate homes are encouraged because the high-income owners need invest only a small part of their own funds, while the impact of the interest cost of borrowed money is substantially reduced by its deductibility. Certainly, a dollar limit should be legislated on the amount of interest on home mortgages that can be deducted on gross income on a single, personal tax return. This measure should be accompanied by a serious federal government review of housing standards.

The third element in the reduction of resources used in housing refers to the maintenance and operations of the housing after it is completed. Here the main emphasis must be on the urban apartment house in which operating expenses have been rising at a far faster rate than the increase in the median income. The Bureau of Labor Statistics, completing a survey of New York City apartment houses, noted that an index of operating costs—labor, fuel, taxes, insurance, contract services—that had stood at one hundred in 1968, had reached one hundred fifty five years later.[13]

No one seems to have systematically studied apartment house operations, but it is clear that as the buildings have become more complicated, a steady trend, they have not merely cost more to build, but more to run. When the old tenement houses of New York City were constructed in the 1870s, the buildings lacked heat, running water in each apartment, and electricity, to say nothing of other systems such as air conditioning, subsequently invented. The addition of a heating system involves not only the capital costs of the boiler, piping, and radiators (to take the model of a steam or hot-water system) but the monthly cost of fuel, too. It involves the maintenance of all this equipment, and the overhead costs of ordering fuel and checking bills, and of insuring the boiler and perhaps adjusting the insurance rate on the building because of the new system.

The systems involved in modern apartment houses grow steadily more complex, stimulated in part by the new concern for the protection of the environment. Incinerating garbage is more expensive than simply stuffing it into cans; incinerating it with high-temperature smoke-reducing units is still more expensive. Compaction, still more. The Department of Housing and Urban Development now demands that FHA-insured urban housing in noisy areas must provide central air conditioning and double-paned windows. These cost more money initially, and to run. A double-paned window is as easy to break as a single-paned window, and is much more expensive to replace. The internal transportation system provided in buildings over four-stories high by the electric elevator takes the place, in part, of a public transportation system, but the public makes no contribution to its operations and repair.

In discussing the urban apartment house, one must also place in the equation the demand by building service employees for a decent wage and good living conditions, an eventuality that no one took into account when building and housing standards for multistory buildings emerged. The result of these unforeseen developments has been so dramatic a rise in cost that the apartment house looks to be economically obsolete, except for wealthy or highly subsidized families. The imposition by the courts of new standards of fairness in dealing with the tenants, whether the owner is private or public, threatens to increase the cost of operations while it may, or may not, improve relationships between the owner and the tenant.

A further increase in operating cost has been mandated by those who insist that housing absorb the social problems of families who have been unable to adjust satisfactorily to the demands of urban life. Though many true believers claim that multiproblem families impose no special burden on public housing management, most public housing managers would disagree, maintaining not only that a few troubled and troublesome families can cause serious physical damage, but that their presence drives many responsible tenant families to leave.

Finally, it is discouraging to report, but must be said, that the cooperative form of ownership, which seemed to offer a solution to the management of large urban apartment houses by making common ground between the residents and the ownership, encounters limits to its usefulness. It was true, and remains so, that families that share a common bond of union membership, or of experience and background, or of belief, can operate a building for their own use at a cost below that experienced by a profit-motivated owner. In their perceived common interest, they have taken splendid care of the property they owned mutually. But experience with large new cooperative developments, filled by many families with little in common but the desire to turn up a housing bargain, are scarcely to be differentiated from owner-operated apartment houses lived in by unrelated tenants. In the large new cooperatives, there is a we and a they. The they may be the board of directors, or another tenant-cooperator faction trying to gain control of the board of directors. It makes little difference—in either case, the long-range interests of building maintenance suffer from the conflict.

Thus, the interest of conserving resources in housing maintenance and operations can be achieved only by proper initial design, which limits the maintenance systems that will require expensive attention over the years. It questions the construction of large apartment complexes in which all maintenance functions become professional, with high costs resulting. It urges that the provision of public services (like interior transportation) be considered as something other than a housing function, or alternatively, that the housing be designed so as not to require such transportation. It stresses the difficulties of dealing with multi-problem tenants and does not blink at the conclusion that some part of every city will remain a permanent slum for those who are beyond the reach of present reclamation services. And it suggests that small buildings in which a resident-owner performs part of the maintenance himself, without keeping track of the value of his own time (or perhaps, expecting that time to be paid for when he sells the house), should become a useful building type for the future.

Objective No. II—The Accumulation of Capital for Housing

Obviously, no partial economies in the use of land or the design and scale of housing will be sufficient to permit complacency as to the rate of capital accumulation that will be necessary for housing purposes. The projection of national housing need in 1968 at 26 million units over a ten-year period implies that a very substantial flow of money into housing will be required, as we have seen. We have also seen that the consumers who will use the housing capital, not to produce goods but simply to provide themselves with homes, are limited in the price that they can pay for the use of the capital. National policies must, therefore, be directed to ensure the flow of money into the institutions that make residential mortgage loans, to ensure that those institutions do, in fact, make mortgages, and to ensure that the mortgages thus written bear interest rates that do not place suitable housing outside the means of every American family who wants it.

To achieve the first of these objectives—to ensure the flow of funds into mortgage-making institutions—someone might suggest the wisdom of originating a new type of mortgage institution. In the 1920s, the savings and loan associations were badly needed, because the mutual savings banks were limited to a relatively small number of states, and the commercial banks did not regard mortgage making as their most interesting activity. At the present time, however, it is difficult to marshall much of a case for the need for a new type of savings intermediary that will make mortgage loans. Many advocates have been urging changes in the relationship between existing intermediaries and a reassessment of their powers and limitations; many suggestions have been made that would adjust or transform the relationship between intermediaries and both the Federal Reserve System and the Federal Home Loan Bank Board, but no one seems to be suggesting that a new type of institution be developed. Because both mutually owned and profit-motivated thrift institutions actively engage in mortgage lending, the only logical addition would appear to be some form of government depository that savers would place their money in and that would directly engage in mortgage lending. No one seems to be advocating this for the very substantial reason that the postal savings system, which once operated as a national savings bank owned by the government, has fallen into desuetude because of the competition from the private depositories. It is difficult to imagine a government savings institution that would operate with greater efficiency than the private institutions; it is equally difficult to believe that Congress would allow it special operating subsidies or other benefits that it would not offer to its private competitors. The experience of socialistic countries in having to prod people to save indicates that socialization of savings banks does not even eliminate the cost of advertising.

If it is unnecessary and perhaps unwise to form a new type of mortgage lender, the demand for mortgage funds must be met by facilitating the flow of money into the existing institutions. Here there is no shortage of suggestions. They fall under several different generic headings.

The first heading might be called Painless Practice, because it seems to hurt no one. The suggestions of this type urge, in one form or another, that savings intermediaries be encouraged in periods of tight money to borrow against their assets in a central bank. If the central bank must, in turn, borrow from the public the money that it would lend to the intermediaries, we have a system of definite but limited value that is already in effect for savings and loan associations. As we saw from the discussion of the savings and loan associations, some of the borrowed money will come directly from savings accounts in thrift institutions. To the extent that these are indeed its origins, it fails to add to the suply of loanable mortgage funds. Even if most of the money that the public uses to buy the obligations of the Federal Home Loan Bank Board comes from some source other than the thrift accounts of the savings and loan associations, the sale by the bank board of its obligations in large quantities at a time of money tightness adds pressure on to the demand side of the money market, pushing interest rates up, and tending to draw down deposit balances as savers shift into the new, higher-interest-bearing investments.

If, contrarily, the suggestion involves the extension of federal reserve credit to savings intermediaries, we have a slightly different suggestion, which infuses new money into the system through bank credit. This might be done directly, through a drastic revision of the relations between these institutions and the Federal Reserve System, or indirectly, as it has been on occasion in the past, through a commercial bank member of the Federal Reserve System. As an emergency measure, to meet demands for funds for withdrawals, the use of Federal Reserve System credit has merit; the major alternative that a savings intermediary has available—the selling of mortgages to the FNMA or the GNMA—requires that these institutions use funds that would otherwise be useful to encourage the origination of new mortgages. To the extent that the secondary market is used for emergency liquidity purposes, the available funds for new mortgages are reduced. This would send the agency—the FNMA or the GNMA—to market, with much the same results that would occur if the Federal Home Loan Bank Board went to market.

Nevertheless, the use of federal reserve credit poses certain risks. It immediately increases the money supply because the effect of the extension of credit is to increase the reserve account of the member bank through which the savings intermediary clears. If the reserves would promptly spread through the banking system, a process that, during a period of high demand (it is taken for granted that that is the period we are talking of, because money stringency, by definition, occurs only at such times), would help to raise prices. If, as some suggest, the savings intermediaries should be drawn into a closer, direct relationship with the Federal Reserve System so that they can borrow money from it by credit to their own reserve accounts, a significantly different banking system will have been designed. The savings and loan associations would resist a requirement to maintain reserves by virtue of their membership in the Federal Reserve System *and* in the Federal Home Loan Bank.

Some special relationship would have to be devised that would combine the two reserve banks in a more intimate embrace. One effect of such a marriage might well be a weakening of the special ties that bind the savings and loan associations, and perhaps the mutual savings banks, to the mortgage market. The ultimate effect might well offset the greater flexibility with which the savings institutions obtain credit help in a time of stress. Although the notion of a direct link between these institutions and the Federal Reserve Bank deserves study and exploration, the attractions remain largely limited to restoring liquidity when the thrift institutions are under withdrawal pressure. Nevertheless, because the fear of withdrawal pressure is the major inhibiting factor in the making of new mortgages in a time of stringency, anything that relieves the feeling of panic is worth analysis.

Another type of painless stimulant to mortgage money flows, not limited in its usefulness to periods of money stringency, involves adjusting the reserve requirements of member commercial banks in the Federal Reserve System. One type of adjustment would reduce reserve requirements for banks that place more than the stipulated percentage of their investments in residential mortgage loans. While such a proposal might be difficult to administer, and would require careful supervision so that it would not seriously threaten bank liquidity, it would seem to have some value in encouraging commercial bank members to make mortgage loans. It would, of course, only be effective with respect to the commercial banks: mutual savings banks and savings and loan associations, not being members of the reserve system, would not be reached by such a device. Similar tax advantages might be given to the commercial banks with respect to income earned on mortgage investment. In both these cases, however, the argument might be made that the effect of stimulating one type of mortgagee—the commercial bank—will be the discouragement of another type of mortgagee—the thrift institution. By making possible the payment of higher interest on thrift accounts, the proposals—both as to the reserve requirement and as to the taxation of income—might simply speed the flow of funds from the present mortgage institutions elsewhere.

The second set of suggestions for increasing the flow of mortgage funds might be called Painful Practice. These suggestions all involve a measure of compulsion: Their thrust is to *require* the investment of a certain part of the assets of any of the fiscal institutions in residential mortgage investments. Typically, union pension and welfare funds have been selected as examples of the financial intermediaries that place little money in the residential mortgage market. The suggestion frequently takes the form of urging the passage of a law that would demand the placement in residential mortgages of, say, 10 percent of each welfare fund's assets.

In commenting on this suggestion, one notes that it has obsolesced. The development of mortgage-backed obligations by the GNMA, and the issuance of many series of notes and other obligations by the FNMA, have provided welcome vehicles for pension fund investment in mortgages. Those who have generally made this suggestion in the past tended to underestimate the complexities of direct mortgage investment. As we have seen, even FHA-insured mortgages expose the lender to a small measure of risk and offer their greatest potential profit to the originator who services them. Although, conceivably, a group of pension funds might, under the pressure of legislation, form a jointly owned mortgage investment entity serving all of them, the GNMA and the FNMA are effectively filling that role and providing guaranteed safety as well.

But even if the issuance of mortgage-backed securities had not brought the pension and welfare funds into the mortgage market, there would be objections to any significant program that would force pension and welfare funds (or any other class of intermediary) to invest in a specific instrument. One must assume for the plainest of reasons that the instrument is itself not attractive. If it were attractive, the compulsion would not be necessary. To the extent that it is not attractive, it must, over the long run at any rate, either offer only a lower return than other instruments or involve a greater risk.

To the extent that it involves a lower yield, the requirement that funds invest in it amounts to a hidden tax on the beneficiaries of those funds. If Congress feels like taxing the pension funds, it might better do so openly; and if it is serious about helping housing, it could earmark the tax funds collected for the purpose of subsidizing mortgage carrying charges on behalf of residents of low or moderate income.

If, on the other hand, the managers of pension funds decide that they require a stipulated rate of return on their entire portfolio, the penalty of having to buy mortgages will lead them to look elsewhere for higher-yield and perhaps higher-risk investments. To an immeasurable extent, perhaps large, perhaps small, this may encourage a wasteful use of capital. It is a fact that housing output depends not only on the amount of mortgage money available—although that surely is the major criterion—but on the general prosperity in the economy, on the development of high technology for housing production and maintenance, and on adequate funding of all of the enterprises that take part in housing production. The imposition of a minimum limit of mortgage investment by each pension fund, furthermore, would tend to reduce the flexibility with which the housing industry responds to demand.

This is not to say that pension and welfare funds should not be more scrupulously supervised than at present. Many observers have noted that these vast concentrations of wealth are subject only to the most cursory supervision, and that the terms of participation in welfare funds should be carefully investigated. To the extent that the funds need fiscal supervision, the supervision should certainly be of the kind that the states and the federal government accord to the other financial institutions. It should not mandate a minimum investment in certain types of securities. The supervisors, rather, should mandate a maximum investment in other types, or specifically delineate which types of investments are forbidden altogether. It would seem that reasonable regulation of this kind would be most persuasive in leading to investment in the mortgage market through the purchase of mortgage-backed government securities, or in Federal Home Loan Bank Board obligations. It might also limit the emphasis on equity positions in common stocks that have been characteristic of many funds and that may have contributed to drastic changes, the ultimate shape of which remains unclear, in the securities market.

The same suggestion of legal minimum investment in residential mortgages that has been made for the pension and welfare funds has been made also for commercial banks with government tax balances. It has, for example, been suggested that the government withdraw its tax accounts from banks that fail to keep a stipulated minimum of their investments in FHA mortgages, or that Federal Deposit Insurance be denied to financial institutions that similarly fail to meet a legislated standard. As in the case of the pension funds, these proposals amount to a tax on the institutions in question: The requirement would be necessary only at times when the mortgages are less attractive than alternative investments.

Perhaps the fundamental difficulty with all proposals that force investment in the residential mortgage market is that they do not clearly distinguish between the needs of a more or less normal economy and those of an economy that is overstraining itself to meet demand at a specific time. To take care of ordinary times, the mortgage market needs little more than the certainty that its offerings will be as attractive as alternative investments. The market does need, and has provided itself with, emergency measures to assure a credit flow in times of extreme stringency. The two should not be confused, nor can the issue of mortgage flow be confused with a problem of the interest rate level in general, or the difference between the mortgage interest rate and the general interest rate at any specific time.

The third set of suggestions made for assuring a flow of funds into mortgages relies on the effort to make the mortgage investment more attractive to the financial intermediaries, and the mortgage-making financial intermediaries more attractive to the saving public.

We have already discussed the most familiar method of making thrift institutions attractive. Government regulations simply permit thrift institutions, which make mortgages, to pay slightly higher rates of interest on their deposits than commercial banks are permitted to pay. This differential is undoubtedly necessary, because the commercial banks are able to offer other services (checking accounts and personal consumer loans) that thrift institutions may not. But the ceilings themselves cause problems, as we have seen, when market interest rates soar above them, and lure depositors into making direct investments in short-term government obligations. Despite the differentiation, commercial banks have generally been able to increase their share of total household savings to 45 percent from the approximately 33 percent that had been maintained in the 1950s. In 1971 and 1972, however, when the credit crunch of 1970 had been overcome, savings institutions found themselves receiving a larger part of the total household savings.[14] It might be surmised that the experience of the high interest rates of 1970 had made savers more conscious of interest rates generally, and had made them quicker to take advantage of differences in rates between commercial banks and thrift institutions. This could have been expected to make them quicker once again to remove their money from deposit accounts and to reenter the government obligation market when the market shifted again, as in 1973. This, indeed, has happened.

A second proposal, which always comes up on behalf of thrift institutions, permits them to offer the same services as commercial banks and gives them wider latitude in making investments of their resources, so that higher yields might be achieved. The higher yields would enable them to pay higher interest rates to their depositors. By 1972, some states had already approved methods by which mutual savings institutions could permit third-party withdrawals, a substitute, within a limited geographic area, for demand deposit checking. New possibilities for transferring funds electronically loomed over the horizon, suggesting to thrift institution managers that the deposit leakage will become more severe if their institutions do not become part of the transfer network. If consumer finance and personal checking—or an electronic equivalent —become widespread among thrift institutions, together with the power to broaden significantly their investment portfolio, the deposit accounts of thrift institutions will grow, but not, perhaps, the amount of money that they actually put into mortgages. If the thrift institutions eventually become merged into the commercial banking industry, it would probably be necessary to start all over again with the development of new thrift institutions specializing in real estate mortgages.

Some people have suggested that the flows of savings into thrift insti-
the mortgage lender a share in the growth of value of the property on
tutions can be accelerated by recasting the mortgage instrument to give
which it is loaned. This would enable mortgage institutions to pass on significantly higher returns to their depositors in an inflationary era, which certainly seems to be the character of the present age. The proposal sounds plausible. With mortgage insurance, thrift institutions are advancing 90 percent or more of the cost of a house. If the owner lives in it for ten years and then sells the house for twice as much as he paid for it, why should the owner keep all of the increment while the institution that loaned him almost all of the money gets none?

From a practical point of view, the proposal becomes more difficult. There is the initial objection that the owner has, in fact, contributed to the ultimate sales price. He maintained the building, and may, indeed, have substantially improved it. The determination of the value of the improvements, and their relevance to the ultimate sales price, would probably cause endless confusion. Furthermore, the participation by the mortgage lender in the resale price of housing would have the effect of inflating all the costs of older buildings; an owner would need the benefit of a higher price if he were selling in the expectation of purchasing a different home. The difficulty of peacefully establishing a fair price grows as the interest of the mortgagee is added to that of the owner. Finally, the process would expose the owner to a great temptation to cheat, accepting part of the sales consideration in some other form than a cash payment made in full view of the mortgagee. To sum up, the change in value results from inflationary conditions. If the selling owner intends to buy himself another house, he has in effect gained nothing from the increase in dollar value. If the owner held his house for rental income, the participation by the mortgagee in rents merely makes necessary the collection of higher rents to cover the same operating costs.

Another proposal for increasing the flow of money into mortgage institutions would use tax stimulus. This proposal would exempt the interest earned on thrift association deposit accounts from income tax, up to a stipulated maximum per return, provided that a stipulated minimum amount of institutional assets are invested in residential mortgages. While such a proposal would be fought by commercial banks, which would regard it as discriminatory, it seems fully as reasonable as offering a tax exemption to money similarly invested in the obligations of state and municipal housing agencies. The state and municipal housing agency bonds are purchased primarily by upper-income investors; a similar tax exemption to thrift institution account holders would extend the benefit to a moderate-income group. British and West German law offers similar tax advantages to those who make deposits in similar institutions—Building Societies in Britain and savings banks in Germany. The proposal would certainly accelerate deposit flows into the thrift institutions and encourage them to make mortgage loans in order that their depositors qualify for the tax relief.

A further suggestion has been made that the government not only grant tax exemption on the interest earned on thrift institution deposits but that the government pay a bonus to those making such deposits, the amount of the bonus to vary inversely with the income of the depositor. A similar scheme has been in use in West Germany. It merely extends the previous suggestion by offering further tax monies to stimulate savings for mortgage purposes. In effect, the promotional schemes put forward by savings banks and their competitors amount to the same thing, except that they are privately financed and discriminate between classes of customers. The premiums, in the form of merchandise, that are given to new bank customers are paid for ultimately by all of the customers, new and old; they—and various types of special dividend accounts—probably don't actually increase the amount of savings as much as they contribute to a confusing churning movement of money from one depository to another. The United States government has moved in to control the premiums given away by banks; surely, a government bonus plan that would affect the depositors as a whole, or that would differentiate between them reasonably on the basis of income, would make a great deal more sense.

Objective No. III—The Need for Effective
Assistance in Lowering Interest Rates

One implicit goal of increasing the supply of mortgage money is that of lowering the effective rate of mortgage interest. In the simplest terms, increasing the amount of money available for mortgage investment means that the mortgage lenders will be in competition to find use for their money. In the competition resulting from oversupply, prices—in this case manifested by the interest rate—drop.

Limiting the public policy interest in mortgages to the assurance of an adequate supply of mortgage money without considering the interest rate does not meet the major challenge to housing. There remain many families who need housing but who cannot afford its monthly cost at the interest rates current in the mortgage market. A number of suggestions have been made for reducing that interest rate. They can be divided into two classes—those that depend on what might be called jawboning—the placing of pressure on institutions making mortgages to persuade or force them to keep interest rates low—and those that provide governmental funds that bridge the gap between the housing cost —assuming high mortgage rates—and effective housing demand.

In the first category, we find the supporters of FHA mortgage interest rate ceilings: those who would pass usury laws, or require by law that lenders lend a stipulated part of their resources for low cost mortgages and those who suggest that the government, as a lender of last resort, make low interest rate mortgages directly, whenever the mortgage rate exceeds 6 percent per annum.

We might discuss the last of these first. Certainly, whenever no banking institution is prepared to make mortgage loans in any part of the country, a government lender should be available. But he relies on myth that would suggest that the government can lend money at below-market interest rates without incurring any expense because it is *the* government. If the government is to step in as a primary lender, it will require vast funds that could not reasonably be produced from tax revenues. Funds would be borrowed, just as the present government institutions in the secondary mortgage market now borrow such funds. The tax cost would be the difference between the interest actually paid by the government on its borrowings and the interest that it would charge on its mortgages, perhaps as little as zero percent, which is Swedish practice on government second mortgage loans. To the extent that the government would make mortgage loans systematically at a below-market interest rate, it would compete very successfully with existing mortgage institutions. It would have to build up its own lending agency, with its own staff, and because it would go out into the market to borrow money, the most likely lenders would be the very institutions that ordinarily would be lending mortgage money directly. With much less effort, they would invest their funds in government bonds, letting the government do the job of deciding which mortgage borrowers are good and which are bad.

Similar conditions obstruct the usefulness of all the schemes that demand that a low rate of interest be charged on mortgage loans. The fact is that mortgage money will always flow to the place where it will get the highest return. The direction of that flow is ultimately not under the control of the managers of the mortgage-making institutions but under the control of the individual savers. If the government believes in the wisdom of allocating resources to housing people who cannot afford decent homes at market interest rates, it must pay for such a program. It has two choices in designing the subsidy pattern. It can develop, as we noted above, its own mortgaging institution, or it can, as heretofore, use the existing privately owned, publicly regulated organs of the money market, and put the subsidies into that system.

Even if it floats its own bonds to set up its own mortgaging institution, it must in the end rely on the private market to absorb the bonds. Unless the government had substantial proof of the corruption of the bond-selling system by collusive practices, a state of affairs that would affect more than the housing industry, the existing system should be utilized. This does not mean that using it avoids all problems. Any scheme for subsidizing housing costs must deal with the question of what are reasonable interest rates, because the size of a reasonable interest rate will determine the size of the subsidy. One should be able to fix a reasonable mortgage interest rate with reference to the Federal Reserve System discount rate at any time.

If that base has been established, and if appropriate measures have been taken to minimize the resources needed for housing, there remain two alternatives for the subsidy flow. It can run to the ultimate consumer, or it can run to the producers of housing, including the mortgagee as well as the builder and the owner, in the case of rental housing.

Lately, much has been made of the possibility of providing special allowances to families with incomes below a stipulated figure, who will then be able to rent housing in the unassisted private market. What happens if they choose not to use the money for housing but continue to demand good housing in any case? What happens if they use the money for housing, but cannot get good housing? Will the existence of such allowances stimulate housing producers to invest time and money in housing, although there can be no assurance that the allowances will continue over the period needed to recoup the owner's initial investment? Is it possible that the allowance-assisted families will be able to (or wish to) distribute themselves throughout the general housing population? Will they not tend to concentrate, as now, in those sections and neighborhoods that provide the services they need?

These questions suggest that income segregation will tend to continue despite housing allowances and that allowances will not stimulate the construction needed to provide decent homes for those whose incomes are not now sufficient to afford it.

Yet the allowance proposal is based on an essential insight: For many families, the gap between housing cost and family means is too great to be bridged by housing production subsidies alone. Their problem is not so much a housing problem (surely not so much a housing problem if mortgage interest rates are to be openly subsidized and housing standards made more economical) as it is an income problem. If the United States is unable to adopt an income program that will ensure that every American family will have the basic means to a fair standard of living, there is no hope whatever of solving the housing problem for what might be called the residual poor. This applies with special force to those low-income families who live in the city, and whose rents incorporate what in a less highly developed environment would be public costs.

The costs of public housing operations include costs that otherwise are absorbed by the city, such as policing, garbage collection, the operation and maintenance (if not the original capital costs) of the internal elevator system, and the social services, such as they are, provided for troubled families. It is also the public housing tenants who have had to pay for the whole fairness system, which assures that tenants are selected in the proper order of priority, that eviction procedures meet the standards set for public housing by the federal courts, and that waiting lists for entry are scrupulously kept. As the original public housing theory that tenants could pay for the maintenance of buildings has broken down, the Brooke and Sparkman amendments to the public housing law have provided a modicum of subsidy for the projects. But no one has as yet been willing to classify the costs of operation.

If the multiple-family apartment house, served by elevators, providing garbage collection, and requiring special policing, costs more to operate than do one- or two-family homes in the suburbs, the added costs should not really be charged against the tenancy but against the whole social order that has made urban living the final resting place, one fears, of poor families who lack the capability—perhaps by their own fault, perhaps not—to become part of the unionized working class.

Once a basically adequate income program has been developed, and the extraordinary services provided in urban housing are charged to the proper account, it is possible to look once again at mortgage interest rates. Then a program for reducing them can be developed. It might be blind—applying by subsidy to all mortgage interest rates or, like the GNMA's special assistance program, applying under certain circumstances to certain classes of mortgage by reducing the discount. Or it might be specifically aimed at individual families, scaled precisely (and, one surmises, requiring an impossible administrative detail) to the needs of each household.

What cannot be hoped is that by some natural event, or by force of argument, interest rates will decline to the point at which no special subsidies will be needed, even for families who have had their incomes raised to a sound minimum. The type of housing makes a tremendous difference; it is fruitless to expect that urban nonworking families can live successfully in a free-standing one-family-home neighborhood where every household must have its car. There is little hope that the nonworking fatherless family can make the repairs that are necessary to keep a one-family house going.

But even beyond this, it is hopeless to expect that mortgage interest rates can be segregated from interest rates generally in the money market. Interest rates reflect the demand for capital, and this reflects the demand for resources. Those who believe that American society already consumes too many resources, and that a slower rate of consumption is desirable, probably also believe that the lower demand for resources would mean lower interest rates, capital having lost its importance. The trouble with this policy is that if capital is not in demand, we have less than full employment, considerably less. Without full employment, we do not get the resources specifically needed to construct housing, or to employ those who need the housing.

All projections of a satisfactory housing output are based on a full-employment economy—a phrase that has hidden elasticity. How many people may be unemployed before the economy loses its qualifying phrase, full employment? But if it is necessary to accept a measure of price inflation to assure at least a reasonable facsimile of a full-employment economy, then it is also necessary to help, by transfer payments, however these may be labeled, those who lack a continuing and expandable claim on the resources of the economy. This, after all, is the moral of the money market: Government has the right to flout its allocations, but only if it is willing to pay for it.

NOTES

Chapter 1

1. Allan A. Twitchell, "Measuring the Quality of Housing in Planning for Urban Development," in *Urban Redevelopment Problems and Practices*, ed. Coleman Woodbury (Chicago: University of Chicago Press, 1953), p. 13.

Chapter 2

1. U.S. Dept. of HUD, *1971 HUD Statistical Yearbook* (Washington, D.C.: U.S. Government Printing Office, 1972), table 353, p. 324.

2. Richard M. Nixon, *Message . . . Transmitting the Fourth Annual Report on National Housing Goals, Pursuant to Section 1603 of the Housing and Urban Development Act of 1968* (Washington, D.C.: U.S. Government Printing Office, 1973), pp. 13, 57–63.

3. Ibid., p. 10.

4. "Report from the Office of Economic Research," *Federal Home Loan Bank Board Journal* 6, No. 4 (April 1973): 7.

5. U.S. Dept. of HUD, *1972 HUD Statistical Yearbook* (Washington, D.C.: U.S. Government Printing Office, 1973), pp. 166, 363.

6. To encourage capital investment, Congress has provided that income from capital gains be taxed at about one-half the rate at which other income—say, salaries—is taxed. Further, there is a maximum rate of about 30 percent.

Chapter 3

1. *Report of the Commission on Mortgage Interest Rates to the President of the United States and to the Congress,* August 1969 (Washington, D.C.: U.S. Government Printing Office, 1969), p. 2.

2. U.S. Department of Housing and Urban Development, *1972 HUD Statistical Yearbook* (Washington, D.C.: U.S. Government Printing Office, 1973), p. 165.

3. Julian H. Zimmerman, *The FHA Story in Summary 1934–1959* (Washington, D.C.: U.S. Government Printing Office, 1959), pp. 13, 17.

4. Glanvil, the earliest recorder of the common law, wrote about mortgages in the twelfth century. See 2 Pollock and Maitland, *History of English Law,* 118.

5. David J. Levidow, "Mortgage Law—Its History and Development," unpublished (1964), p. 12 ff.

6. Ibid., p. v.

7. Ibid., p. i.

8. Ibid., p. v.

Chapter 4

1. Housing and Urban Development Act of 1968, Title XVI.
2. For example, when veterans needed housing the result was the Housing (production) Act of 1948.
3. U.S. Department of Commerce, Bureau of the Census, *U.S. Census of Population and Housing 1960: Census Tracts,* Final Report PHC (1)–104, Part 1 (Washington, D.C.: U.S. Government Printing Office, 1972), p. 7.
4. Ibid.
5. William G. Grigsby, "Housing Markets and Public Policy," in *Urban Renewal, the Record and the Controversy,* ed. James Q. Wilson (Cambridge, Mass.: MIT Press, 1966), p. 26.
6. U.S. Department of Commerce, Bureau of the Census, *Census of Population and Housing 1970: General Demographic Trends for Metropolitan Areas, 1960 to 1970* (Washington, D.C.: U.S. Government Printing Office, 1971), p. 16.
7. U.S. Department of Commerce, Bureau of the Census, *Housing Special Reports,* Series H-46 No. 1 (Washington, D.C., 1946), p. 12.
8. Idem., *General Demographic Trends 1960–1970,* p. 16.
9. See the *Encyclopedia Britannica Atlas* for density figures.
10. Richard M. Nixon, *Message . . . Transmitting the Fourth Annual Report on National Housing Goals, Pursuant to Section 1603 of the Housing and Urban Development Act of 1968* (Washington, D.C.: U.S. Government Printing Office, 1973), p. 104.
11. Ibid., p. 73.
12. Ibid.
13. Ibid., p. 99.
14. Ibid.
15. U.S. Savings and Loan League, *Fact Book 1971,* p. 9.
16. Nixon, *Message,* pp. 52–92.
17. Ibid., p. 52.

Chapter 5

1. Federal Reserve Bank of Richmond, *Readings on Money* (pamphlet), 6th ed., 1967, p. 19.
2. Federal Deposit Insurance Corporation, *Call Reports* (Washington, D.C., 1971).
3. Ibid.
4. Board of Governors, *The Federal Reserve System,* 5th ed. (Washington, D.C., 1963), p. 26.
5. Ibid., p. 27.
6. Ibid., pp. 196–197.
7. Interest payments are deductible from net income which (for large corporations) is taxed at about 52 percent.

Chapter 6

1. Richard M. Nixon, *Message . . . Transmitting the Fourth Annual Report on National Housing Goals, Pursuant to Section 1603 of the Housing and Urban Development Act of 1968* (Washington, D.C.: U.S. Government Printing Office), pp. 66–68. In fact, commercial bank real estate loans were projected to surpass insurance

company mortgage holdings and to become the second largest source of real estate capital.

2. Ibid., p. 66.

3. National Association of Mutual Savings Banks, *1973 National Fact Book of Mutual Savings Banking* (New York, 1973), p. 27.

4. U.S. Department of Housing and Urban Development, *1971 HUD Statistical Yearbook* (Washington, D.C.: U.S. Government Printing Office, 1972), p. 176; Nixon, *Message,* pp. 10, 12.

5. Association of Mutual Savings Banks, *1973 National Fact Book,* p. 31.

6. Ibid., pp. 26, 52–53.

7. In dollar terms: Nixon, *Message,* p. 13.

8. National Association of Mutual Savings Banks, *1971 National Fact Book of Savings,* 1971, p. 53.

Chapter 7

1. National Association of Mutual Savings Banks, *1972 National Fact Book of Mutual Savings Banking* (Washington, D.C., 1972), p. 14.

2. Ibid.

3. Ibid.

4. Ibid.

5. Ibid., p. 13.

6. "Regulation Q" established these interest limits. For more detail, see *Report of the President's Commission on Financial Structures and Regulation* (Washington, D.C.: Government Printing Office, 1971), p. 23 ff.

7. Association Mutual Savings Banks, *1972 Fact Book,* p. 14.

8. Ibid. (This is in dollar terms.)

9. Ibid. (The year was 1969.)

10. Ibid., p. 41.

11. Ibid., p. 27.

12. Ibid., p. 32.

13. Ibid.

14. Ibid., pp. 14, 27.

15. Ibid.

16. Ibid.

17. Ibid., p. 29.

18. Ibid.

19. Ibid.

20. Ibid., p. 56.

21. Ibid.

22. United League of Savings Associations, *'74 Savings and Loan Fact Book* (Chicago, 1974), p. 9.

23. Ibid.

24. Association and Mutual Savings Banks, *1972 National Fact Book,* p. 17.

25. Ibid., p. 20.

26. Ibid., p. 15.

27. League of Savings Associations, *Fact Book,* p. 54.

28. Ibid., p. 15.

29. Association of Mutual Savings Banks, *1973 National Fact Book,* p. 24.

30. Ibid., p. 36.

31. Ibid., p. 39.

32. *Report of the President's Commission on Financial Structure and Regulation* (Washington, D.C.: Government Printing Office, 1971).

Chapter 8

1. United League of Savings Associations, *'74 Savings and Loan Fact Book* (Chicago, 1974), p. 53. In fact, by this time, S and L's are probably the second largest percentage date on mortgages: Ibid., p. 96.

2. See Note 12, Chapter 7.

3. League of Savings Associations, *'74 Fact Book*, pp. 35, 53.

4. Ibid., p. 37.

5. Ibid., p. 40.

6. Ibid., p. 55. The average assets per capita figure was $1298.

7. Ibid., p. 67.

8. Ibid., p. 79.

9. United League of Savings Associations, *'73 Savings and Loan Fact Book* (Chicago, 1973), p. 59.

10. Ibid., pp. 56, 59.

11. Ibid.

12. National Association of Mutual Savings Banking (Washington, D.C., 1972), p. 14.

13. League of Savings Associations, *'74 Fact Book*, p. 144.

14. Ibid., p. 114.

15. Association of Mutual Savings Banks, *1973 National Fact Book*, p. 12.

16. Ibid., p. 36; *1971 National Fact Book*, Section "Federal Government Agencies."

17. Federal Home Loan Bank Board, *Thirty-seventh Annual Report* (Washington, D.C.: 1969), p. 55.

18. League of Savings Associations, *'74 Fact Book*, p. 58.

19. Idem., *'72 Fact Book*, p. 15.

20. Ibid.

21. This is consistent with the behavior of other assets during the deflation of 1930 and after.

22. League of Savings Associations, *'74 Fact Book*, p. 53.

23. Association of Mutual Savings Banks, *'73 National Fact Book*, p. 12.

24. League of Savings Associations, *'74 Fact Book*, p. 15.

25. Ibid.

26. Ibid.

27. Loan Bank Board, *Thirty-seventh Annual Report*, p. 43.

28. Ibid.

29. James A. Coles, "The Federal Home Loan Bank System," *Federal Home Loan Bank Board Journal*, Vol. 5, No. 4 (April 1972): 26.

30. Ibid., p. 25.

31. Title I of the Emergency Home Finance Act of 1970; Part 527 (new), FHLB Regulations Sec. 545.6–1(a)(6), March 1971.

Chapter 9

1. United League of Savings Associations, *'72 Savings and Loan Fact Book* (Chicago, 1972), p. 53.

2. Institute of Life Insurance, *1971 Life Insurance Fact Book* (New York, 1971), p. 68.

3. Ibid., p. 82.

4. Guttentag and Beck, *New Series on Home Mortgage Yields since 1951* (New York: National Bureau of Economic Research, 1970), p. 5.

5. Institute of Life Insurance, *1971 Life Insurance Fact Book*, p. 85.

6. Raymond Vernon, "A Sceptic Looks at the Balance of Payments," *Foreign Policy*, No. 5 (Winter 1971–72): 52.

7. Guttentag and Beck, *New Series*, p. 51.

8. Ibid.

9. Ibid.

10. Ibid.

11. Ibid.

12. Ibid.

13. Ibid., pp. 53–54.

14. Ibid., p. 58.

15. Ibid., p. 60.

16. Ibid., pp. 101–103.

17. Ibid., p. 103.

18. Ibid.

19. Institute of Life Insurance, *1971 Life Insurance Fact Book*, p. 80.

20. Ibid.

21. Louis Winnick, *Rental Housing* (New York: McGraw-Hill, 1958).

22. Institute of Life Insurance, *1973 Life Insurance Fact Book*, p. 84.

23. Chapter 845 of the Laws of 1942, McKinney's Unconsolidated Laws, Secs. 3401–3426, repeal effective 3/1/62.

24. Guttentag and Beck, *New Series*, p. 108.

25. Ibid.

Chapter 10

1. Saul B. Klaman, *The Postwar Rise of Mortgage Companies* (New York: National Bureau of Economic Research, 1959).

2. Ibid., p. 48.

3. Robert Deforest and Laurence Veiller, *The Tenement House Problem*, V.I. (1903).

4. Public Relations Committee of the Mortgage Bankers' Association, *If Mortgage Banking Isn't Banking, What Is It?* (Washington, D.C., 1971), p. 1.

5. Ibid.

6. Klaman, *The Postwar Rise*, p. 7.

Chapter 11

1. The Limited Dividend Housing Companies Law of 1926.

2. Chapter 407 of the Laws of 1955, repealed by Chapter 803 of the Laws of 1962 (which is not dissimilar).

3. See Article 12-A of Public Housing Law, as added by Chapter 671 of 1960, as repealed by Chapter 803 of the Laws of 1961.

4. Chapter 803, Laws of 1961, effective 3/1/62.

5. Article XII, Secs. 650–67. Private Housing Finance Law Chapter 551, Laws of 1971.

6. A.C.I.R., *State Action on Local Problems 1971* (Washington, D.C., 1972), p. 5.

7. Bureau of National Affairs, *Housing and Development Reporter* (Washington, D.C., 1973), p. 50:0017.

8. *New York State Housing Finance Agency Annual Report 1971*, p. 5.

9. W. H. Morton and Co., *The Bond Buyer's Municipal Finance Statistics* 10 (April 1972): 17.

10. Ibid.

Chapter 12

1. 12 United States Code 1702 (1934).
2. 38 U.S. Code 1801 *et. seq.* (1944).
3. *Report of the Commission on Mortgage Interest Rates to the President of the U.S. and to the Congress* (Washington, 1969).
4. 42 U.S. Code 1401 *et. seq.*
5. Section 221 of the National Housing Act, 12 U.S.C. 1715 (1).
6. Amendment P.L. 90–448 to U.S.C. 1715, Sections 235 and 236.
7. See, for example, Brian Boyer, *Cities Destroyed for Cash: The FHA Scandal at HUD* (Washington, D.C.: Follet, 1973).
8. Julian H. Zimmerman, *The FHA Story in Summary 1934–1959* (Washington, D.C., 1959), pp. 13–14.
9. Ibid., p. 19.
10. U.S. Dept. of HUD, *1972 HUD Statistical Yearbook* (Washington, D.C.: U.S. Government Printing Office, 1972), p. 281.
11. Ibid.
12. Ibid., p. 284.
13. Ibid., p. 292.
14. They only exceeded 2 percent on a few occasions. Ibid., p. 204.
15. Dept. of HUD, *1972 Yearbook,* p. 276.
16. U.S. Dept. of HUD, *1971 HUD Statistical Yearbook* (Washington, D.C.: U.S. Government Printing Office, 1971), p. 120.

Chapter 13

1. Carl Burke, *Background and History 1970–FNMA* (Washington, D.C., 1971), p. 7.
2. U.S. Dept. of HUD, *1972 HUD Statistical Yearbook* (Washington, D.C., Government Printing Office, 1972), p. 368.
3. Hunter, *Background and History 1970,* p. 2.
4. Ibid.
5. Ibid., p. 3.
6. Ibid.
7. Ibid., p. 4.
8. Harry Bivens, *Background and History 1938–69 FNMA* (Washington, D.C., 1970), p. A–6.
9. Barke, *Background and History 1970,* p. 50.
10. Ibid.
11. Ibid.
12. Ibid.
13. Ibid.
14. Public Law 83–560 (1954).
15. Barke, *Background and History 1970,* p. 50.

Chapter 14

1. In 1974 you could buy a share of "FedNMt" for from 11-⅛ to 20-¾ dollars.
2. These include housing for: disaster areas, Guam, neighborhood conservation, Alaska, defense areas, coops, the elderly. Section 203(b), 203(i), or 222 of under $10,000, Section 221(d)(3), Section 233 Experimental Housing, Indian housing, Rent Supplement housing, NASA/AEC employees, Servicemen's Readjustment Act Housing.

3. *GNMA Annual Report* (Washington, 1970), p. 8.
4. *GNMA Annual Report* (Washington, 1972), p. 10.
5. *GNMA Annual Report*, 1972, p. 11.
6. Ibid.
7. Ibid., p. 7.
8. Ibid., p. 9.

Chapter 15

1. U.S. Department of Commerce, Bureau of the Census, *1970 Census of Population and Housing* (Washington, D.C.: U.S. Government Printing Office, 1971), p. 16.
2. Ibid.
3. Ibid.
4. Bureau of Labor Statistics, *Consumer Price Index for Urban Wage Earners and Clerical Workers U.S. City Average: Shelter* (1967 = 100), 1955–67.
5. Idem., *Consumer Price Index for Urban Wage Earners and Clerical Workers U.S. City Average: Shelter* (1967 = 100), 1968–1971.
6. U.S. Dept. of HUD, *1972 HUD Statistical Yearbook* (Washington, D.C.: U.S. Government Printing Office, 1972), p. 213.
7. Ibid., pp. 344–345.
8. Ibid.
9. Ibid., p. 213.
10. Ibid., p. 213 ff.
11. Ibid., p. 213.
12. Henry Aaron, "Income Taxes and Housing," *The American Economic Review*, Vol. 60, No. 5 (December 1970).
13. Bureau of Labor Statistics, *1973 Price Index of Operating Costs for Rent Stabilized Apartment Houses in NYC* (1973), p. 3.
14. United League of Savings Associations, *Savings and Loan Fact Book* (1972), p. 14.

INDEX

Aaron, Henry, 220
Accounts receivable financing, 66–67
Advance commitments in mortgage banking, 146
Air conditioning, 218, 221
Alaska, 36, 139
Amalgamated Bank of New York, 62
Amalgamated Clothing Workers Union, 62
American Public Health Association, 219
Amortization: apartment house mortgages and, 31; depreciation allowances and, 17; income tax credits and, 16; interest rate changes and, 30–31; mortgage debt size and, 17; release of sellers in transfer of, 25; self-amortizing, see Self-amortizing mortgages; size of repayments under, 29–31
Apartment houses: amortization schedules for, 31; availability of, 41; capital gains in sale of, 17–18; cooperative, see Cooperative apartment houses; development of, 18–19; elevator costs in, 5, 221; financing of, 13, 16, 42; garbage collection costs in, 5; life insurance companies and, 128–135; maintenance operations in, 43–44, 133–134, 220–221; mutual nonprofit ownership of, 95; mutual savings banks and, 101; rental percentages for, 24; savings and loan associations and, 108; tenant movement and, 133; useful life of, 40
Appraisers, real estate, 28, 85–86
Apprenticeship program in trade unions, 49
Architects and architecture, 10, 26
Asbestos products manufacture, 53

Asphalt tile manufacture, 53
Auctions of FHA mortgages, 193–197
Automobiles: dependence on, 210, 212; loans for, 66

Bank of England discount rate, 30
Banknotes, 59, 187
Banks, see Commercial banks; Mutual savings banks; Savings and loan associations; Thrift institutions
Bathrooms, and construction costs, 42
Beck, Morris, 122, 125, 126, 127
Belgium, 36, 52
Blacks: building trade unions and, 48; credit worthiness of, 24; in New York City apartment developments, 129–130, 132–133; political problems and housing for, 39; public housing densities and, 47
Bonds, in construction loans, 91; of housing authorities; individual investment in, 8, 103, 107, 124–126, 162–163; of New York State agencies, 153–154, 157–158, 161; tax-exempt nature of, 159–163, 164
Bowery Savings Bank, New York City, 6, 98, 109–110
Bricks, importation of, 36, 52
Brookings Institution, 220
Bryan, William Jennings, 60
Building codes: concrete requirements in, 51; European housing and, 211; Federal Housing Administration and, 174–175; price of materials and, 52–53
Building materials, as housing resource, 35, 49–53

Building Societies (England), 230
Building trade unions, 48–49
Bureau of Domestic Commerce, 50
Bureau of Labor Statistics, 212, 220
Bureau of Standards, 53
Bureau of the Census, 50; housing standards of, 40–41; housing surveys of, 10, 210
Business mortgage retirement rates, 85–86

California, 80, 109, 111, 118
Call Reports of Federal Deposit Insurance Corporation, 68
Canada, 127
Capital gains: reforms in, 159, 161; rental property sales under, 17–18
Carrying charges in cooperatives, 105, 134
Census Bureau, see Bureau of the Census
Certificates of deposit, 64–65
Charter Act, 192, 198
Chase Manhattan Bank, New York City, 98–99
Checks, and money supply, 59–60
Chicago, 47, 73, 130, 133
China, 45
Cities: as service centers 216–217; subsidized housing location in, 47
Class, and housing choice, 4
Codes, see Building codes
Commercial banks, 85–92; assest (1970) of, 96; construction financing by, 90–91; determination of policy of, 66–68; Federal Deposit Insurance Corporation and, 113; Federal Housing Administration and, 169; Federal National Mortgage Association and, 195; Federal Reserve System and, 64, 68–73; interest rate regulation of, 80–81, 96–97, 115, 228; money supply and, 62–65; 121; mortgage banks and, 146, 186; mortgage investment by, 6–7, 68, 108; mutual savings banks and, 96, 97–99; as national lenders, 126; percentage of savings in, 56; policies for changes in, 228–229; Real Estate Investment Trusts and, 88–89; reserves maintained by, 64–65; total loans and investments (1971) of, 68; treasury bill investment by, 65–66; warehousing of mortgages by, 87–88
Commitment fees, for Federal National Mortgage Association, 189, 194–195, 196
Committee on the Hygiene of Housing, 219
Common law theory of mortgages, 32
Competition: among banks, 97–99; in concrete industry, 51–52; among life insurance companies, 123–124; price of materials and, 52

Concrete, in construction, 50–52
Condominiums: debt-to-value ratio for, 16; equity requirements for, 33
Congress: deposit-insurance legislation in, 113; federal agencies and, 99; Federal National Mortgage Association and, 191, 193; Federal Reserve System and, 68; Government National Mortgage Association and, 198, 199, 200, 202, 203; housing goals set by, 4, 38, 47; mortgage rates regulated by, 105, 106; mutual savings banks and, 102; savings and loan associations and, 115, 120; tax reforms before, 158, 160
Construction costs: inflation and, 152; utility package and, 41–42
Construction labor, as housing resource, 47–48
Construction mortgage financing: by commercial banks, 67, 90–91; by mortgage bankers, 139
Construction Review, 50
Consumer advocates, and tenants, 44
Consumer goods: environmental conservation and demand for, 213–214; savings and, 57
Consumer loans, 66
Conventional mortgages: life insurance companies and, 127–128; mortgage bankers and, 139
Cooperative apartment houses: carrying charges in, 105, 134; debt-to-value ratio in, 16; equity requirements for, 33; Federal Housing Administration and, 167; limits to, 221–222
Corporate loans, 67–68
Corporate securities, 99, 163
Correspondent banks in corporate loans, 67–68
Costs: of adequate housing, 3–4; to builder, under governmental supervision, 157–158; building codes and, 52; land and, 45; operating, in apartment buildings, 220–221; percentage of income for, 212–213; of public housing operations, 233–234; savings for housing and, 57; shelter package and, 5; size of mortgage loan and, 27–28; of state lending agencies, 156–157; utility package and, 5, 41–42
Courts of Equity (England), 32
Currency, as Federal Reserve System asset, 70
Current Industrial Reports (Bureau of Census), 70
Customer relations of banks, 67

Dakota (apartment building), New York City, 40
Debt-to-value ratio in equity financing, 15–16

Index

Defense expenditures, and money supply, 61
DeForest, Robert, 141–142
Demand deposits: in commercial banks (1971), 68; in Federal Home Loan Bank, 112; as Federal Reserve System asset, 70, 73; money supply and, 59–60, 62
Density: of housing, 46; of population, 44–45, 161, 215
Department of Housing and Urban Development (HUD): air conditioning requirements of, 221; Federal National Mortgage Association and, 188; FHA mortgage premiums and, 170; FHA 236 programs and, 201, 202; housing surveys of, 10, 43; low-rent public housing and, 7; mortgage interest ceilings and, 199; subsidized housing criteria of, 47
Depletion allowances, 158, 161
Depreciation: double-declining-balance, 17–18; reforms in, 158–159, 161; recapture of, 18; straight-line, 16–17
Deteriorating housing, definition of, 40
Detroit, 177
Differential rates for mortgage interest, 23
Dilapidated housing, definition of, 40–41
Disaster housing, provisions for, 201
Discount rate in Federal Reserve System, 77–78, 89–90, 232
District of Columbia, 110
Domes, in housing construction, 49
Doomsday Book, 32
Double-declining-balance depreciation, 17–18
Dry Dock Savings Bank, New York City, 98

Earnings, see Income (personal)
Economic integration, 168
Educational institutions: housing choice and, 4, 211; land values and, 45; loans for, 106
Elevators in apartment houses, 5, 221
Energy industries, and environment, 53
England: amortization in, 30–31; Building Societies in, 230; common law theory of mortgages in, 32; gold standard in, 59; housing in, 211–212, 219; new towns in, 45–46, 215, 216; population density in, 45
Environmental standards: apartment houses and, 221; demand for consumer goods and, 213–214; housing materials and, 53; land use and, 46
Equitable Life Assurance (company), 133
Equity, 10–20; debt-to-value ratio in, 15–16; homeownership and, 33; life insur-

ance companies and, 128, 130, 135; nonprofit housing programs and, 19–20
Europe: gold standard in, 59; goods and services for house builders in, 36; housing in, 211–212, 217; population density in, 45

Factory assembly of housing components, 48
Family savings, 97
Faulkner, William, 10
Federal Deposit Insurance Corporation (FDIC): Call Reports of, 68; commercial banks and, 113; minimum investment legislation and, 227; mutual savings banks under, 96
Federal funds (reserves at Federal Reserve Banks), 73, 77
Federal Home Loan Banking System, 205; accounts in, 111–112; history of, 112–116; loans by, 112, 116–117; national lender defined by, 126; obligation system of advances in, 116–118; policies for change in, 223–226; savings and loan associations and, 110, 111, 112–120, 225; subsidies under, 119; variable rate mortgages under, 104
Federal Home Loan Mortgage Corporation (FHLMIC), 119, 205–206
Federal Housing Administration (FHA), 167–181; debt service subsidies under, 157; development of, 141, 183–184; Federal Home Loan Mortgage Corporation and, 206; Federal National Mortgage Association and, 182; local bonds insured by, 163; long-term mortgages developed by, 31; net losses of, 178; 221(d)3 programs of, 176, 192, 201; 235 and 236 programs of, 176, 201–202, 203
Federal Housing Administration (FHA) insured mortgages, 28, 167, 170; air conditioning requirements of, 221; auctions of, 193–197; commercial banks and, 86; changes in type of home under, 218–219; for construction, 91; default on, 192; Federal National Mortgage Association and, 185, 186, 187–191, 193–197; interest ceiling on, 74, 124, 171–174, 199, 231; life insurance companies and, 127–128, 135; mortgage bankers and, 139, 142–143, 144; nontransferability of, 184–185; percentage of income for, 212; for rehabilitation, 175
Federal National Mortgage Association (FNMA), 147, 182–197; assets (1971) of, 182; auctions held by, 193–197; construction loan insurance under, 91; Government National Mortgage Asso-

245

FNMA *(continued)*
ciation and, 198; 200, 201–202, 203, 207; tandem plan of, 201–202, 203
Federal Reserve Act of 1913, 85
Federal Reserve System: commercial banks and, 64, 68–73; discount rate of, 77–78, 89–90, 232; Federal Home Loan Bank System and, 118; interest rates and, 71–72, 73, 213, 232; money supply and, 55–56, 75, 76–78; money supply restriction by, 79–80, 99; money supply stimulation by, 78–79, 193; mutual savings banks and, 96; open market operations of, 78, 116, 197; policies for change in, 223–226; reserve requirements of, 76–77, 98; Treasury and, 69, 124, 125, 190, 213
Federal Savings and Loan Insurance Corporation (FSLIC), 110, 113
FHA, *see* Federal Housing Administration (FHA)
First National City Bank of New York, 98
FNMA, *see* Federal National Mortgage Association (FNMA·)
Fordham Hill (apartments), New York City, 130, 133
Forest Hills, Queens, New York City, housing dispute, 47
Forward commitments in mortgage banking, 146–147
France, 32
Fresh Meadows development, New York City, 130, 133
Full-employment economy, 234–235

Gage concept in common law theory of mortgages, 32
Garbage collection, and; housing costs, 5
Geographic factors: in antiusury laws, 22; in building trade union monopolies, 48–49; mortgage funds and, 13; in money supply, 80; in portland cement industry monopoly, 51–52
George, Henry, 45
Gold standard, 59
Golden Age apartment houses, 42
Government National Mortgage Association (GNMA), 198–208; Federal Housing Administration and, 178; Federal National Mortgage Association and, 186; local government bond guarantees under, 163; mortgage banking and, 105–106, 145, 147–148; policies for change in, 224, 226; special assistance programs of, 198, 199, 201, 208, 234
Government National Mortgage Corporation, 144
Governors of Federal Reserve System, 69

Great Britain, *see* England
Guam, 201
Guttentag, Jack, 122, 125, 126, 127
Gypsum products in housing construction, 50

Holy Roman Empire, 182
Home Owners' Loan Act (1933), 110
Home Owners Loan Corporation (HOLC), 183
Home Savings and Loan of California, 109
Homesteading grants in Alaska, 36
Hoover, Herbert, 182
Housing, 3–9; length of life of, 5–6; raising funds for, 7–9; as resource for further housing development, 35, 37–44; shelter provided by, 3–4, 5; social package in, 4–5; utility package in, 4, 5
Housing Act of 1949, Title I, 131
Housing and Home Finance Administration, 192
Housing authorities, and debt obligations, 176
Housing Development Corporation (New York City), 154–155
Housing Finance Agency (New York State), 153–154, 155, 156, 157–158, 163
Housing Opportunity Allowance Program, 119
HUD, *see* Department of Housing and Urban Development (HUD)

Imports of construction material, 36, 50, 52
Income (personal): credit worthiness and, 24; mortgage interest limits and, 74; percentage of, for housing (1965), 212; property maintenance and, 43; savings and, 55
Income tax: apartment house ownership and, 16, 19; depreciation deductions on, 16–17; interest deductions on, 13, 66, 219–220; savings interest under, 103
India, 36
Industry: environmental standards and, 53; new towns and, 215–217; zoning and, 215
Inflation: FHA programs and, 179; money supply and, 61; rent and, 152
Institute of Life Insurance, 121
Insurance: construction loan, 91; default, 14; Federal Deposit Insurance Corporation and, 96; mortgage, *see* Federal Housing Administration insured mortgages, Veterans Administration insured mortgages; savings and loan associations and, 110, 113; title, 26

Insurance companies, *see* Life insurance companies

Interest on loans: consumer loans, 66; for Federal Home Loan Bank System, 112, 116–117, 118; Federal Reserve System and, 56, 71–72, 73, 77; government obligations and, 66; on interbank loans, 73; life insurance policies and, 123; treasury bill sales as indicator of, 66

Interest on mortgages: amortization schedules and, 30–31; ceilings for, 22–23, 171–174, 199; costs of loan and, 27; credit worthiness and, 23–24; Department of Housing and Urban Development and, 199; differential rates for, 23, 104–105; Federal National Mortgage Association and, 197; Federal Reserve System and, 213; fluctuations in, 21–22; Government National Mortgage Association and, 199–200; housing costs and, 213; income tax deductions for, 13, 16, 219–220; limits on, 74; long-term mortgages and, 14, 29; mortgage debt size and, 17; policies for lowering, 231–232; safety objectives of lenders and, 23; self-amortizing mortgages and, 31; warehousing of mortgages and, 87–88

Interest on savings: bonds and, 163; certificates of deposit and, 65; income tax law and, 103, 230; regulation of, 80–81, 96–97, 115, 228; time accounts and, 64

Internal Revenue Service, 40, 103, 161

Jobs, and housing choice, 45, 211
Johnson, Lyndon B., 38, 175

Kennedy, John F., 125
Kitchen space standards, 219
Klaman, Saul, 122, 139–140, 142, 144
Korean War veterans, 171

Labor for housing industry, 35, 36, 47–49
Labor unions, *see* Unions
Lake Meadows project, Chicago, 130, 133
Land: automotive dependence and, 210; building and increase in value of, 15–16; as resource for housing, 35, 44–47; for settlement, 36; urban reconstruction and, 135
Laws: common law theory of mortgages under, 32; property maintenance under, 43–44; rent control under, 132
Leases for apartments, 44
Life insurance companies, 121–127; credit creation system and, 118; mortgage bankers and, 147; mortgages and, 108, 143–144, 148, 196; tax exempt bonds and, 162

Limited partnerships for apartments, 19
Limited Profit Housing Company Bill (New York State), 150, 151
Loans: availability of money and, 63–64; to commercial banks, 64, 66, 67, 71, 77–78; from commercial banks, 68; educational, 106; from Federal Home Loan Bank System, 112, 116–117, 118; from Federal Reserve System, 77–78; rehabilitation, 169–170; resource allocation and, 6; to savings and loan associations, 112, 116–117; *see also* Mortgages
Loan-to-value ratio, 31, 33
Local governments: bonds issued by, 66, 157–164; building codes of, 52–53; land use policies of, 215
Location, and land utilization, 45–46
Lotteries, for raising housing funds, 8
Low-income housing: Congressional action for, 7; construction loan defaults and, 92; costs of, 233–234; difficulty of providing, 3; equity requirements for, 33; Federal Housing Administration programs for, 175–177; housing allowances for, 232–233; housing densities and, 47; improvement of American housing and, 41; local government bonds for, 164; nonprofit character of, 11; seed money grants for, 19–20; standards for, 219; subsidies for, 150
Lumpers, in tenement construction, 141–142

Maintenance: apartment building, 220–221; cooperative apartments and, 105, 134; income level and, 43
Manhattan House, New York City, 130
Massachusetts, 106, 110
Metropolitan Life Insurance Company, 133; Parkchester; constructed by, 128–130; Stuyvesant Town and, 130–132
Millwork in housing construction, 50
Mitchell-Lama Law, 150
Mobile housing, 218
Monaco, 45
Money: availability and lending of, 63–64; Federal Reserve Board and supply of, 55–56; lack of housing resources and, 37; limits to supply of, 58–62; major elements in, 6; market for, 58–81; as resource for housing, 35, 53–57; universal acceptability of, 7
Mortgage bankers, 138–148; Government National Mortgage Association and, 204–205; as national lenders, 126
Mortgage Bankers Association, 138, 143, 144

Mortgage Guaranty Insurance Corporation, 180

Mortgages, 11, 21–34; amortization of, see Amortization; bank assets and, 65; commercial banks and, 68, 85–87; construction financing through, 67, 90–91; continuing market for, 29; Federal Home Loan Banking System and, 116–119; Government National Mortgage Association and, 203–206; insurance on, see Federal Housing Administration insured mortgages, Veterans Administration insured mortgages; interest on, see Interest on mortgages; lender's objectives in, 21, 23–24, 26–27; life insurance companies and, 121–124, 126–128, 135–137; life of, 13–14, 29; liquidity of investments and, 74–75; loan-to-value ratio and, 27–29; mutual savings banks and, 95, 96, 101; nonprofit housing programs and, 19–20; origin of term, 32; ownership under, 25–26; personal savings compared with, 12–13; refinancing through, 42–43; release of seller in transfer of, 24–25; saving flow swings and, 99; self-amortizing, see Self-amortizing mortgages; servicing fees for, 144–145, 147, 186, 196; warehousing of, 87–88

Multiple Dwelling Law (New York State), 175

Multiple dwellings, see Apartment houses; Condominiums; Cooperative apartment houses

Municipal Loan Program (New York City), 91–92

Mutual funds, 93

Mutual savings banks, 93–107; assets (1970) of, 95–96; commercial banks in competition with, 97–99; credit creation systems and, 118; credit worthiness for mortgages and, 23–24; Federal Deposit Insurance Corporations and, 113; Federal Housing Administration and, 169; Federal Reserve System and, 89–90; growth rates for, 99–101, 113, 114; largest, 109–110; mortgages from, 108; as national lenders, 127; Regulation "Q" on interest from, 81; savings in, 56, 103–104; see also Thrift institutions

Nassau County, New York, 177

National Fact Book of Mutual Savings Banking (1972), 99

National Housing Act, 110, 216

National Housing Act of 1934, 168, 169, 170, 175, 183, 185

National Housing Act of 1937, 176

National Housing Act of 1949, 4

National Housing Act of 1954, Title III, 192

National lenders, definition of, 126–127

Netherlands, 45

New towns: British, 45–46, 215, 216; Federal Housing Administration and, 167; financing for, 15–16

New York City: apartment house boom in, 101; bank competition in, 98; building codes in, 175; cooperatives in, 134; Forest Hills housing dispute in, 47; importation of housing resources by, 36; as lending institution, 151–152, 154–155; life insurance companies in, 128–132; Municipal Loan Program of, 91–92; mutual savings banks in, 103; open market operations in, 78; rent control in, 132; tax exemptions for housing construction in, 149; tenements in, 18, 141–142, 220; thrift institutions in, 74, 115; treasury bill market in, 73; United Housing Foundation and, 102; useful life of apartments in, 40

New York Federal Reserve Bank, 66

New York Life (company), 128, 133

New York State: housing codes in, 175; as lending institution, 149–158, 161; rent control in, 132; savings banks in, 90, 106; Stuyvesant Town development and, 131

New York State Housing Finance Agency, 153–154, 155, 156, 157–158, 163

New York State Division of Housing and Community Renewal, 156

New York State Limited Profit Housing Mortgage Corporation, 153

New York Stock Exchange, 198

Nixon, Richard M., 201

Norman period of English history, 32

Notes issued by banks, 59, 187

Oklahoma, 80

Open Market Committee, Federal Reserve System, 78, 197

Open market operations, 78, 116

Oregon, 187

Overcrowding in housing, 41, 210

Ownership: condition of mortgaged property and, 31–33; equity investment and, 11–12; mortgages and feelings of, 25–26

Panics, 69–70

Parkchester (apartments), New York City, 128–130

Parker-Morris Standards, 219
Parkmecede development, San Francisco, 130
Pass-through type of security, 207
Patman, Wright, 171
Payment bonds, for construction loans, 91
Pension funds: Federal Home Loan Bank obligations and, 117; investment policies of, 226–227; life insurance companies and, 122
Performance bonds, in construction loans, 91
Plastic, in housing construction, 49
Plumbing facilities, in housing standard definitions, 40–41, 209–210
Poland, 8
Population densities, 44–45, 161, 215
Portland cement industry, 50, 51–52, 53
Presidential appointment of Federal Reserve Board governors, 69
Profits for builders: debt-to-value ratio and, 15; land value increases and, 15–16; as motive for building houses, 11
Prudential Life (company), 128
Public housing, see Low-income housing
Public Law 89–597, 115, 116
Puerto Rico, 96, 109

Racial factors: credit worthiness and, 24; Federal Housing Administration and, 168, 176; housing and, 4, 39, 41; in mortgage evaluations, 26; universal acceptability of money and, 7
Rate control Act, 115
Real estate appraisers, 28, 85–86
Real Estate Investment Trusts, 146; commercial banks and, 88–89; construction loans by, 29; income tax policies and, 19
Reconstruction Finance Corporation (RFC), 177, 182, 183, 184, 186, 189
Reconstruction Finance Corporation Mortgage Association, 185
Recreation areas, and land values, 45
Redevelopment Companies Law (New York), 131
Regulation "Q" Federal Reserve Board, 80–81
Rehabilitation of housing: factors in, 42; Federal Housing Administration and, 167, 169–170, 175; mortgage bankers and, 140–141; Municipal Loan Program and, 91–92; mutual savings banks and, 101–102; surge of interest in, 39; useful life of buildings and, 40; see also Urban renewal
Releases, mortgages, in transfers, 24–25
Renaissance, 59, 60

Rent: concessions in, 24; control statutes for, 132; economic integration and supplements for, 168; equity requirements and, 33; inflation and, 152; leases and, 44; maintenance and, 43; ownership rights and, 12; profits of builders and, 16
Rental property, see Apartment houses
Report on National Housing Goals (Fourth, 1972), 12, 45, 47–48, 56
Reserve requirements of Federal Reserve System, 76–77, 98
Resources for housing, 35–57; building materials as, 49–53; labor as, 47–49; land as, 44–47; money as, 7–8, 53–57; policies for reduction in demand on, 214–222; stockpile of existing housing as, 37–44
Retirement funds, 117
Riverton Houses, Harlem, New York City, 131, 132
Rockefeller, Nelson A., 153
Romney, George, 203
Roosevelt, Franklin D., 183
Rumania, 8
Russia, see Soviet Union

San Francisco, 130
Saulnier, Raymond J., 132
Savings: capacity of economic system and, 55–57; mortgages as outlets for, 8, 12–13, 55; rates of, 55; shifts in patterns of, 161–162
Savings and loan associations, 108–120; Federal Housing Administration and, 169; growth of, 99, 104, 109, 111, 113, 114; mortgages and, 121; as national lenders, 127; percentage of savings (1972) in, 56; reserve requirements for, 225; savings interest regulation and, 55, 81, 96–97, 115; see also Thrift institutions
Saxon period in English history, 32
Second mortgages, 174
Seed money grants for nonprofit housing, 19–20
Self-amortizing mortgages: apartment houses and, 213; FHA mortgages and, 170–171; servicing fees for, 144
Senate, 69
Servicing fees for mortgages, 144–145, 147, 186, 196
Shares, in savings and loan associations, 109
Shelter package in housing, 3–4, 5
Shopping centers, 15
Siberia, 45
Smith, Alfred, 149, 150, 155
Social package in housing, 4–526, 164, 211, 217

Soviet Union, 36; housing in, 8, 217; population density in, 44–45

Special assistance programs, Government National Mortgage Association, 198, 199, 201, 208, 234

Standards in housing, 40–41

Standby commitment in mortgage banking, 147

State Mutual Life Insurance Company, Worcester, Massachusetts, 128

States: bonds of, 8; commercial banks and, 68; housing authorities within, 176; interest rate ceilings of, 22–23; land use policies of, 215; leases under, 44; as lending institution, 149–164; loan-to-value ratios in, 33; mortgage insurance in, 180, mutual savings banks in, 96, 101; obligations of, 66; savings and loan associations in, 109, 110; uniform building codes in, 52; university housing in, 19

Steel in housing construction, 50

Stock Exchange, New York City, 198

Stock market investments, 93–94, 103, 107

Stock-ownership associations, 109, 111, 118

Straight-line depreciation, 16-17

Stuyvesant Town development, New York City, 130–132

Substandard housing, definition of, 40

Sullivan, Leonor K., 171

Surety companies, 91

Tandem plan, and Government National Mortgage Association, 201–202, 203

Taxation: bonds under, 159–163, 164; commercial banks and, 87; construction exemptions under, 131, 132, 149; interest; under, 66, 106; land improvement and, 45; money supply and, 61, 230; resource allocation through, 7–8

Tenant movement, 133, 221

Tenement House Law (1901, New York City), 40

Tenements, 18, 40, 41, 141–142, 220

Texas, 80

Thatching, in housing construction, 49

Thoreau, Henry David, 4, 10

Thrift accounts, 62, 64

Thrift institutions: competition with, 74; interest rate regulation in, 80–81, 228; policies for change in, 228–230; see also Mutual savings banks; Savings and loan associations

Time accounts, 62, 64, 68, 112

Title insurance, 26

Transfers of mortgages, 24–25

Treasury (United States): Federal Home Loan Bank System and, 113, 114, 115- 116, 118; Federal Housing Administration and, 177, 180; Federal National Mortgage Association and, 187, 188, 192, 193; Federal Reserve System and, 69, 124, 125, 190, 213; Government National Mortgage Association and, 199–203; Home Owners Loan Corporation and, 183; money supply and, 75

Treasury bills, 77; commercial banks and, 65–66, 68, 71, 73–74; individual investment in, 103, 107

Twitchell, Allan A., 5

221(d)3 programs (FHA), 176, 192, 201

234 programs (FHA), 176, 201, 202, 203

236 programs (FHA), 176, 201–202, 203

Underwriting firms, 146

Unions: apartment house workers and, 134; building trade, 48–49, 53; commercial banks and, 62; investment policies of, 19, 226–227

United Housing Foundation, 102

United States Savings and Loan League, 109

University buildings, 19

Urban Development Corporation, 18, 157–158

Urban renewal: apartment houses and, 134–135; Federal Housing Administration and, 167; Government National Mortgage Association and, 201; origin of term, 131; see also Rehabilitation

Utility package in housing, 4, 5, 41–42, 49, 164

Veiller, Laurance, 141–142

Vermont, 187

Vernon, Raymond, 124

Veterans Administration insured mortgages, 86, 127, 171; defaults on, 192; FHA-insured mortgages and, 187; Government National Mortgage Association and, 207; life insurance companies and, 127; mortgage bankers and, 139, 142, 144

Vietnam war, 98, 125, 171, 193

Warehousing of mortgages, 87–88

West Germany, 106, 230

William the Conqueror, 32

Winnick, Louis, 128

Women, and credit worthiness, 24

Working class: money supply changes and, 59, 60; savings by, 93, 94

World War II, 39, 81, 100, 124, 190

Zoning: industry and, 215; land utilization and, 46, 47; Urban Development Corporation and, 157–158